PERSONAL HOROSCOPES 2013

DAN LIEBMAN

PERSONAL HOROSCOPES 2013

Personal Horoscopes 2013
Copyright © 2011, 2012 by Dan Liebman.
All rights reserved.

Published by Collins, an imprint of HarperCollins Publishers Ltd.

First edition

HarperCollins books may be purchased for educational, business, or sales
promotional use through our Special Markets Department.

HarperCollins Publishers Ltd
2 Bloor Street East, 20th Floor
Toronto, Ontario, Canada
M4W 1A8

www.harpercollins.ca

Library and Archives Canada Cataloguing in Publication
information is available upon request.

ISBN 978-1-44341-691-7

Printed and bound in Canada

WEB 9 8 7 6 5 4 3 2 1

MIX
Paper from
responsible sources
FSC® C004071

CONTENTS

PERSONAL HOROSCOPES 2013

INTRODUCTION

THE
BASICS OF
ASTROLOGY

Welcome to 2013, and to a personal horoscope guide that will take you on an astrological journey through the year ahead.

Astrology, the study of interactions among the stars and the planets, has long fascinated humankind. ("We like to think of ourselves as the second-oldest profession," said astrologer Richard Brown.) Its history can be traced back to the early Babylonians, who introduced the concept of the zodiac in the third millennium BC. Astrology predates not only psychology but also astronomy.

We look to our horoscopes to answer an array of questions and to aid us in understanding our strengths and weaknesses. Astrology provides us with a feeling of how events might unfold, gives direction as we approach our goals, and helps us to better comprehend relationships. It assists us in connecting with others and examining our feelings. If we are prone to secrecy, for example, an awareness of the traits associated with our sign can encourage us to open up. We can discover a lot about our personality as well as our potential.

Personal Horoscopes 2013 begins with a brief introduction of the basics of astrology, explaining some of the tools used to create the zodiac profiles and the weekly forecasts. Part One provides a snapshot of each zodiac sign—personality traits, information on health and career, and associations (including numbers, colours, and gemstones)—followed by a list of famous (and some infamous) people born in each sign and on every day of the year. You'll discover some fascinating trends when you see who shares your sign.

Part Two is a complete compatibility guide, which offers ratings on and explanations about every possible pairing between you and your significant others (romantic and other partners, family members, and associates). You'll find it interesting to see not only *how* you get along (or don't) with others but *why* you do (and don't).

Part Three is the heart of the book—weekly forecasts for all zodiac signs that will guide you through the entire year. As you navigate your journey, you'll become aware of what lies ahead in the different areas of your life, including events taking place behind the scenes. You'll be able to watch for possible stumbling blocks and then see when the road looks clearer. Keywords for each month indicate your general approach, attitude, and mood. Key days are pinpointed so you'll know when the time is right to make your move in the areas of romance, friends and family, career and status, and finance.

Part Four is devoted to the Chinese zodiac, which is based on a different tradition from the Western zodiac. You'll find out about your animal sign—what it means, its most (and least) favourable relationships, and what's in store for the Year of the Snake (2013). Because the Chinese year does not coincide exactly with our calendar, we've included a chart that indicates the precise dates of every Chinese year over the past century. You'll also see each Chinese sign's equivalent in the Western system.

As a final note, this book is "personal" in another important way. In addition to providing information and guidance, it does so from a Canadian perspective. What that means is that, when you read about events that may happen during Thanksgiving, it will be Canadian Thanksgiving (in October, not the U.S. holiday in November). You'll find references to other Canadian holidays such as Boxing Day, Canada Day, and Victoria Day (a.k.a., May Two-Four), as well as to Canadian people, Canadian activities and events, and, yes Canadian seasons (both of them).

We hope you'll find *Personal Horoscopes 2013* to be informative, enlightening, and even entertaining.

THE BASICS

"Astrology is a language," wrote the astrologer and author Dane Rudhyar. "If you understand this language, the sky speaks to you."

Many excellent books and articles have been written to explain the language of astrology. Some of the vocabulary is, by necessity, complex and technical. We've chosen to concentrate on the basic information used in creating the profiles, compatibility guides, and forecasts in this book.

First, it's important to remember that *Personal Horoscopes 2013* is based on your Sun sign, which is one of several factors involved in creating a comprehensive astrological profile. To provide other astrological influences, we would have to factor in the time, date, and place of your birth (something obviously impossible to do in a book of this scope). Many good resources are available to help you determine your rising sign, Moon sign, and other influences.

Sun Signs

ARIES
March 21–April 20

TAURUS
April 21–May 21

GEMINI
May 22–June 21

CANCER
June 22–July 22

LEO
July 23–August 22

VIRGO
August 23–September 23

LIBRA
September 24–October 23

SCORPIO
October 24–November 22

SAGITTARIUS
November 23–December 21

CAPRICORN
December 22–January 20

AQUARIUS
January 21–February 19

PISCES
February 20–March 20

Over the years, the dates for each sign have shifted. The Sun doesn't move into a new sign at precisely the same moment each year, so the first and last dates of a Sun sign may vary by a day or so. If you are born at the cusp (the beginning or end of an astrological sign), check an astrological table (some are available online) for the dates for your sign in the year you were born. Cusp people, not surprisingly, often feel the influence of both signs, although one sign is always stronger. *Note:* If you were born prematurely and wonder whether astrological signs apply to when you were born or when you were expected to be born, the answer is the former. An astrological chart is based on the time of a newborn's first breath.

The twelve signs of the zodiac are arranged in two columns to show that each sign has an opposite. What affects one sign also affects the opposite sign. In determining compatibilities, we see that opposite signs are attracted because of similarities as well as differences. When reading this book, also consider your neighbouring sign because it's likely that you share planetary influences and have some common qualities.

The Planets

The planets, including the Sun and the Moon (in astrology, these heavenly bodies are considered planets), are associated with the twelve zodiac signs. In understanding the different facets of our personality, it is helpful to know the nature and the role of the planets. Taurus, for example, is ruled by Venus, a planet that represents love and beauty.

A planetary transit is the passage of one of the planets through a zodiac sign. Some of these passages occur quickly while others are in effect over longer periods. For example, Saturn entered the sign of Scorpio in October 2012 and will occupy it until December 2014. Transits affect all the signs, so Saturn's transit through Scorpio will have an impact not just on Scorpio.

A sign and its ruling planet share characteristics. The following brief descriptions of each planet's attributes also apply to the corresponding sign or signs mentioned here.

The *Sun* is related to health, energy, willpower, achievement, and advancement toward goals. It rules flamboyant, egotistical, extravagant Leo.

The *Moon* affects moods, feelings, and emotions. It symbolizes home and intuition and relates to the subconscious. It rules emotional and romantic Cancer, the sign of home and family.

Mercury affects the mind and movement, how we think, and how we communicate. It rules Gemini (chatty, adaptable) and Virgo (picky, conscientious). Both signs are intellectually oriented, but Gemini seeks knowledge for its own sake and Virgo uses it for practical purposes.

Venus is connected to art, beauty, material possessions, and feelings of love and enjoyment, and is a peaceful planet that promotes generosity. It rules Taurus (dependable, stubborn) and Libra (charming, diplomatic, and indecisive). Taurus is the primary money sign of the zodiac. Libra emphasizes harmony.

Mars energizes different areas of life, inspiring diligence but promoting tension. It relates to leadership, initiative, and aggressiveness. It rules impulsive, courageous, decisive Aries and co-rules (with Pluto) intense Scorpio.

Jupiter, the largest planet, is identified with growth, expansion, and beneficial influences—it is commonly called the planet of good luck (though it brings opportunities rather than increased possessions). It rules freedom-loving, optimistic, outspoken Sagittarius.

Saturn represents limitation and consolidation. It is connected to hard work and caution and helps us make choices. It rules ambitious, rigid, disciplined Capricorn.

Uranus is related to sudden changes and areas of life that need change. It represents nonconformity and experimentation and is connected to discovery as well as disruptions. It rules independent, idealistic, eccentric Aquarius.

Neptune, the most spiritual planet, represents creativity and the imagination. It is also connected with deception and confusion. It represents imaginative, compassionate, emotional Pisces.

Pluto brings about significant transformations and unexpected and disruptive events. It is subtle and secretive, like the sign it co-rules (with Mars)—mysterious, intuitive Scorpio.

Note: Despite Pluto's demotion to "dwarf planet" status by astronomers, it remains a significant planet in astrology. As for the "new" thirteenth Zodiac sign, a focus of discussion in the media, the consensus among experts is that Ophiuchus, a constellation that falls between Scorpio and Sagittarius, is simply that—a constellation.

Finally, a note on terminology: When a planet is retrograde, it *appears* to be travelling backwards through the zodiac (but this is actually an optical illusion). The effects vary according to the planet and the individual chart, but during this time, the planet's influence is felt in a more internal way. Direct or forward-moving motion represents a planet's normal course.

The Qualities and the Elements

Zodiac signs are classified in two ways: by quality and by element. Simply put, qualities refer to the way in which we deal with the world. Elements reflect our personality traits. It's helpful to understand the qualities and elements, especially when looking at the Snapshots and Compatibility sections of this book, as well as the weekly forecasts.

The three qualities are cardinal, fixed, and mutable.

Cardinal signs: Aries, Cancer, Libra, Capricorn. These are the action signs. Action isn't used in the "aggressive" or "militant" sense of the word. It means that an effort is taken to change circumstances. For example, if you're strapped for cash, you don't buy a lottery ticket and wait for your Lotto 6/49 ship to come in. You follow a plan, perhaps taking a self-improvement course; or you have a serious talk with the person in charge of your salary; or you take on a part-time job. Examples of people who were born in cardinal signs include Nellie McClung (Libra), who fought for women's voting rights, and the fourteenth Dalai Lama (Cancer), a Nobel Peace Prize winner who has devoted his life to compassionate work. Other examples include singer Susan Boyle (Aries) and comedian/actor Jim Carrey (Capricorn).

Fixed signs: Taurus, Leo, Scorpio, Aquarius. As the name suggests, people born under these signs are fixed in their ways. They're not ornery; they are patient, persistent, and determined—and believe that others will have to accept them for who and what they are. For example, if you're being challenged at work for going too slowly, you won't sacrifice your standards for the sake of speed. You'll continue to be thorough and expect others to ultimately appreciate the care you take in your job. Examples of people who were born in fixed signs include singer/actor Barbra Streisand (Taurus), who, early in her career, refused to get a nose job—firmly believing that it could affect the quality of her singing; and hockey commentator Don Cherry (Aquarius), who emphatically won't tone down his flamboyant dress style and outspoken manner. Other examples include author Margaret Atwood (Scorpio) and U.S. president Bill Clinton (Leo).

Mutable signs: Gemini, Virgo, Sagittarius, Pisces. These are the zodiac's adaptable signs. They're flexible and not set in their ways, and will change themselves rather than their circumstances. For example, if you feel a relationship has hit an impasse, you will first evaluate your own role in the situation. If you're unhappy in a job, you'll try a new approach before sending out a resumé. Examples of people who were born in mutable signs include Britain's King George VI (Sagittarius), who conquered his stammering and became an effective world leader; and actor Michael J. Fox (Gemini), who, since being diagnosed with Parkinson's disease, has become an activist for research. Other examples include singer/songwriter Shania Twain (Virgo) and actor Al Waxman (Pisces).

The four elements are fire, air, water, and earth.

Fire signs: Aries, Leo, Sagittarius. The fire signs are characterized by enthusiasm, passion, self-confidence, and strong will. People born under these signs take the initiative—they are leaders and motivators and go after goals. People born under the fire signs include singer Céline Dion (Aries), cancer activist Terry Fox (Leo), and astronaut Roberta Bondar (Sagittarius).

Air signs: Gemini, Libra, Aquarius. The air signs are linked to abstract thinking. Air signs are the communicators of the zodiac—they exchange ideas, find it easy to write or speak (or both), and are always on the move. They're intelligent and quick studies. People born under the air signs include singer/songwriter Bob Dylan (Gemini), Prime Minister Pierre Elliott Trudeau (Libra), and author Mordecai Richler (Aquarius).

Water signs: Cancer, Scorpio, Pisces. The water signs are all about feelings and emotions. They are empathetic, intuitive, creative, imaginative, and highly sensitive of their surroundings.

They also tend to be secretive and may have psychic leanings. People born under the water signs include author Alice Munro (Cancer), singer/songwriter Joni Mitchell (Scorpio), and poet Elizabeth Barrett Browning (Pisces).

Earth signs: Taurus, Virgo, Capricorn. The earth signs are practical, with a materialistic side. They are stable, diligent, and ambitious, and they seek out financial security (but are generally modest). They are persistent, as well as rigid and inflexible. People born under the earth signs include comedian Jerry Seinfeld (Taurus), investor Warren Buffett (Virgo), and Prime Minister John A. Macdonald (Capricorn).

The Ascendant (Rising Sign) and Houses of Your Horoscope

The twelve houses of a horoscope correspond to different areas of a person's life. Each house is ruled by a different zodiac sign. The line that divides each house is known as a cusp. The cusp, or start, of the first house is called the Ascendant. Once the Ascendant is determined, the "house rulers" can easily be identified. In a hypothetical example, you are a Capricorn and your Ascendant is Virgo. That means your first house is ruled by Virgo, your second house by Libra, your third house by Scorpio, and so on—the order of the signs remains constant. At the end of the book, you'll find information and a chart that will help you identify your Ascendant and the houses of your horoscope. (See page 545.)

Your Ascendant is the sign that was rising over the eastern horizon at the time of your birth. (That's why the Ascendant is also known as your rising sign.) This marks the moment at which you made your appearance in the world. To calculate the Ascendant sign, you need to know the location and exact time you were born. It is useful to understand the different areas of a person's life that the houses relate to and, generally, how the houses work.

If, using the above hypothetical example, you determine your Ascendant is Virgo, it means your second house will be ruled by Libra. Librans are known for their innate good taste and love of all things beautiful. The second house covers the money you earn. Therefore, given Libra's influence on your second house, it is likely that you'll spend a lot of your income on the finer things in life.

Your Ascendant determines how others view you, not your actual nature. It indicates the manner in which you interact with people. The following list summarizes the areas of your life that the houses govern.

The first house. This is the house of self, and it represents appearance, instincts, attitude, temperament, and disposition.

The second house. This is the house of your own income. It rules money you earn yourself, not from other sources, and also involves your attitude toward possessions.

The third house. This is the house of communication and learning. It relates to diverse matters, including siblings, aunts, uncles, cousins, neighbours, and acquaintances; short-distance travel; educational activities; and hobbies.

The fourth house. This is the house of home life, property, and domestic affairs. It rules some conditions involving early life, some related to the end of life, and endings in general.

The fifth house. This is the house of creativity, love, and romance. It also covers a variety of other recreational activities, as well as financial speculation.

The sixth house. This is the house of health and service, covering well-being and illness. It also includes work (but not career), interactions with employers/employees and colleagues, and pets.

The seventh house. This is the house of partnerships (including business partnerships), marriage, and commitment. It also includes rivals and competitors.

The eighth house. This is the house of rebirth and regeneration—it covers birth, death, and money other than what you earn yourself (for example, it includes inheritances, shared finances, and partner's money).

The ninth house. This is the house of intellectual growth and long-distance travel. It includes other types of explorations, including journeys into religious, spiritual, philosophical, and occult areas.

The tenth house. This is the house of career, professional accomplishments, and reputation.

The eleventh house. This is the house of friendship, influential people, and group activities. It is often referred to as the house of hopes and wishes.

The twelfth house. This is the house of behind-the-scenes, secret, and hidden activities. It is linked to the past and relates to research, places of confinement, and privately made arrangements.

We hope the above summaries have provided some useful and insightful information that will help you explore the following parts. We also hope that *Personal Horoscopes 2013* will serve not only as a guide to the next fifty-two weeks but also as an opportunity to learn something about your goals, motivations, relationships, and talents.

Finally, if you have any doubts, remember the words of Sir Arthur C. Clarke, who said, "I don't believe in astrology. I'm a Sagittarius, and we're skeptical."

PART ONE

SNAPSHOTS OF YOUR ZODIAC SIGN

ARIES

March 21–April 20

The Ram

First sign in the zodiac

Strengths to play up: leadership, courage, affection

Weaknesses to watch out for: possessiveness,

impatience, and excessive behaviour

Behind the name and the symbol of your sign:

Your astrological symbol is the ram—known for being hard-driving, powerful, and aggressive. In Greek mythology, the constellation of Aries is associated with the flying ram, whose skin came to be known as the Golden Fleece. Rams butt their heads—and those born under the sign of Aries are said to take life "head on." A ram's horn is part of the cornucopia—the horn of plenty—which represents abundance.

Your element:

The four elements in astrology are air, earth, fire, and water. Your element is fire. Fire signs are upbeat, generous, and fired with enthusiasm. They're more aggressive than assertive, but they don't have hidden motives. What you see is what you get.

Your quality:

Three qualities are found in the zodiac: cardinal, fixed, and mutable. You're a cardinal sign, which means you have initiative and take immediate action when required, according to your preferred style.

Your ruling planet and what it means:

Mars, your ruling planet, is named for the god of war. Mars is the action planet, connected to initiative, aggression, conflict, competitiveness, and drive.

Personality traits identified with Aries:

Aries is the first sign of the zodiac. You're sure to be number one out of the starting gate—and the first to complete whatever you do. Here are some of the words that describe you. (They're not broken down by positive traits and negative traits because some can fall in either category.)

Acquisitive
Adventure-seeking
Affectionate
Authoritarian
Decisive
Disappointed in people (because they lack your standards)
Driven
Emotionally vulnerable (you fall in love at first sight)
Energetic (your energy level is extremely high)

Excessive

Forthright

Fun (you add life to any party)

Generous

Gullible (as a result of your idealism)

Idealistic

Impulsive

Loving (you're deeply committed in love)

Not detail-oriented (you see the forest rather than the trees)

Obstinate

Overachieving

Overdoing

Pioneering (you're the first to take a chance)

Possessive

Quick-witted

Self-centred

Single-minded

Spontaneous

Take-charge (leadership is your operative word)

What you see is what you get (you don't hide your intentions or your motives)

Relationships and compatibilities:

You're the most compatible with: Sagittarius, Gemini, and Aquarius.

You're the least compatible with: Virgo, Pisces, Capricorn, and Cancer.

See also the Aries Compatibility Guide on page 99.

Associations with your sign:

Numbers: 6, 7, 9

Colours: Red (carmine, scarlet, and other shades)

Flowers: Wild rose, thistle

Gemstones: Bloodstone, amethyst

Day of the week: Tuesday

Health and well-being for your sign:

You could be susceptible in the area of the body that relates to your sign. Aries rules the head (including the brain, the face, and the eyes). You could be prone to headaches. Take time to refresh yourself (you tend to overwork your mind), and make sure you get sufficient sleep. You're generally vigorous and have lots of stamina. But you need to realize you're vulnerable—not always easy for impatient types like you.

Careers suited to your sign:

Regardless of your career choice, you want to make your mark in it. Your ruling planet, Mars, is associated with action and determination—and you focus your energy on your work. You need a job that keeps you busy and lets you take charge—leadership is what drives you. But you also need to develop qualities that are not strong in your sign.

Aim to expand your attention span and to see things through rather than changing direction once you lose interest. Many Aries people work well with their hands, becoming architects, sculptors, or painters. Others are entrepreneurs. A surprising number of singers are born under this sign, among them Elton John, Jann Arden, Céline Dion, and Susan Boyle. *See also* Who Was Born in Your Sign and on Your Birthday? (page 82).

TAURUS

April 21–May 21
The Bull
Second sign in the zodiac
Strengths to play up: loyalty, determination, compassion
Weaknesses to watch out for: self-indulgence,
stubbornness

Behind the name and the symbol of your sign:
In Greek mythology, the constellation Taurus is associated with Zeus, the father of the gods who transformed himself into a white bull so he could approach a beautiful Phoenician princess. The bull symbolizes tenacity and strength. Like the bull, people born under its sign will graze peacefully in a pasture. But if it's disturbed, watch out. It will charge!

Your element:
The four elements in astrology are air, earth, fire, and water. Your element is earth. Your feet are planted firmly on the ground, and you're practical, dependable, and unpretentious. You do what's

needed to keep your reputation untarnished. You're goal-oriented—and that goal generally involves financial security.

Your quality:
Three qualities are found in the zodiac: cardinal, fixed, and mutable. You're a fixed sign. That means you don't try to change things. It's open to interpretation, but you're seen as patient, determined, or stubborn.

Your ruling planet and what it means:
Venus, the goddess of love, art, and beauty, gives her name to your ruling planet. Venus is associated with peacefulness and harmony, money and luxuries, shared pleasure, and tranquility.

Personality traits identified with Taurus:
Taurus has a reputation for being stubborn and bull-headed—but that's hardly fair. There's far more to Taurus's personality. And remember, one person's stubbornness is another's determination. Here are some of the words that describe you. (They're not broken down by positive traits and negative traits because some can fall in either category.)

Cautious (you don't take risks, and you weigh decisions carefully)
Celebrity-seeking (you like high-end types)
Complacent
Conservative (you resist change)
Conventional (some may think you're boring)
Dependable, determined, dogged
Entertaining (you're lively and fun and you love to entertain—
    you're a gourmet cook and throw great dinner parties)

Grounded (roots are important)

Hard-working

Loyal (unwaveringly so)

Materialistic

Methodical

Modest (you often live and dress below your means)

Money smart (you're the main money sign; you're cautious
with cash [low-risk investments])

Multi-talented (you do many things well)

Nature-loving (a born gardener)

Nurturing (you're especially good with kids and pets)

Opinionated

Patient

Peace-loving

Persevering and strong (but can become bull-headed)

Placid

Possessive

Powerful (but your pace can be plodding)

Quick-tempered (you're like the bull who grazes peacefully . . .
until enraged)

Scrupulous (you have high standards and strong convictions)

Security-seeking (you want stability and like to be in a permanent relationship)

Self-indulgent (you find it hard to diet)

Sensual

Stingy (you're not always the best tipper)

Tactile (you love to touch things, you love fragrances too—
everything from roses to coffee)

Tenacious

Tender

Trustworthy

Well-groomed (you're concerned with appearance—yours and everyone else's)

Relationships and compatibilities:

You're the most compatible with: Scorpio, Pisces, and Cancer.

You're the least compatible with: Sagittarius, Virgo, Libra, and Aquarius.

See also the Taurus Compatibility Guide on page 108.

Associations with your sign:

Numbers: 1, 6, 9

Colours: Red, dark green, yellow

Flowers: Violet, freesia, lilac

Gemstones: Sapphire, emerald

Day of the week: Friday

Health and well-being for your sign:

You could be susceptible in the area of the body that relates to your sign. Taurus rules the neck, throat, thyroid gland, and vocal chords, so be cautious about those areas. You may be prone to laryngitis. Be sure to wear a scarf under your parka on cold winter days. You can be docile—you're something of a couch potato—and should become more active. And watch out for your tendency to enjoy too many of life's good things (especially the high-caloric ones).

Careers suited to your sign:

Taurus is the main money sign of the zodiac. You want to accumulate possessions *and* maintain your wealth—you need to have money in the bank. If you had to choose between a prestigious position and a hefty salary, you'd choose the latter. You find it difficult to delegate authority. You have a tendency to start a new job and think you're smarter than your boss.

You may be drawn to a finance-related position. Being Venus-ruled, you show an artistic side and find yourself working in the arts. Your nurturing personality makes you suited to a career in social work. And because you are earthy, you're interested in earth-related work and may be suited to a job in architecture, gardening, or real estate. In Canada, earth would include ice—and there are quite a few prominent Taurus figure skaters, among them Jamie Salé, Tessa Virtue, and Barbara Ann Scott. *See also* Who Was Born in Your Sign and on Your Birthday? (page 82).

GEMINI

May 22–June 21

The Twins

Third sign in the zodiac

Strengths to play up: charm, ability to
communicate, versatility

Weaknesses to watch out for: short attention span,
unwillingness to commit yourself

Behind the name and the symbol of your sign:
The constellation Gemini includes the stars Castor and Pol-
lux—the twins of Greek mythology who sailed with Jason in
the quest for the Golden Fleece. (Gemini is Latin for "twins.")
Like the twins, those born under this sign are said to have a dual
nature. The symbol for Gemini shows two lines joined together.
The constellation, as well as those born under the sign, is associated with communication and the exchange of ideas.

Your element:
The four elements in astrology are air, earth, fire, and water.

Your element is air. You circulate easily, exchanging ideas and mingling with people of all ages and backgrounds. You're all about mental stimulation, not emotional involvement. You form relationships but enjoy simultaneous light-hearted friendships. Intensity is not in your vocabulary.

Your quality:

Three qualities are found in the zodiac: cardinal, fixed, and mutable. You're a mutable sign. That means adaptability is your middle name. You're flexible and willing to change your approach when necessary.

Your ruling planet and what it means:

Mercury, your ruling planet, is named for the messenger of the gods. Mercury is associated with communication, the thought process, observation, curiosity, and flexibility.

Personality traits identified with Gemini:

Gemini, the twins, has a dual nature. Those born under this sign are associated with communication and the exchange of ideas. You're flexible and adaptable, and you circulate so very quickly as you work a room that people may think you have two personalities—or that there are two of you. Here are some of the words that describe you. (They're not broken down by positive traits and negative traits because some can fall in either category.)

Adaptable and flexible
Amusing (you can cheer up even the most downbeat types)
Analytical

Articulate (you love to engage in debates and wordplay; are you ever at a loss for words?)

Chameleonlike (you're the most versatile of all the signs)

Communicator (you're by far the zodiac's top exchanger of information)

Curious

Cynical

Edgy

Expressive (you always come up with the perfect word or phrase)

Fickle

Fidgety

Gracious (you're not domestic but are an excellent host)

Hammy (you're a born actor)

Impatient (with a short attention span)

Indecisive

Intellectual (you're ruled by your mind, not your emotions)

Investigative

Lively (you live life fully)

Logical

Multi-faceted

Multi-talented (you have diverse interests)

Noncommittal

Perceptive

Quick to anger (you can change moods at the blink of an eye, but you generally return to your cheery self quickly)

Resilient (you bounce back quickly)

Resourceful (you're a storehouse of knowledge and can pull bits of information out of your hat)

Spontaneous

Superficial (you skim the surface of things rather than probe
  deeply)
Volatile, changeable
Witty

Relationships and compatibilities:
You're the most compatible with: Leo, Aries, Libra, and Sagittarius.
You're the least compatible with: Scorpio, Pisces, and Virgo.
See also the Gemini Compatibility Guide on page 118.

Associations with your sign:
Numbers: 3, 4, 5
Colours: Yellow, light blue
Flowers: Rose, daffodil, snapdragon
Gemstones: Agate, aquamarine
Day of the week: Wednesday

Health and well-being for your sign:
You could be susceptible in the area of the body that relates to
your sign. Gemini rules the arms (including the fingers and
hands), shoulders, nervous system, and respiratory system, so
be cautious in all those areas. (For example, watch your hand
when you close the car door.) Yoga is something that could benefit both your nerves and your breathing. Mainly, slow down—
you tend to do several things at once, and all of them too quickly.

Careers suited to your sign:
Gemini is all about communication, and your sign leans toward professions that involve the use of words. There are many
to choose from—broadcasting, journalism, teaching, and real

estate are a few possibilities. (Mercury, your ruling planet, governs education and transportation, as well as communication.) Sales suit you, too, given your charming nature. And because of your dual nature, it wouldn't be surprising to take on twin careers.

Any job that allows little variety would frustrate you. In short, there is an exciting range of possibilities, but the key is to find something that lets you exchange ideas. Among the many members of your sign who express themselves through words are actors Mike Myers, Michael J. Fox, and Michael Cera; poet William Butler Yeats; singer/songwriters Alanis Morissette and Bob Dylan; and authors Joyce Carol Oates, Robert Munsch, and Sir Arthur Conan Doyle. *See also* Who Was Born in Your Sign and on Your Birthday? (page 82).

CANCER

June 22–July 22

The Crab

Fourth sign in the zodiac

Strengths to play up: imagination, loyalty, intuition

Weaknesses to watch out for: possessiveness, moodiness

Behind the name and the symbol of your sign:
According to Greek mythology, the goddess Hera (Zeus's wife)
placed the image of a crab in the night sky. In Greek mythology,
Hercules crushed the crab that Hera sent to distract him in his
battle with the monster Hydra. The crab, like those ruled by its
sign, has a tough and protective shell. Within their shell, Cancer
people are emotional, intuitive, secretive, and moody.

Your element:
The four elements in astrology are air, earth, fire, and water.
Your element is water. You probe life's deeper mysteries and
operate on an emotional rather than intellectual level. Secretive
and intuitive, you look for hidden meanings beneath the surface

of things. You are persistent, and your personality often has a jealous side.

Your quality:

Three qualities are found in the zodiac: cardinal, fixed, and mutable. You're a cardinal sign. That means you have initiative and take immediate action when required, according to your preferred style.

Your ruling planet and what it means:

The Moon, second to the Sun in importance, rules Cancer. The Moon is associated with the home and the family, nurturing, intuition, motivation, and the subconscious.

Personality traits identified with Cancer:

Cancer is the sign of home and feelings. You have an urge to nurture and a need to protect, and you never let go of your ties to the past. Here are some of the words that describe you. (They're not broken down by positive traits and negative traits because some can fall in either category.)

Committed (you need permanence and are not flirtatious)
Defensive (just like the crab is)
Dependent
Family-loving (you're your family nurturer and caregiver)
Grouchy (when Cancer gets grumpy, the world should back off)
Hesitant (you reveal your feelings gradually)
Home-loving (your home is the focus of your life)
Imaginative
Inhibited (you're reserved and don't communicate freely)

Insightful

Intuitive (you may even have psychic abilities)

Melancholy (you can become remote and even jealous)

Moody and sulky (though you try to conceal your touchiness)

Nostalgic (you're very much tied to the past)

Not confident (it's easy for you to develop an inferiority complex)

Peace-loving (you mediate to achieve compromise)

Perceptive

Possessive (and even clingy—it's hard for you to say goodbye easily)

Protective (you're not a risk-taker)

Resourceful

Rooted (you're the one who'll research the family tree)

Sarcastic (your way of expressing your displeasure)

Sensitive

Shrewd

Stable (you tend to stay at one place and in one job—and improve your position there)

Successful (you enjoy earning money—not for its own sake but to provide for your family)

Sympathetic

Relationships and compatibilities:

You're the most compatible with: Pisces, Taurus, Libra, and Capricorn.

You're the least compatible with: Aries, Virgo, and Leo.

See also the Cancer Compatibility Guide on page 129.

Associations with your sign:

Numbers: 2, 3, 7, 8

Colours: Silver, grey, indigo

Flowers: Chrysanthemum, hydrangea

Gemstones: Moonstone, pearl

Day of the week: Monday

Health and well-being for your sign:

You could be susceptible in the area of the body that relates to your sign. Cancer rules the stomach, breasts, chest, and lungs, so be cautious about those vulnerable areas and be sure to get regular checkups. Like the crab, you have a tough outer shell. But within that exterior, you're tender, sensitive, and temperamental. Engage in activities that can distract or de-stress you—anything from a game of curling to dog-walking. As well, avoid high-fat foods.

Careers suited to your sign:

Although your sign is attached to home and family, and many people born under the sign of Cancer work successfully from home, you have a need to be seen and recognized by the broader public. A service-oriented job suits your personality—the field of medicine is particularly appropriate. So does work that involves the family—you would be a natural as a genealogist, historian, or biographer. Being a collector, you could find yourself working in a library or, especially, a museum. Many successful artists (Rembrandt and Degas, to name two)—and, especially, designers—are born under the sign of the crab.

You can, in fact, apply your understanding of human nature to an assortment of careers. Not surprisingly, two prominent authors whose stories often focus on the family—Margaret Laurence and Alice Munro—share your sign. *See also* Who Was Born in Your Sign and on Your Birthday? (page 82).

LEO

July 23–August 22

The Lion

Fifth sign in the zodiac

Strengths to play up: loyalty, ambition, idealism

Weaknesses to watch out for: self-centred, scene-stealing

Behind the name and the symbol of your sign:

The first on the list of Hercules' twelve labours was the task of killing the Nemean Lion—a giant beast that roamed the villages of ancient Greece. Hercules wrestled the lion, which found its way to the night sky to commemorate the great battle. (*Leonis* is Latin for "lion.") Like the lion, Leos are flamboyant, regal, and powerful—and inclined to think they're the centre of the universe.

Your element:

The four elements in astrology are air, earth, fire, and water. Your element is fire. Fire signs are upbeat, generous, and fired with enthusiasm. They're more aggressive than assertive, but they don't have hidden motives. What you see is what you get.

Your quality:
Three qualities are found in the zodiac: cardinal, fixed, and mutable. You're a fixed sign. That means you don't try to change things. It's open to interpretation, but you're seen as patient, determined, or stubborn.

Your ruling planet and what it means:
The Sun, which rules your sign, is connected to self-confidence, the quest for goals, health, vigour, dignity, and one's ego. (Leos know the world revolves around the Sun but think it revolves around them.)

Personality traits identified with Leo:
Leo epitomizes self-confidence and theatricality. You want to put your stamp on everything, and you haven't yet met a stage that you don't like. *Dominant* and *regal* are two adjectives that are often attached to the name of your sign. Here are some of the other words that describe you. (They're not broken down by positive traits and negative traits because some can fall in either category.)

Ambitious
Arrogant
Attention-seeking
Bossy
Broad-minded (you're open to suggestions and are willing to try something new)
Charismatic (you cultivate a following of fans)
Charming

Dramatic (even when not performing for an audience you're showing off)

Egotistical

Fair (you appreciate a good challenge)

Fiery

Fun-loving

Good-hearted (your intentions are always the best)

Gracious (you're appreciative of others)

Honourable

Hot-tempered

Idealistic

Inflexible (you don't like to concede a point in discussions or debates)

Kind (kindness is your best quality)

Loyal and devoted (your friends are for a lifetime)

Majestic and dignified

Noble (you're a natural leader)

Orderly (you're a strong organizer)

Overbearing

Passionate

Protective

Proud

Romantic (yes, you are a *true and hopeless* romantic)

Self-centred (you're so involved with your own appearance, you often don't notice others; yet you aren't selfish)

Self-confident

Self-sufficient

Straightforward (your attitude is "what you see is what you get"; you don't understand deception)

Strutting (you were born to show off)

Stylish (you have panache, do everything with flair, and, of course, love bold colours)

Theatrical (you have star quality, the world is your stage, and you command applause)

Tyrannical

Vain

Vivacious

Warm-hearted

Relationships and compatibilities:

You're the most compatible with: Gemini, Libra, and Capricorn.

You're the least compatible with: Scorpio, Pisces, and Cancer.

See also the Leo Compatibility Guide on page 140.

Associations with your sign:

Numbers: 1, 4, 5, 9

Colours: Golden yellow, orange

Flowers: Marigold, sunflower

Gemstones: Onyx, amber

Day of the week: Sunday

Health and well-being for your sign:

You could be susceptible in the area of the body that relates to your sign. Leo rules the heart, chest, back, and spine, so be cautious about and attentive to those areas. You have a bottomless pit of energy and sometimes ignore your own needs, notably a good night's sleep (Leo needs lots of sleep) and a balanced diet. (You're inclined to eat rich foods). You need to take things less personally, and you need time to recharge your batteries.

Careers suited to your sign:

Named for the lion and ruled by the Sun, your sign seeks status and wealth and enjoys being in the public eye. Whatever position you choose, you need room to grow and thrive in a position of authority. You have a strong ego but aren't selfish, and though demanding, you're a generous boss.

You love an audience, so a career in the theatre would suit you from an early age. (Actor Daniel Radcliffe is a Leo.) A career in law is also appropriate. But your creative talents shine too. You lean toward being a writer or an artist—and definitely not a starving one. (Author J. K. Rowling is on the list of the world's wealthiest people.) Other Leo artists include Tom Thomson. Finally, you can also make your mark in the world of sports. Hockey alone boasts several great Leos, among them Marcel Dionne, Maurice Richard, and Sidney Crosby. *See also* Who Was Born in Your Sign and on Your Birthday? (page 82).

VIRGO

August 23–September 23

The Virgin

Sixth sign in the zodiac

Strengths to play up: teaching skills,

creativity, eye for detail

Weaknesses to watch out for: preachiness,

obsession with detail

Behind the name and the symbol of your sign:
Virgo (from the Latin word meaning "a maiden") has been attributed to different female deities, including the goddess of justice, Astraea. Astraea was placed among the stars by Zeus along with her scales of justice (the constellation Libra). Virgo, the only female figure among the zodiac's constellations, represents careful planning, curiosity, subtlety, and an analytical mind.

Your element:
The four elements in astrology are air, earth, fire, and water. Your element is earth. Your feet are planted firmly on the ground, and

you're practical, dependable, and unpretentious. You do what's needed to keep your reputation untarnished. You're goal-oriented—and that goal generally involves financial security.

Your quality:
Three qualities are found in the zodiac: cardinal, fixed, and mutable. You're a mutable sign. That means adaptability is your middle name. You're flexible and willing to change your approach when necessary.

Your ruling planet and what it means:
Mercury, your ruling planet, is named for the messenger of the gods. Mercury is associated with communication, the thought process, observation, curiosity, and flexibility.

Personality traits identified with Virgo:
Virgo is associated with personal integrity, the work ethic, order, and precision. You're analytical and precise. You set impossible standards for yourself and expect—or at least hope—that everyone else will meet them. Here are some of the words that describe you. (They're not broken down by positive traits and negative traits because some can fall in either category.)

Analytical (and self-analytical too)
Cautious (you lack spontaneity)
Conservative
Critical/hypercritical
Curious
Cynical
Design-oriented (your decor and wardrobe are always tasteful)

Detail-oriented (but you neglect some of the larger issues)

Discriminating

Dissatisfied (your standards are so high that you easily get turned off)

Education-oriented (you enjoy teaching, formally and informally)

Encouraging (you have a knack for bringing out the best in others)

Finicky

Growth-oriented (you seek to improve yourself)

Methodical

Meticulous (even your car is spiffy)

Observant (you don't miss anything that's said . . . or *not* said)

Orderly (your motto: everything in its place)

Organized (you're a natural planner and will check the weather report a week ahead of time)

Pedantic (you're a born teacher, but when you feel uneasy or unsure, you become preachy)

Perfection-oriented (you are, in fact, an ultra-perfectionist)

Pet-friendly (you're concerned with the well-being of all creatures)

Practical

Precise

Refined

Reliable (you take direction well—even when you're not happy with the instructions)

Reserved

Self-conscious

Service-oriented (you're often a community leader)

Soft-spoken

Subtle

Tasteful

Thrifty

Unrealistic (sometimes *nothing* is good enough for your standards)

Witty

Worrying (you can turn a molehill into the Rockies)

Relationships and compatibilities:

You're the most compatible with: Pisces, Virgo, Scorpio, and Capricorn.

You're the least compatible with: Aries, Taurus, Gemini, and Cancer.

See also the Virgo Compatibility Guide on page 150.

Associations with your sign:

Numbers: 4, 5, 8

Colours: Blue, green, ochre

Flowers: Lily, gladiolus

Gemstones: Agate, carnelian

Day of the week: Wednesday

Health and well-being for your sign:

You could be susceptible in the area of the body that relates to your sign. Virgo rules the digestive system, the stomach, and the intestines, so be especially attentive to those areas. You're generally health-conscious and cautious, and you strive to keep fit. Being a perfectionist, you're inclined to be germ-phobic. You're a worrier and, when upset or feeling exploited, can be vulnerable to various stress-related ailments.

Careers suited to your sign:

Virgo is service-minded and detail-oriented. Not surprisingly, you excel in careers that include teaching and accounting, and involve organization, analysis, and research. You prefer to work within a company rather than being head honcho, but that doesn't mean you shouldn't aim high. (Remember that missionary Mother Teresa was a Virgo; so is journalist and former governor general Michaëlle Jean.) Unfortunately, you're inclined not to give yourself enough credit for all that you do. Rather than complain to family about being overworked and under-appreciated, you need to speak up and make a point of being noticed by those in high places.

Ruled by Mercury, the planet of intellect, you have a natural curiosity and collect all sorts of interesting facts that can prove highly valuable. With your logical mind and eye for detail, you make an excellent scientist, health-care worker, or journalist. You also work well with your hands and excel at jobs that require dexterity. *See also* Who Was Born in Your Sign and on Your Birthday? (page 82).

LIBRA

September 24–October 23

The Scales

Seventh sign in the zodiac

Strengths to play up: diplomacy, adaptability, intellect

Weaknesses to watch out for: indecisiveness,

self-absorption, fickleness

Behind the name and the symbol of your sign:
The symbol for Libra is the scales. In mythology, Libra depicts the scales held by the goddess of justice. Libra is the only zodiac symbol that's neither a human being nor an animal. Libra is from a Latin word meaning "balance" or "poise"—and those are the qualities identified with people born under the sign of the scale: they strive for harmony, and they balance every pro against every con.

Your element:
The four elements in astrology are air, earth, fire, and water. Your element is air. You circulate easily, exchanging ideas and

mingling with people of all ages and backgrounds. You're all about mental stimulation, not emotional involvement. You form relationships but enjoy simultaneous light-hearted friendships. Intensity is not in your vocabulary.

Your quality:
Three qualities are found in the zodiac: cardinal, fixed, and mutable. You're a cardinal sign. That means you have initiative and take immediate action when required, according to your preferred style.

Your ruling planet and what it means:
Venus, the goddess of love, art, and beauty, gives her name to your ruling planet. Venus is associated with peacefulness and harmony, money and luxuries, shared pleasure, and tranquility.

Personality traits identified with Libra:
Libra starts the second half of the year. Your opposite sign is Aries—the "I" sign. You're the first of the "we" signs—you develop your strengths by relating to others, and you need others in your life. *Balance* is your keyword. You strive for harmony and are the unofficial diplomat of the zodiac. Here are some of the words that describe you. (They're not broken down by positive traits and negative traits because some can fall in either category.)

Adaptable
Affectionate
Ambitious
Appearance-conscious

Approval-seeking

Artistic (you enjoy all the arts, seek out beauty, and decorate tastefully)

Balanced (you're not obsessive about things)

Calm

Changeable

Charitable (you volunteer your time for good causes)

Compromising (you'll give more than 50 percent to achieve an agreement)

Conscientious

Considerate

Cooperative (you deal in compromise)

Courteous (manners are important)

Cultured

Devoted (especially to family and the elderly)

Diplomatic

Discreet

Distracted (you like to daydream)

Easygoing

Elegant

Fair-minded, with a sense of justice

Flirtatious (you use charm to your advantage)

Frivolous

Genteel (you shy away from anything offensive)

Graceful and gracious

Gregarious (you need to circulate and are happiest when you socialize)

Idealistic

Image-conscious (you crave admiration)

Indecisive

Intellectual

Intuitive

Lazy (particularly in your eating habits)

Mature (you dislike pettiness)

Objective and non-judgmental (you understand several view-
points, often including those you don't agree with)

Partnership-oriented (you have an urge to merge)

Peaceable (you will arbitrate, mediate, and strategize to keep
the peace)

Poised

Refined

Responsible (you have a sense of duty to family)

Romantic

Self-absorbed

Self-indulgent

Slow to anger (but given to sudden, short-lived outbursts)

Tactful

Tender

Tense (your struggle to settle disputes can lead to stress)

Tranquil

Urbane and sophisticated

Versatile (you can't handle monotony)

Witty (you have a way with words—verbally and in writing)

Relationships and compatibilities:

You're the most compatible with: Leo, Aquarius, Gemini, and
Sagittarius.

You're the least compatible with: Taurus, Virgo, and Capricorn.

See also the Libra Compatibility Guide on page 161.

Associations with your sign:

Numbers: 6, 8, 9

Colours: Primary colours (red, blue, yellow), violet

Flowers: Violet, daisy, gardenia

Gemstones: Opal, sapphire

Day of the week: Friday

Health and well-being for your sign:

You could be susceptible in the area of the body that relates to your sign. Libra rules the kidneys, the skin, and the buttocks, so be particularly attentive to those areas. Protect your skin not just in the summer but also against the effects of a typical Canadian winter. Everything you do needs to be balanced, and that involves more than diet. Be cautious not to be knocked off balance—physically as well as emotionally.

Careers suited to your sign:

Because of your need for harmony and balance, and the importance of the arts in your life, career choices may range from diplomat to administrator in one of the artistic professions. You could find yourself working behind the scenes for a dance troupe or music ensemble. Partnership arrangements in particular appeal to you. (You generally prefer working with other people than on your own.)

Your tact and composure would be assets in any job in which you deal with the public, and you would do well as a politician, teacher, lawyer, or judge. Many Libras have achieved renown in the arts, among them artist A. Y. Jackson, pianist Glenn Gould, and actor/singer Julie Andrews. Prime Minister Pierre Elliott

Trudeau, another prominent Libra, is remembered for his diplomatic and political achievements. *See also* Who Was Born in Your Sign and on Your Birthday? (page 82).

SCORPIO

October 24–November 22

The Scorpion

Eighth sign in the zodiac

Strengths to play up: intuition, resourcefulness,

determination

Weaknesses to watch out for: jealousy,

extremism, sarcasm

Behind the name and the symbol of your sign:

In Greek mythology, Scorpius, the scorpion, killed Orion, the giant huntsman. (The two constellations were then set at opposite ends of the night sky to avoid further trouble.) Unlike the scorpion's sting, Scorpio's isn't lethal. But it can be biting. The sign, like the scorpion, is intense, subtle, and mysterious. And it will wait patiently—even a lifetime—to get even with its enemies.

Your element:

The four elements in astrology are air, earth, fire, and water. Your element is water. You probe life's deeper mysteries and operate on an emotional rather than intellectual level. Secretive and intuitive, you look for hidden meanings beneath the surface of things. You are persistent, and your personality often has a jealous side.

Your quality:
Three qualities are found in the zodiac: cardinal, fixed, and mutable. You're a fixed sign. That means you don't try to change things. It's open to interpretation, but you're seen as patient, determined, or stubborn.

Your ruling planet and what it means:
Mars and Pluto co-rule Scorpio. Mars, named for the god of war, is the action planet—connected to initiative, aggression, conflict, competitiveness, and drive. Pluto is named for the ruler of the underworld. It is associated with intuition and transformation, and all things mysterious, hidden, subtle, and secretive. (Before Pluto was discovered, Scorpio was ruled by Mars, who remains the co-ruler. Although Pluto has been demoted as a planet, it remains co-ruler.)

Personality traits identified with Scorpio:
The words that best describe Scorpios are *intense*, *intuitive*, and *passionate*. You have an extraordinary depth of feeling—little wonder yours is known as the sign of extremes. And you have a gift for reading people. Here are some of the words that describe you. (They're not broken down by positive traits and negative traits because some can fall in either category.)

Accident prone
Analytical

Compulsive

Cool (you have a calm exterior, yet manage to keep your cool
and seethe at the same time)

Courteous (even when you're angry)

Determined

Distrusting

Easily hurt (you're injured when your pride suffers)

Energetic (your energy—and you have more reserves than
the Alberta tar sands—can be harnessed in a constructive or
destructive manner)

Intense and powerful

Intuitive (reading people is one of your talents)

Jealous

Judgmental

Loyal (many of your friendships are from childhood, even
though circumstances have changed over the years)

Magnetic

Mature (even when young, you're often the kid who helps out
the family)

Motivated

Mysterious (you uncover mysteries and are yourself mysterious)

Not to be taken lightly

Observant

Obsessive

Passionate (you have strong feelings about the things, and the
people, in which you believe)

Perceptive (you can read motives)

Possessive

Powerful

Probing (you go far beneath the surface to solve mysteries)

Protective (you will defend even your most unpopular friends)

Proud (your great pride is both an asset and a liability)

Pushy (you seem to know everyone's pressure points)

Resentful

Resourceful

Responsible

Revenge-hungry

Sarcastic

Skeptical (your favourite expression: "Fool me once, shame on you . . . but fool me twice, shame on me.")

Security-minded (you strive for emotional and financial security)

Seductive

Sensual

Sexy

Stinging (with Scorpio as your sign, a biting tongue is a given)

Striking (a) (appearance-wise; you have intense eyes)

Striking (b) (you will strike out if provoked)

Strong (you're a survivor—you have inner strength plus the strength of your convictions)

Subtle

Supportive

Tenacious

Treacherous (*if* you forgive, you never forget what you forgave)

Unforgiving

Unpredictable

Relationships and compatibilities:

You're the most compatible with: Taurus, Virgo, and Pisces.

You're the least compatible with: Gemini, Leo, and Sagittarius.

See also the Scorpio Compatibility Guide on page 171.

Associations with your sign:

Numbers: 0, 3, 5, 9

Colours: Burgundy, maroon, violet

Flowers: Gerbera, hibiscus

Gemstones: Bloodstone, malachite

Day of the week: Tuesday

Health and well-being for your sign:

You could be susceptible in the area of the body that relates to your sign. Scorpio rules the reproductive system, the sexual organs, and the bowels, so be attentive to those areas in particular. Intense and passionate, you need to introduce the words *flexibility* and *moderation* into your vocabulary. You also need to pay special care to directions, including medical instructions. You can be accident prone—it may be a good idea to carry a flashlight. Lighten up on spicy foods, which often don't agree with your temperament.

Careers suited to your sign:

Scorpios are driven people, and many begin working seriously at an early age. Given your intensity, you take any job seriously—as long as you have an opportunity to shine. Your understanding of human nature and your intuitive strengths draw you to professions that range from psychology to public speaking to investigative reporting. You do well in the entertainment field, both as a writer and a performer. Joni Mitchell, k.d. lang, Diana Krall, Bryan Adams, Neil Young, and Gordon Lightfoot are all Scorpios, as is Margaret Atwood.

With the confidence you exude and your skills at researching information, you also lean to a career in police work and real estate. (Scorpios are said to make good crooks too.) A word of caution: you are protective and possessive about your work, an attitude that may alienate less-than-secure colleagues. *See also* Who Was Born in Your Sign and on Your Birthday? (page 82).

SAGITTARIUS

November 23–December 21

The Archer

Ninth sign in the zodiac

Strengths to play up: thirst for knowledge,

upbeat nature, compassion

Weaknesses to watch out for: outspokenness,

carelessness

Behind the name and the symbol of your sign:
Sagittarius, the archer, is often thought to represent a centaur—half-man and half-horse. (Sagittarius is derived from the Latin word meaning "arrow.") In some legends, the centaur was Chiron, said to have changed himself into a horse in order to escape his jealous wife. Chiron was celebrated for his gentleness and skills as an archer, musician, and physician. Similarly, those born under the sign of Sagittarius are skilled in many areas. They are the zodiac's eternal students—ever on a quest to learn something new before moving on.

Your element:

The four elements in astrology are air, earth, fire, and water. Your element is fire. Fire signs are upbeat, generous, and fired with enthusiasm. They're more aggressive than assertive, but they don't have hidden motives. What you see is what you get.

Your quality:

Three qualities are found in the zodiac: cardinal, fixed, and mutable. You're a mutable sign. That means adaptability is your middle name. You're flexible and willing to change your approach when necessary.

Your ruling planet and what it means:

Jupiter (Jove) was the king of the gods, and the planet named for him is associated with good luck, expansiveness, opportunity, optimism, and risk-taking.

Personality traits identified with Sagittarius:

Jupiter, your ruler, gives you optimism and good luck. The latter quality is helpful, given your tendency to take risks. You're competitive—but a friendly competitor. And you're known as the zodiac's eternal student, ever on a quest for knowledge. Here are some of the words that describe you. (They're not broken down by positive traits and negative traits because some can fall in either category.)

Adventurous

Boastful (you've been known to take credit for other people's accomplishments)

Care-giving (you're the one that relatives call on)

Careless (you misplace stuff)

Curious (you want to learn about everything)

Easygoing and not possessive

Energetic

Ethical

Exaggerating (as a rule of thumb, one can divide your statistics in half)

Forgiving (you truly *do* forgive and forget . . . with occasional exceptions)

Frank

Freedom-loving (but faithful)

Friendly ("Join the party!" is one of your mottos)

Funny (often hilarious)

Generous (you'll give someone the shirt off your back . . . and off my back too)

Groundbreaking

Honest and honourable (there's nothing phony about you)

Idealistic

Impatient

Independent (you have a need to be free of restrictions)

Intellectual (your goal is to acquire wisdom)

Irresponsible (you're well intentioned, but . . .)

Jovial

Lively (you have a zest for life)

Lucky ("Make your own luck" is one of your mottos, but it helps that you're ruled by Jupiter, the opportunities planet)

Mobile (you're perpetually on the go and like to wander from place to place and hop from job to job)

Open-minded

Outspoken (that's an understatement; just ask a Virgo)

Philosophical

Problem-solver (crosswords rather than the problems of the world)

Resilient

Sarcastic (with a biting tongue)

Sports-oriented

Tolerant

Unfocused (your energies can be scattered)

Unrealistic (you make light of serious issues—often turning mountains into molehills)

Upbeat (you bring laughter to a room)

Versatile (you're lost without variety—and activity—in your life)

Volatile (you have a short fuse—but the flame is quick to extinguish)

Relationships and compatibilities:

You're the most compatible with: Aries, Gemini, and Libra.

You're the least compatible with: Taurus, Scorpio, Capricorn, and Pisces.

See also the Sagittarius Compatibility Guide on page 182.

Associations with your sign:

Numbers: 3, 9

Colour: Purple

Flowers: Tulip, carnation, azalea

Gemstones: Topaz, turquoise, amethyst

Day of the week: Thursday

Health and well-being for your sign:

You could be susceptible in the area of the body that relates to your sign. Sagittarius rules the thighs, the hips, and the liver, so be sensitive to those areas. You tend to be restless and even reckless. You need to slow down and exercise more caution. You're sports-inclined, but, again, you tend to take risks. You also tend to have an addictive personality, doing everything on overdrive—overextending yourself and overindulging. Your temper, though it flares up only briefly, can venture into hot-headed territory, playing havoc with your blood pressure.

Careers suited to your sign:

Sagittarius is the zodiac's perpetual student. No sooner do you master one area of expertise than you pursue another area—for the pure joy of learning something new. This tendency may not be practical in the real-life world where one has to earn a living, but a surprising number of Sagittarians have excelled in more than one profession. Because of your interest in learning and your deeply caring nature, the professions most suited to your sign are teacher, health professional, and philosopher. Sagittarians who dislike the sight of blood often turn to law. You're not interested in a power position or a big paycheque, but because of your strong work ethic and your charisma, you advance easily (well, to others it *appears* like it's easy).

A job that includes travel appeals to your interest in seeing new places and learning about different cultures. You're also adept at languages and would make a good translator. But given your blunt approach, don't expect to be named Canada's ambassador to anywhere. Theatre appeals to the ham in you, and you do well in comedy roles. Not surprisingly, the list of career possibilities for Sagittarius is a long one. To sample this variety, look at some famous people born under your sign: author Lucy

Maud Montgomery, actor Christopher Plummer, artist Emily Carr, comedian Woody Allen, sprinter Donovan Bailey, singer Frank Sinatra, and astronaut Roberta Bondar. *See also* Who Was Born in Your Sign and on Your Birthday? (page 82).

CAPRICORN

December 22–January 20
The Goat
Tenth sign in the zodiac
Strengths to play up: perseverance,
ambition, consideration
Weaknesses to watch out for: rigidity,
vindictiveness when hurt

Behind the name and the symbol of your sign:
The constellation Capricorn is in an area of the night sky known as the sea. (Capricornus translates as "sea goat.") The myth behind the name may involve the goat-god Pan, who escaped the monster Typhon by diving into the Nile. The part of Pan that was submerged turned into a fish tail; his top half remained that of a goat. Like the goat, people born under the sign of Capricorn climb steadfastly toward the goal—determined to reach it despite the obstacles and challenges along the way.

Your element:

The four elements in astrology are air, earth, fire, and water. Your element is earth. Your feet are planted firmly on the ground, and you're practical, dependable, and unpretentious. You do what's needed to keep a good reputation. You're goal-oriented—and that goal generally involves financial security.

Your quality:

Three qualities are found in the zodiac: cardinal, fixed, and mutable. You're a cardinal sign. That means you have initiative and take immediate action when required, according to your preferred style.

Your ruling planet and what it means:

Saturn, your ruling planet, is named for the god who was Zeus's father. Saturn is associated with ambition and diligence, responsibility, the conscience, and restriction.

Personality traits identified with Capricorn:

Capricorns are said to grow younger as they grow older. As a child, you're already mature—you take on responsibilities at an early age. Your ambitious climb continues throughout your life, but you become more relaxed and less rigid as the journey continues. Here are some of the words that describe you. (They're not broken down by positive traits and negative traits because some can fall in either category.)

Achieving (you tackle what interests you, then advance toward your goal)

Ambitious (this is the adjective that consistently accompanies
   your sign)
Attractive (you have a stately, dignified appearance, and you
   may begin to look more youthful as you age)
Bossy
Brave
Business-oriented
Calculated
Cautious (you're not impulsive)
Challenge-seeking
Condescending
Considerate
Courteous (yes, you have excellent manners)
Diligent
Disciplined
Fatalistic
Focused
Funny (you have a wry sense of humour)
Goal-oriented
Grouchy
Impatient
Industrious
Inhibited
Nimble (yet not graceful; you can, in fact, be clumsy)
Oblivious (your mind is made up, and you really don't fuss
   over what others think)
Organized (you manage things in all areas—home, career, rela-
   tionships; you're the one who takes charge in an emergency)
Overbearing
Patient (yes, one of your qualities is impatience too)

Persevering (you think big, and you never give up)

Pessimistic (you need a positive environment)

Pleasure-loving (just because you work hard doesn't mean you don't enjoy life)

Refined and refining (your manners are excellent; as well, you excel at taking ideas and finessing them)

Relentless

Resourceful

Rigid (yours is the sign of restriction and consolidation)

Selective (you have a few close, carefully chosen friends)

Solid (as a rock)

Vindictive (when hurt)

Relationships and compatibilities:

You're the most compatible with: Leo, Capricorn, and Aquarius.

You're the least compatible with: Aries, Libra, and Sagittarius.

See also the Capricorn Compatibility Guide on page 194.

Associations with your sign:

Numbers: 3, 7, 8, 9

Colours: Brown, silver, indigo

Flowers: Carnation, poinsettia

Gemstones: Ruby, onyx

Day of the week: Saturday

Health and well-being for your sign:

You could be susceptible in the area of the body that relates to your sign. Capricorn rules the knees, joints, bones, and skin, so be particularly attentive to those areas. Given the long hours you devote to work, exercise and relaxation should be at the top of your priority list. Apply your disciplined approach to a fitness regime. Your competitive nature necessitates that you keep your energy level high, so don't shortchange yourself on sleep and relaxation, and watch that your diet is properly balanced.

Careers suited to your sign:
Yours is the sign of ambition. Not surprisingly, occupations that suit you often involve money. You may find yourself working in finance, economics, banking, or real estate. You are also drawn to teaching, and may advance to the position of principal. Because of your talent as a debater, you make an excellent politician. (Two of Canada's prime ministers—Sir John A. Macdonald and Jean Chrétien—not only share a sign but a birthday, January 11.) You enjoy any kind of work that involves long-term planning—you have a need to organize. Public service appeals to you, as does entertaining (you have a dry wit) and work involving your hands.

But everything comes back to your determination, drive, and ambition, and the career possibilities are wide open, as you'll see from these individuals who rose to the top of their game: Patrick Chan (figure skater), Stephen Hawking (physicist), Stephen Leacock (humorist), Jim Carrey (comedian/actor), and Mary Tyler Moore (actor). *See also* Who Was Born in Your Sign and on Your Birthday? (page 82).

AQUARIUS

January 21–February 19
The Water Bearer
Eleventh sign in the zodiac
Strengths to play up: idealism, courtesy, inventiveness
Weaknesses to watch out for: aloofness,
crankiness, bluntness

Behind the name and the symbol of your sign:
In Greek mythology, Aquarius was the cup bearer to the gods.
It is said that Aquarius poured water from the heavens, inun-
dating the earth. Aquarius appears in the night sky near Pisces
and other water constellations. People born under this sign are
inventive, individualistic, and great humanitarians—they carry
the cup of human kindness and pour generously from it.

Your element:
The four elements in astrology are air, earth, fire, and water.
Your element is air. You circulate easily, exchanging ideas and
mingling with people of all ages and backgrounds. You're all

about mental stimulation, not emotional involvement. You form relationships but enjoy simultaneous light-hearted friendships. Intensity is not in your vocabulary.

Your quality:

Three qualities are found in the zodiac: cardinal, fixed, and mutable. You're a fixed sign. That means you don't try to change things. It's open to interpretation, but you're seen as patient, determined, or stubborn.

Your ruling planet and what it means:

Uranus, the powerful planet named for the husband of Gaia (Mother Earth in Greek mythology), rules independence and is connected with innovation, change, independence and freedom, and individuality.

Personality traits identified with Aquarius:

Aquarius is known as "the reformer." You champion causes. You're also a groundbreaker. Along with *humanitarian*, the adjective that most accompanies the name of your sign is *eccentric*, and you march to your own drummer. Here are some of the words that describe you. (They're not broken down by positive traits and negative traits because some can fall in either category.)

Active and lively
Aloof (sometimes you can be hard to get close to . . . though
  sometimes you're warm)
Analytical
Attractive

Bright (you're a very quick study)

Compassionate

Contemplative (you're more a thinker than a doer)

Cranky

Eccentric

Enigmatic (aloof/warm, exhibitionist/shy, outgoing/retiring)

Exhibitionist . . . or shy (there's no middle ground in this area)

Experimental (you find it hard to do anything routine)

Fair (you want for others what you want for yourself)

Frank, outspoken

Freedom-loving

Humanitarian (some think you care more for humanity as a
   whole than for individuals)

Idealistic

Imaginative

Independent (when you require it, you demand independence)

Individualistic

Innovative

Inventive

Logical

Nonconforming

Non-controlling (you're happy to delegate jobs rather than taking control of everything)

Objective (you try to stay detached and won't take sides based
   on friendship, yet you remain concerned)

Outgoing (there are two types of Aquarius: retiring is the other)

Outspoken

Progressive

Quirky

Retiring (there are two types of Aquarius; outgoing is the other)

Rude (when angered, you're a master at the silent treatment)

Selfless

Set in ways (your opinions are firmly fixed)

Shy . . . or exhibitionist (there's no middle ground in this area)

Solitude-seeking (you need quiet time)

Tactless

Take-charge (you're quick to respond in an emergency)

Technical (you keep up with changes, regardless of your age)

Trustworthy

Unconventional

Warm (but sometimes aloof)

Relationships and compatibilities:

You're the most compatible with: Libra, Aquarius, Sagittarius, and Capricorn.

You're the least compatible with: Taurus, Virgo, and Scorpio.

See also the Aquarius Compatibility Guide on page 205.

Associations with your sign:

Numbers: 2, 4, 8

Colours: Violet, green, electric blue

Flowers: Orchid, bird of paradise

Gemstones: Garnet, sapphire

Day of the week: Saturday

Health and well-being for your sign:

You could be susceptible in the area of the body that relates to your sign. Aquarius rules the ankles and the circulatory system, so be both cautious (wear sensible shoes) and proactive. Keep your blood flowing through proper exercise, and improve your eating habits (garlic is said to be good for the circulation). Uranus, which rules your sign, is the planet of nervous tension, so try to tune out when the stress level peaks. You tend to exhaust yourself when working on a project. Balance things out with rest and relaxation.

Careers suited to your sign:

Aquarius and routine work do not often find themselves in the same sentence. You are an individualist and need something that includes a large measure of creativity, independence, inventiveness (Aquarius is the sign of the inventor), and originality. You bring immense energy to projects that appeal to you but need time to recharge in between. Many Aquarians excel in theatre, movies, and literature. You're the zodiac's humanitarian. Even if you don't work for a specific cause or charity, you bring your idealism to the job—fighting for better conditions and pay. With your way with words, you do well in professions involving writing, including journalism, biographical and historical writing, and editing. You also keep up with technology and are well-suited to jobs involving computers, cameras, and scientific study.

You don't like show-offs and have no use for phonies or office politics. Many Aquarians are happy working on their own, even in an office setting. Two other professions associated with your sign are pilot (you're an air sign, after all) and comic (you're a particularly good mimic). And regardless of their chosen careers, Aquarians will work for the betterment of others. Little wonder that well-known water bearers include Paul Newman and Oprah Winfrey. *See also* Who Was Born in Your Sign and on Your Birthday? (page 82).

PISCES

February 20–March 20

The Fishes

Twelfth sign in the zodiac

Strengths to play up: imagination, creativity, compassion

Weaknesses to watch out for: melancholy, laziness,
being out of touch with reality

Behind the name and the symbol of your sign:

In Greek mythology, Pisces represents the fish into which the goddess Aphrodite (Venus) and her son Eros (Cupid) transformed themselves to escape the fire god. To make sure they didn't lose each other as they swam to safety, their tails were tied with a cord. Like the fish, people born under the sign of Pisces live beneath the surface. They probe for the hidden and the mysterious, and live in a fluid world of emotion and creativity.

Your element:

The four elements in astrology are air, earth, fire, and water. Your element is water. You probe life's deeper mysteries and operate on an emotional rather than intellectual level. Secretive and intuitive, you look for hidden meanings beneath the surface of things. You are persistent, and your personality often has a jealous side.

Your quality:

Three qualities are found in the zodiac: cardinal, fixed, and mutable. You're a mutable sign. That means adaptability is your middle name. You're flexible and willing to change your approach when necessary.

Your ruling planet and what it means:

Neptune, the most spiritual planet, is named for the god of the sea. It is associated with imagination, creativity, transformation, deception, and illusion.

Personality traits identified with Pisces:

Pisces' theme is "Imagine this!" You do best when your imagination is allowed—or permits itself—to wander. *Empathetic* is another adjective that's frequently used for those born under your sign. Here are some of the words that describe you. (They're not broken down by positive traits and negative traits because some can fall in either category.)

Absent-minded
Adaptable (you adapt to different surroundings)
Artistic
Charitable (with your rose-coloured glasses, you see the best in
  others)
Charming

Compassionate (your ruling planet, Neptune, is responsible for
that quality, and you're the zodiac's best Samaritan)

Creative (you survive through your creativity)

Curious (you enjoy experiencing new things)

Dreamy

Easily wounded

Easygoing

Ecological

Emotional (you're the most emotional of the signs)

Empathetic (your concern for others is deep—you're the most
empathetic of the signs)

Escapist

Ethereal (not surprising, with your water influence)

Fidgety

Gentle

Gullible

Imaginative

Impractical

Inconsistent (your sign shows two fish tied together and swimming in opposite directions)

Indiscreet (you tend to blab)

Insecure (you often tend to cling)

Instinctive

Intuitive—probing

Malleable (you're known to take on other people's qualities)

Melancholy

Passive (you're more a spectator than a participant)

Patient

Peace-loving

Perceptive

Prophetic

Psychic

Rebellious (against the norm)

Secretive

Self-sacrificing

Sensitive (you're the most sensitive sign in the zodiac)

Shy

Solitude-seeking (you require private time)

Spiritual

Subtle (sometimes so subtle that your message doesn't get across)

Tenacious (about your spirituality)

Thoughtful (you like to spoil people with little gifts; and you like to be spoiled with luxurious ones)

Trusting

Uncompetitive

Unrealistic (you often believe what you want to)

Unreliable

Vague

Relationships and compatibilities:

You're the most compatible with: Virgo, Taurus, Scorpio, and Cancer.

You're the least compatible with: Aries, Gemini, Leo, and Sagittarius.

See also the Pisces Compatibility Guide on page 217.

Associations with your sign:

Numbers: 5, 6, 8

Colours: Sea green, lilac, pink

Flowers: Violet, zinnia

Gemstones: Amethyst
Day of the week: Thursday

Health and well-being for your sign:

You could be susceptible in the area of the body that relates to your sign. Be particularly attentive to the feet and the immune system, which Pisces rules. Pisces is so empathetic that you're known to take on the ailments of others. Being acutely sensitive and impressionable, it's easy to slip into bad habits and despondency. Sunshine is important during the long Canadian winter. You're not a sporty sign (other than water-related sports), but you do need exercise. A large number of Pisceans are vegetarians—so be sure you're getting enough protein and iron.

Careers suited to your sign:

Pisces is the sign of the poet, and you bring a poetic sensibility to your work. Yes, you excel in a job that involves the arts. You're interested in human nature and you probe what happens behind the scenes. A job in psychology, the occult, research, and even police work would appeal to you.

Despite your moodiness, you add optimism to your work and enjoy dealing with the public. But most of all you're a caregiver and are drawn to social work and the medical profession in general (including veterinary work, given your attachment to animals). You want a meaningful job, but often you're the one who makes it meaningful. As an example, the most thoughtful waiters and bartenders are often Pisces. As well, your sign is connected with religion, and regardless of your own beliefs you could find yourself working for a religious organization. Most of all, you add imagination, and compassion, to whatever you take on. It is hardly surprising that Elizabeth Taylor, who will be remembered not only for her acting but also for her style and great kindness, was born under the sign of the fishes. *See also* Who Was Born in Your Sign and on Your Birthday? (page 82).

WHO WAS BORN
IN YOUR SIGN AND ON
YOUR BIRTHDAY?

The following lists include famous (and some infamous) individuals born on each day of the year. As explained in the introduction, over the years the dates for each sign have shifted. Some names appearing at the cusp (the beginning or end) of a sign may belong to the preceding or following sign.

Aries
March 21–April 20

March 21, 1962, actor Matthew Broderick

March 22, 1931, actor William Shatner

March 23, 1904, actor Joan Crawford

March 24, 1976, football player Peyton Manning

March 25, 1947, singer/songwriter Elton John

March 26, 1950, actor Martin Short

March 27, 1962, singer/songwriter Jann Arden

March 28, 1951, dancer Karen Kain

March 29, 1964, supermodel Elle Macpherson

March 30, 1968, singer Céline Dion

March 31, 1928, hockey player Gordie Howe

April 1, 1961, singer Susan Boyle

April 2, 1914, actor Alec Guinness

April 3, 1961, actor Eddie Murphy

April 4, 1956, dancer Evelyn Hart

April 5, 1908, actor Bette Davis

April 6, 1866, folk hero Butch Cassidy

April 7, 1964, actor Russell Crowe

April 8, 1892, actor Mary Pickford

April 9, 1971, racing driver Jacques Villeneuve

April 10, 1932, actor Omar Sharif

April 11, 1932, actor Joel Grey

April 12, 1947, TV host David Letterman

April 13, 1906, playwright Samuel Beckett

April 14, 1996, actor Abigail Breslin

April 15, 1990, actor Emma Watson

April 16, 1927, Pope Benedict XVI

April 17, 1984, Soviet leader Nikita Khrushchev

April 18, 1963, actor Eric McCormack

April 19, 1981, actor Hayden Christensen

April 20, 1949, figure skater Toller Cranston

Taurus
April 21–May 21

April 21, 1977, figure skater Jamie Salé

April 22, 1937, actor Jack Nicholson

April 23, 1564, playwright William Shakespeare

April 24, 1942, singer/actor Barbra Streisand

April 25, 1940, actor Al Pacino

April 26, 1785, artist John James Audubon

April 27, 1791, inventor Samuel Morse

April 28, 1908, humanitarian Oscar Schindler

April 29, 1970, tennis player André Agassi

April 30, 1959, Prime Minister Stephen Harper

May 1, 1939, singer/songwriter Judy Collins

May 2, 1975, soccer player David Beckham

May 3, 1947, magician Doug Henning

May 4, 1929, actor Audrey Hepburn

May 5, 1818, revolutionary Karl Marx

May 6, 1972, hockey player Martin Brodeur

May 7, 1933, football player Johnny Unitas

May 8, 1949, author Peter Benchley

May 9, 1928, figure skater Barbara Ann Scott

May 10, 1960, singer/songwriter Paul "Bono" Hewson

May 11, 1943, skier Nancy Greene

May 12, 1921, author Farley Mowat

May 13, 1950, singer/songwriter Stevie Wonder

May 14, 1969, actor Cate Blanchette

May 15, 1953, baseball player George Brett

May 16, 1966, singer Janet Jackson

May 17, 1989, figure skater Tessa Virtue

May 18, 1970, actor Tina Fey

May 19, 1941, writer/movie director Nora Ephron

May 20, 1949, actor Dave Thomas

May 21, 1904, musician Fats Waller

Gemini
May 22–June 21

May 22, 1859, author Sir Arthur Conan Doyle

May 23, 1933, actor Joan Collins

May 24, 1941, singer/songwriter Bob Dylan

May 25, 1963, actor Mike Myers

May 26, 1907, actor John Wayne

May 27, 1945, singer/songwriter Bruce Cockburn

May 28, 1944, singer/songwriter Rita MacNeil

May 29, 1917, U.S. president John F. Kennedy

May 30, 1909, bandleader Benny Goodman

May 31, 1950, Beatle George Harrison

June 1, 1974, singer/songwriter Alanis Morissette

June 2, 1924, author/activist June Callwood

June 3, 1926, actor Colleen Dewhurst

June 4, 1975, actor Angelina Jolie

June 5, 1971, actor Mark Wahlberg

June 6, 1799, author Alexander Pushkin

June 7, 1988, actor Michael Cera

June 8, 1927, architect Frank Lloyd Wright

June 9, 1961, actor Michael J. Fox

June 10, 1922, singer/actor Judy Garland

June 11, 1910, undersea explorer Jacques Cousteau

June 12, 1959, actor Scott Thompson

June 13, 1865, poet William Butler Yeats

June 14, 1946, magnate Donald Trump

June 15, 1964, actor Courteney Cox

June 16, 1938, author Joyce Carol Oates

June 17, 1980, tennis player Venus Williams

June 18, 1966, figure skater Kurt Browning

June 19, 1902, bandleader Guy Lombardo

June 20, 1945, singer Anne Murray

June 21, 1982, Prince William, Duke of Cambridge

Cancer
June 22–July 22

June 22, 1949, actor Meryl Streep
June 23, 1927, choreographer Bob Fosse
June 24, 1958, Quebec premier Jean Charest
June 25, 1946, General Roméo Dallaire
June 26, 1974, baseball player Derek Jeter
June 27, 1880, author/activist Helen Keller
June 28, 1948, actor Kathy Bates
June 29, 1900, author Antoine de Saint-Exupéry
June 30, 1917, singer/actor Lena Horne
July 1, 1952, actor Dan Aykroyd
July 2, 1986, actor Lindsay Lohan
July 3, 1962, actor Tom Cruise
July 4, 1927, playwright Neil Simon
July 5, 1943, singer/songwriter Robbie Robertson
July 6, 1935, the Dalai Lama
July 7, 1940, Beatle Ringo Starr
July 8, 1949, celebrity chef Wolfgang Puck
July 9, 1956, actor Tom Hanks
July 10, 1931, author Alice Munro
July 11, 1949, guitarist Liona Boyd
July 12, 1930, actor Gordon Pinsent
July 13, 1942, actor Harrison Ford
July 14, 1918, movie director Ingmar Bergman
July 15, 1606, artist Rembrandt van Rijn
July 16, 1967, actor Will Ferrell
July 17, 1935, actor Donald Sutherland
July 18, 1950, politician Jack Layton

July 19, 1834, artist Edgar Degas

July 20, 1971, actor Sandra Oh

July 21, 1926, movie director Norman Jewison

July 22, 1940, TV host Alex Trebek

Leo
July 23–August 22

July 23, 1989, actor Daniel Radcliffe

July 24, 1969, singer/actor Jennifer Lopez

July 25, 1930, opera singer Maureen Forrester

July 26, 1964, actor Sandra Bullock

July 27, 1922, producer Norman Lear

July 28, 1958, humanitarian/athlete Terry Fox

July 29, 1938, journalist Peter Jennings

July 30, 1941, singer/songwriter Paul Anka

July 31, 1965, author J. K. Rowling

August 1, 1936, fashion designer Yves Saint Laurent

August 2, 1932, actor Peter O'Toole

August 3, 1951, hockey player Marcel Dionne

August 4, 1921, hockey player Maurice (Rocket) Richard

August 5, 1877, artist Tom Thomson

August 6, 1911, actor Lucille Ball

August 7, 1987, hockey player Sidney Crosby

August 8, 1937, actor Dustin Hoffman

August 9, 1964, hockey player Brett Hull

August 10, 1902, actor Norma Shearer

August 11, 1922, author Mavis Gallant

August 12, 1979, speed skater Cindy Klassen

August 13, 1926, Cuban leader Fidel Castro

August 14, 1945, actor/author Steve Martin

August 15, 1925, pianist/composer Oscar Peterson

August 16, 1954, movie director James Cameron

August 17, 1943, actor Robert De Niro

August 18, 1936, actor Robert Redford

August 19, 1946, U.S. president Bill Clinton

August 20, 1974, actor Amy Adams

August 21, 1956, actor Kim Cattrall

August 22, 1862, composer Claude Debussy

Virgo
August 23–September 23

August 23, 1912, actor Gene Kelly

August 24, 1920, artist Alex Colville

August 25, 1954, singer/songwriter Elvis Costello

August 26, 1910, Mother Teresa

August 27, 1969, actor Chandra Wilson

August 28, 1965, singer/songwriter Shania Twain

August 29, 1986, actor Lea Michele

August 30, 1930, investor Warren Buffett

August 31, 1931, hockey player Jean Béliveau

September 1, 1939, actor Lily Tomlin

September 2, 1964, actor Keanu Reeves

September 3, 1810, artist Paul Kane

September 4, 1981, singer Beyoncé Knowles

September 5, 1916, comedian Frank Shuster

September 6, 1957, journalist/governor general Michaëlle Jean

September 7, 1533, Queen Elizabeth I

September 8, 1937, journalist Barbara Frum

September 9, 1975, singer Michael Bublé

September 10, 1960, actor Colin Firth

September 11, 1885, author D. H. Lawrence

September 12, 1943, author Michael Ondaatje

September 13, 1941, singer David Clayton-Thomas

September 14, 1983, singer Amy Winehouse

September 15, 1984, Prince Harry

September 16, 1982, actor Alexis Bledel

September 17, 1935, author Ken Kesey

September 18, 1895, Prime Minister John Diefenbaker

September 19, 1948, actor Jeremy Irons

September 20, 1951, hockey player Guy Lafleur

September 21, 1934, singer/songwriter Leonard Cohen

September 22, 1958, opera singer Andrea Bocelli

September 23, 1930, musician Ray Charles

Libra
September 24–October 23

September 24, 1962, actor/movie director Nia Vardalos

September 25, 1932, pianist Glenn Gould

September 26, 1898, composer George Gershwin

September 27, 1984, singer/songwriter Avril Lavigne

September 28, 1955, politician Stéphane Dion

September 29, 1547, author Miguel de Cervantes

September 30, 1939, actor Len Cariou

October 1, 1935, actor/singer Julie Andrews

October 2, 1869, Indian leader Mahatma Gandhi

October 3, 1882, artist A.Y. Jackson

October 4, 1946, actor Susan Sarandon

October 5, 1965, hockey player Mario Lemieux

October 6, 1866, inventor Reginald Fessenden

October 7, 1923, artist Jean-Paul Riopelle

October 8, 1970, actor Matt Damon

October 9, 1940, Beatle John Lennon

October 10, 1813, composer Giuseppe Verdi

October 11, 1925, author Elmore Leonard

October 12, 1935, opera singer Luciano Pavarotti

October 13, 1941, singer/songwriter Paul Simon

October 14, 1939, fashion designer Ralph Lauren

October 15, 1959, Sarah Ferguson, Duchess of York

October 16, 1854, author Oscar Wilde

October 17, 1969, comedian Rick Mercer

October 18, 1919, Prime Minister Pierre Elliott Trudeau

October 19, 1937, swimmer Marilyn Bell

October 20, 1873, feminist Nellie McClung

October 21, 1833, Nobel Prize founder/inventor Alfred Nobel

October 22, 1844, Métis leader Louis Riel

October 23, 1885, artist Lawren Harris

Scorpio
October 24–November 22

October 24, 1947, actor Kevin Kline

October 25, 1881, artist Pablo Picasso

October 26, 1947, Secretary of State Hillary Clinton

October 27, 1914, poet Dylan Thomas

October 28, 1967, actor Julia Roberts

October 29, 1953, hockey player Denis Potvin

October 30, 1885, poet Ezra Pound

October 31, 1950, actor John Candy

November 1, 1972, actor Toni Collette

November 2, 1961, singer/songwriter k.d. lang

November 3, 1953, actor Kate Capshaw

November 4, 1960, comedian Kathy Griffin

November 5, 1959, singer/songwriter Bryan Adams

November 6, 1946, actor Sally Field

November 7, 1943, singer/songwriter Joni Mitchell

November 8, 1966, chef Gordon Ramsay

November 9, 1988, actor Nikki Blonsky

November 10, 1925, actor Richard Burton

November 11, 1974, actor Leonardo DiCaprio

November 12, 1945, singer/songwriter Neil Young

November 13, 1955, actor Whoopi Goldberg

November 14, 1954, rower Silken Laumann

November 15, 1932, singer Petula Clark

November 16, 1964, pianist/singer Diana Krall

November 17, 1938, singer/songwriter Gordon Lightfoot

November 18, 1939, author Margaret Atwood

November 19, 1942, fashion designer Calvin Klein

November 20, 1841, Prime Minister Wilfrid Laurier

November 21, 1945, actor Goldie Hawn

November 22, 1974, figure skater David Pelletier

Sagittarius
November 23–December 21

November 23, 1992, singer Miley Cyrus

November 24, 1978, actor Katherine Heigl

November 25, 1968, actor/musician Jill Hennessy

November 26, 1939, singer Tina Turner

November 27, 1942, musician Jimi Hendrix

November 28, 1962, TV anchor Jon Stewart

November 29, 1955, actor Howie Mandel

November 30, 1874, author Lucy Maud Montgomery

December 1, 1935, actor/movie director Woody Allen

December 2, 1978, singer/songwriter Nelly Furtado

December 3, 1968, actor Brendan Fraser

December 4, 1945, astronaut Roberta Bondar

December 5, 1968, comedian Margaret Cho

December 6, 1967, movie director Judd Apatow

December 7, 1932, actor Ellen Burstyn

December 8, 1953, actor Kim Basinger

December 9, 1934, actor Judi Dench

December 10, 1960, actor/director Kenneth Branagh

December 11, 1838, brewer John Labatt

December 12, 1915, singer/actor Frank Sinatra

December 13, 1929, actor Christopher Plummer

December 14, 1895, England's King George VI

December 15, 1832, architect Gustave Eiffel

December 16, 1967, sprinter Donovan Bailey

December 17, 1946, actor Eugene Levy

December 18, 1980, singer/actor Christina Aguilera

December 19, 1980, actor Jake Gyllenhaal

December 20, 1946, paranormal Uri Geller
December 21, 1966, actor Kiefer Sutherland

Capricorn
December 22–January 20

December 22, 1962, actor Ralph Fiennes
December 23, 1943, actor Harry Shearer
December 24, 1971, singer Ricky Martin
December 25, 1899, actor Humphrey Bogart
December 26, 1956, author David Sedaris
December 27, 1822, inventor Louis Pasteur
December 28, 1763, brewer John Molson
December 29, 1936, actor Mary Tyler Moore
December 30, 1869, author Stephen Leacock
December 31, 1990, figure skater Patrick Chan
January 1, 1919, author J. D. Salinger
January 2, 1920, author Isaac Asimov
January 3, 1939, hockey player Bobby Hull
January 4, 1937, opera singer Grace Bumbry
January 5, 1642, astronomer Sir Isaac Newton
January 6, 1883, author Kahlil Gibran
January 7, 1964, actor Nicolas Cage
January 8, 1935, singer/actor Elvis Presley
January 9, 1982, Catherine, Duchess of Cambridge
January 10, 1943, singer/songwriter Jim Croce
January 11, 1815, Prime Minister John A. Macdonald
January 12, 1930, hockey player Tim Horton
January 13, 1986, figure skater Joannie Rochette

January 14, 1956, opera singer Ben Heppner

January 15, 1947, actor Andrea Martin

January 16, 1974, supermodel/singer Kate Moss

January 17, 1962, comedian/actor Jim Carrey

January 18, 1961, hockey player Mark Messier

January 19, 1946, singer/songwriter Dolly Parton

January 20, 1946, movie director David Lynch

Aquarius
January 21–February 19

January 21, 1941, opera singer Placido Domingo

January 22, 1957, hockey player Mike Bossy

January 23, 1957, Princess Caroline of Monaco

January 24, 1949, actor John Belushi

January 25, 1981, singer/songwriter Alicia Keys

January 26, 1961, hockey player Wayne Gretzky

January 27, 1931, author Mordecai Richler

January 28, 1968, singer/songwriter Sarah McLachlan

January 29, 1954, TV host Oprah Winfrey

January 30, 1937, actor Vanessa Redgrave

January 31, 1964, diver Sylvie Bernier

February 1, 1882, Prime Minister Louis St. Laurent

February 2, 1882, author James Joyce

February 3, 1907, author James Michener

February 4, 1913, activist Rosa Parks

February 5, 1934, broadcaster Don Cherry

February 6, 1895, baseball player Babe Ruth

February 7, 1812, author Charles Dickens

February 8, 1994, singer Nikki Yanofsky
February 9, 1936, singer/songwriter Stompin' Tom Connors
February 10, 1939, journalist/governor general
  Adrienne Clarkson
February 11, 1926, actor Leslie Nielsen
February 12, 1938, author Judy Blume
February 13, 1933, actor Kim Novak
February 14, 1946, actor/dancer Gregory Hines
February 15, 1954, cartoonist Matt Groening
February 16, 1953, hockey player Lanny McDonald
February 17, 1938, actor Martha Henry
February 18, 1954, actor John Travolta
February 19, 1473, astronomer Nicolas Copernicus

Pisces
February 20–March 20

February 20, 1941, singer/songwriter Buffy Sainte-Marie
February 21, 1987, actor Ellen Page
February 22, 1963, golfer Vijay Singh
February 23, 1949, astronaut Marc Garneau
February 24, 1975, fiddler Ashley MacIsaac
February 25, 1943, Beatle George Harrison
February 26, 1928, singer Monique Leyrac
February 27, 1932, actor Elizabeth Taylor
February 28, 1929, architect Frank Gehry
February 29, 1916, singer Dinah Shore
March 1, 1994, singer Justin Bieber
March 2, 1935, actor Al Waxman

March 3, 1890, humanitarian Norman Bethune

March 4, 1954, actor Catherine O'Hara

March 5, 1958, singer/songwriter Andy Gibb

March 6, 1806, poet Elizabeth Barrett Browning

March 7, 1875, composer Maurice Ravel

March 8, 1923, actor/dancer Cyd Charisse

March 9, 1976, TV host Ben Mulroney

March 10, 1947, Prime Minister Kim Campbell

March 11, 1931, media magnate Rupert Murdoch

March 12, 1946, singer/actor Liza Minnelli

March 13, 1914, author W. O. Mitchell

March 14, 1933, actor Michael Caine

March 15, 1943, film director David Cronenberg

March 16, 1951, actor Kate Nelligan

March 17, 1938, dancer Rudolf Nureyev

March 18, 1970, actor Queen Latifah

March 19, 1947, actor Glenn Close

March 20, 1939, Prime Minister Brian Mulroney

March 20, 1948, hockey player Bobby Orr

PART TWO

COMPATIBILITY
GUIDE FOR
EVERY MATCH

ARIES
COMPATIBILITY GUIDE

The following descriptions, based on your Sun sign, provide a broad picture of how you relate to members of all twelve signs (including your own) in the different spheres of life.

Aries and Aries

Compatibility rating: **** (6 out of 10)**
You are two strong people who understand each other. Both of you are self-confident, so neither is likely to cramp the other's style. You excel in your chosen field. While supportive and not possessive, you are highly competitive. And although a competition between two Aries brings out the best in each person, it doesn't take much for a friendly battle to turn fierce. In romance, Aries is a deeply committed partner. But there's a stumbling block: because Aries is self-absorbed, each partner can be oblivious to what is going on in the other's life. If a relationship is in trouble, you may be the last to know. Aries–Aries relatives tend to vie for the spotlight in family situations. Sometimes the results can be highly entertaining, but often this competition leads to friction . . . and then fireworks. Aries who work together need to have their roles and responsibilities clearly defined, and each Aries needs to be in charge of something. The key to avoiding a battle over turf is for each Aries to have a position of authority plus a very well-massaged ego. *Celebrity couple: Sarah Jessica Parker (March 25, 1965) and Matthew Broderick (March 21, 1962).*

Aries and Taurus

Compatibility rating: **** (6 out of 10)**

Because Aries and Taurus are neighbouring signs—Taurus follows Aries—the odds are that you share some planetary influences and have some common qualities. But judging by Sun signs alone, you are, in many ways, opposites. Depending on circumstances, you may complement each other. On the other hand, you may find each other's traits difficult to deal with. Aries is impulsive, while Taurus is slow but steady. Aries is blunt and has a thick skin, while Taurus is ultra-sensitive and doesn't deal well with criticism. You look at the forest, and Taurus sees the trees. In a romantic relationship, good-natured Taurus is comfortable letting Aries enjoy the spotlight. Taurus is a naturally sociable sign, and there can be tense domestic situations when Taurus, rather than Aries, initiates a family-related event. In the career environment, Aries is generally the independent, bold, decisive leader of the team. Taurus adds a creative touch and, as the principal money sign, makes sure that Aries' budgets are not out of control. Job-wise, this can be a successful pairing. *Celebrity couples: Spencer Tracy (April 5, 1900) and Katharine Hepburn (May 12, 1907); Victoria Beckham (April 17, 1974) and David Beckham (May 2, 1975); Alison Hewson (March 23, 1961) and Bono (May 10, 1960).*

Aries and Gemini

Compatibility rating: ****** (8 out of 10)**

Aries and Gemini have a great deal in common—both are communicators, neither one stands still for very long, and both enjoy adventure. As a couple or a team, you complement and have the potential to bring out the best in each other. You're ruled by action-oriented Mars, planet of excitement. Gemini is ruled by Mercury, renowned for wit and charm. Your motto is "I do"; and Gemini thinks rather than initiates things. In a romantic, domestic, or professional relationship, each one provides what the other needs without stealing any thunder from the other. You're both impulsive and, as the two of you circulate, you make the decisions and Gemini provides the entertainment. Each of you is an independent spirit, rarely feeling threatened. The two signs thrive on each other's optimism and provide an upbeat mood to family events. In a working relationship, you're self-centred. But Gemini, the most adaptable of the signs, is willing to let you enjoy centre stage as long as he or she can handle the communications and PR. *Celebrity couple: Mary Pickford (April 8, 1892) and Douglas Fairbanks (May 23, 1883).*

Aries and Cancer

Compatibility rating: ***** (5 out of 10)
Both Aries and Cancer are cardinal signs, meaning that they're active players, not spectators, in the game of life. But you are independent, while Cancer is insecure and possessive. You seek adventure, while Cancer's sign is related to home and familiarity. You're a pioneer—keen to try something new. Cancer, in contrast, is conservative and a creature of habit. But there are certain qualities that make this a potentially harmonious pairing. Cancer, in fact, is the most varied of the signs. While

other signs include an unusually large percentage of singers or athletes or authors, Cancer includes such an assortment of notables as Pamela Anderson, the Dalai Lama, Alice Munro, Alex Trebek, and Rembrandt! In a romantic pairing, Cancer has to be willing to defer to your independence, while Aries has to be more involved in family matters. On the domestic front, no one is more supportive than Cancer. Of course, you may confuse supportive with clingy or stifling. At work, Cancer is happy to leave the leadership role to you. In turn, you need to accept that Cancer avoids risks and will try to rein in your reckless tendencies. *Celebrity couple: Shirley Douglas (April 2, 1934) and Donald Sutherland (July 17, 1935).*

Aries and Leo

Compatibility rating: ***** (7 out of 10)**
Both you and Leo are competitive, congenial, and generous. Leo, who rules the theatre, is the drama king, or queen, of the zodiac. You are an achiever—or, more accurately, an overachiever. You like the limelight but don't always require an audience. Both signs are affectionate, and both adore parties and good food. But you are tolerant and idealistic, while Leo can be interfering. In a romantic relationship, you're both loyal and enthusiastic participants. Each one will defend the other. Both signs are extravagant with money and share the philosophy that one can always earn more. Neither holds a grudge for long. The difficulty this pairing faces lies in Leo's domination and your quest for independence. These needs don't necessarily compete, but they can present a definite conflict that may

prove problematic in domestic as well as professional environ-
ments. In family as well as professional relationships, Aries
and Leo do best when each of the two has a specific place. And
that place, in the eye of its beholder, is, of course, number one.
*Celebrity couple: Jennifer Garner (April 17, 1972) and Ben Affleck
(August 15, 1972).*

Aries and Virgo

Compatibility rating: **** (4 out of 10)
Virgo is modest and cautious. You are expansive and reckless.
Virgo is detailed and thrifty. You focus on the big picture—and
you're the zodiac's big spender. In other words, your views
of the world are diametrically opposed. Virgo looks within
and is critical. You're an adventurer and, unless your pride
is injured, you don't make waves. You "get over it," while
Virgo may forgive but never forgets. A relationship is possible
because Virgo is witty and affectionate and is happy to let
action-oriented Aries look after life's major decisions. Virgo
is sometimes perceived as cool, but that's not a fair assessment. There is genuine warmth to the Virgo personality—but
it's often concealed. In domestic relationships, every family
needs a Virgo, but Aries—always heading for the next adventure—rarely acknowledges Virgo's contributions. By the same
token, Virgo feels under siege when Aries charges in when
the mood strikes. For this relationship to have success at any
level, you need to become aware of Virgo's talents. Virgo,
meanwhile, would do well to learn a couple of words from
the Aries vocabulary: *spontaneity* and *self-confidence.*

Aries and Libra

Compatibility rating: ******* (7 out of 10)

Aries and Libra are opposite signs, with birthdays half a year apart (more or less). Opposite signs indicate an attraction based on similarities and differences. The Sun sign opposite yours has the same quality (cardinal, fixed, or mutable) as you, but the elements (air, earth, fire, or water) are different. Although opposite signs often share the same goals, each sign has its own reasons for going after those goals and its own methods in reaching them. Both Aries and Libra are cardinal signs—you both love action and aren't passive. If anyone can handle your bluntness, it is diplomatic Libra. And Libra admires Aries' independent streak and free spirit. You are rambunctious and Libra is peace-loving, but one is as determined as the other. Libra's greatest gift is to weigh all sides of a matter before making a decision. You value Libra's sense of fairness and will enjoy the sense of beauty that Libra introduces. Libra admires your assertiveness and will benefit from your direct approach. You know that you can reach a common objective, whether in love, domestic harmony, or a professional relationship. In other words, you can always negotiate a harmonious arrangement. *Celebrity couple: Deryck Whibley (March 21, 1980) and Avril Lavigne (September 27, 1984).*

Aries and Scorpio

Compatibility rating: ****** (6 out of 10)

Both signs are ruled by Mars (Scorpio is co-ruled by Pluto), meaning that you each take a "make war, not love" approach to negotiations. Scorpio takes control by being possessive, intense, and emotional. You are the more aggressive and spirited of the two. While you are resilient and cheerful, Scorpio's jealousy can be oppressive. You're decisive, while Scorpio can be underhanded, mysterious, and secretive. There's another difference in your personalities: spontaneity (you) versus premeditation (Scorpio). Scorpio is a planner who will wait until the time is right to strike. Some signs respond to Scorpio's drive and passion, and depending on other planetary influences you can interact successfully. You're capable of inspiring Scorpio with your optimism, and in a time of crisis Scorpio will provide the strength that a family needs. Scorpio's powerful nature can overwhelm less self-confident signs. It does help that Scorpio has a great head for business and an intuitive sense for money matters—qualities that offset your tendency to take risks. *Celebrity couple: Elton John (March 25, 1947) and David Furnish (October 25, 1962).*

Aries and Sagittarius

Compatibility rating: ****** (8 out of 10)**
Both Aries and Sagittarius are fire signs. Sagittarius is secure, never possessive, and is usually delighted to let you take charge of things. And while both signs are prone to a quick temper, Sagittarius's anger, though intense and sometimes nasty, is short-lived, as is yours. A potential drawback in this relationship is that you and Sagittarius are both less than willing to make a commitment, and in a romantic union especially, neither one is in a hurry to bite the bullet. But when a commitment is made, each sign is willing to respect the other's need for independence.

In other areas, such as family and career, you and Sagittarius are equally enthusiastic. Sagittarius is always eager to learn, and you're a willing teacher. As a bonus, Aries is usually amused rather than put off by Sagittarius's outspokenness. Sagittarius is wise in business and can help implement Aries' ideas. Since there is generally no battle over turf—there is never a question that Aries will lead the way—the potential for achievement is strong indeed.

Aries and Capricorn

Compatibility rating: *** (5 out of 10)**
Both Aries and Capricorn are cardinal signs, indicating at least a minimum of attraction. Capricorn, an earth sign, is the achiever of the zodiac. You, a fire sign—assertive and a force to be reckoned with—have nothing but admiration for Capricorn's perseverance. In fact, you feel protective toward a Capricorn partner, relative, or associate without smothering him or her. The connection may end there, however, because in outlook the two signs are, in many ways, opposites. Capricorn is devoted to business and appreciates the value of a loonie. You, in contrast, are the idea person—happy to give the family fortune away and then start over again. Capricorn's symbol is the goat and, like that animal, will climb over hurdles, determined to reach a goal. Aries the ram is eager to arrive at its destination and then move on to newer, or greener, pastures. There is nothing conservative or conventional about Aries. Unfortunately, those are the two adjectives that best sum up a Capricorn. *Celebrity couple: Céline Dion (March 30, 1968) and René Angélil (January 16, 1942).*

Aries and Aquarius

Compatibility rating: ******** (8 out of 10)

The two signs, if not initially attracted to each other, can easily grow to like each other. Their differences are complementary rather than conflicting. You and Aquarius are one of the zodiac's mutual admiration societies, with Aries the strong, fiery, and independent partner and Aquarius the friendly, cool, and non-aggressive half. Aquarius is inventive, a quality that you—always willing to try something new—admire. Aries is also comfortable with Aquarius's independent nature. In personal relationships, both signs are happy to be alone or together, as their moods dictate. Aquarius is a progressive thinker and a great humanitarian, qualities that Aries respects and encourages. A possible stumbling block is created by Aquarius's emotional coolness, but Aries—as a boss, co-worker, or subordinate—is often oblivious to that trait and is grateful for Aquarius's tenacity. And while some relatives may be embarrassed by their Aquarius cousin's eccentricities, you find these qualities endearing and know that Aquarius's heart is always in the right place. *Celebrity couples: Gordie Howe (March 31, 1928) and Colleen Howe (February 17, 1933); Ryan O'Neal (April 20, 1941) and Farrah Fawcett (February 2, 1947).*

Aries and Pisces

Compatibility rating: **** (4 out of 10)

Pisces is a mutable water sign—emotional, sensitive, and often needy. Aries, in contrast, is self-confident and passionate. On a romantic level, this pairing needs an ample supply of TLC. You have little patience for Pisces' overindulgences and moods. Pisces, ruled by Neptune, the spiritual planet, has little understanding of your self-centred disposition and never-ending desire for action. Pisces is certainly compassionate, but its need for security threatens your independent style. Empathetic Pisces is a valued family member, providing a shoulder to lean on. But Aries doesn't always want a shoulder. What you need is an audience. In a work setting, Pisces is creative (and some members of the sign have scientific skills) and flexible. But a no-nonsense Aries co-worker may find Pisces' need for approval annoying. As for a Pisces boss and an Aries subordinate, that combination is, frankly, rare. But if it exists, generous Pisces will let Aries think he or she is in control—and such an odd coupling may actually work.

TAURUS COMPATIBILITY GUIDE

The following descriptions, based on your Sun sign, provide a broad picture of how you relate to members of all twelve signs (including your own) in the different spheres of your life.

Taurus and Aries

Compatibility rating: **** (6 out of 10)**
Because Taurus and Aries are neighbouring signs—Taurus follows Aries—the odds are that you share some planetary influ-

ences and have some common qualities. But judging by Sun signs alone, you are, in many ways, opposites. Depending on circumstances, you may complement each other. On the other hand, you may find each other's traits difficult to deal with. Aries is the first sign in the zodiac—a leader. You're a builder. Aries is impulsive, while you are slow but steady. Aries is blunt and has a thick skin, while you are ultra-sensitive and don't handle criticism well. You look at the trees, and Aries checks out the forest. In a romantic relationship, your good nature will allow Aries to enjoy the spotlight. You're a naturally sociable sign, and there can be tense domestic situations when you take over a family-related event from an Aries relative. In the career environment, Aries is generally the independent, bold, decisive leader of the team. Taurus adds a creative touch and, as the principal money sign, makes sure that Aries' budgets are not out of control. Jobwise, this can be a profitable pairing. *Celebrity couples: Katharine Hepburn (May 12, 1907) and Spencer Tracy (April 5, 1900); David Beckham (May 2, 1975) and Victoria Beckham (April 17, 1974); Bono (May 10, 1960) and Alison Hewson (March 23, 1961).*

Taurus and Taurus

Compatibility rating: ****** (6 out of 10)

When two members of the same sign get together, you have two people who understand each other's strengths and foibles. But you also wind up with a concentration of negative traits. In the case of Taurus and Taurus, stubborn meets ornery. Fortunately, you also find two people who have generous hearts and common goals—and in this pairing, those goals involve acquisition.

You are among the most materialistic members of the zodiac. You're also among the most cautious, so in a romantic relationship one might wonder who will make that all-important first move and when. If a relationship evolves, both partners will surround the home with beauty and elegance. (Is it any surprise that figure skaters Tessa Virtue, Barbara Ann Scott, and Jamie Salé—all renowned for their grace and style—are born under the sign of the bull?) But there is a lazy streak at work, and while the two of you are pampering each other, chores pile up. At work, each Taurus may want results without paying all the dues. If the job involves creativity, however, the results can be breathtaking.

Taurus and Gemini

Compatibility rating: *** (5 out of 10)**

What's going for this pair is that both Taurus and Gemini are peace-loving, like to make new friends, and have a way with words. As well, being neighbours in the zodiac, it is likely that you share a number of planetary influences. There's friction in this partnership, however, because Gemini is restless and enjoys flitting about the globe—or at least the neighbourhood. You have a possessive streak and may be resentful of witty Gemini's immense popularity. And while Gemini is adaptable, it is also superficial—a quality that irks you. You want a partner with both feet planted on the ground. In a family setting, you are the nurturing one, a quality Gemini appreciates and often requires. But Taurus's stubbornness and Gemini's indecisiveness result in inflexibility—and usually another relative needs to kick-start things. At work, both

Taurus and Gemini are artistic and bring lovely finishing touches to a project. But sometimes both sacrifice substance for style. The best thing is that, when Taurus and Gemini tackle something, there's usually laughter in the room. *Royal couple: Queen Elizabeth II (April 21, 1926) and Prince Phillip (June 10, 1921).*

Taurus and Cancer

Compatibility rating: ***** (7 out of 10)**

Taurus and Cancer share enough interests and have sufficient differences to allow for a successful pairing. There's a sense of comfort plus a stimulation factor. Neither of you has a great deal of self-confidence, yet each provides support for the other—together you're stronger than alone. Among the things you share is an interest in acquiring things. You can be found bidding side by side at an auction or bargaining at a flea market. You both have an interest in old things—and chances are you prefer a fix-it-upper to a spanking new condo. Cancer is the sign of home, and Taurus is the zodiac's interior designer. In a family relationship, Taurus, the nurturer, will provide a listening ear, while Cancer will be able to confide in Taurus. The reverse holds true to a point, but generally Cancer talks and Taurus listens. Taurus and Cancer work best together if Taurus is in charge. Taurus has been known to undermine a Cancer boss's authority. And while there's initial camaraderie when you work in tandem, you have a habit of feeling a little superior and a lot underappreciated. *Celebrity couple: Barbra Streisand (April 24, 1942) and James Brolin (July 18, 1940). Celebrity dance team: Fred Astaire (May 10, 1899) and Ginger Rogers (July 16, 1911).*

Taurus and Leo

Compatibility rating: ****** (6 out of 10)

Both you and Leo are fixed signs, meaning you are stable, determined, and will persevere to reach a goal—whether personal or professional. And while you are an earth sign and Leo is fire, you're both affectionate. The difficulty lies in the fact that stubborn Taurus may lack an open mind—your opinions are fixed. Leo, in contrast, is generous and broad-minded—a born romantic who is ruled by the Sun. For you, more inclined toward nurturing than passion, romance is an acquired art. Both of you are stylish—you like your surroundings comfortable and snazzy. Neither of you has a restless streak. But while Taurus and Leo are comfortable staying close to home and family, you are possessive and can resent Leo's flamboyance. Leo needs to be the centre of attention. Leo also needs to lead, but in a fashion that is tempered with kindness. The things you share are meaningful. If you understand a Leo's hidden vulnerability, then a relationship—whether romantic, domestic, or professional—has a chance of growing and thriving. *Celebrity couple: Bianca Jagger (May 2, 1945) and Mick Jagger (July 26, 1943).*

Taurus and Virgo

Compatibility rating: ***** (5 out of 10)

Both Taurus and Virgo are earth signs, so to start, the two of you are cautious and neat. However, you're laid-back and more demonstrative than Virgo, who is thoughtful but quiet. Both signs prefer a small group to a large circle of acquaintances. Both work hard and are careful with their money—it's not uncommon for both signs to live beneath their means. You and Virgo both take a traditional approach to courtship and romance, and so you make an affectionate if not particularly passionate couple. The difficulty is that both signs will wait for the right moment to strike— and neither one is inclined to make the first, or second, move. Although loving and reliable, you can be jealous. Virgo has high standards—sometimes impossibly high—and can be hypercritical. Taurus's jealousy and Virgo's pickiness, if not kept in check, can bring down a relationship. In family situations, you will provide the warmth while Virgo tends to practicalities. If an elder relative is ailing, for example, you'll offer the compassion and Virgo the medications. Work-wise, Virgo is obsessed with the details that Taurus detests (or ignores), so if you don't get on each other's nerves you will complement each other in a business arrangement. *Celebrity couple: Jerry Seinfeld (April 29, 1954) and Jessica (Sklar) Seinfeld (September 21, 1971). Celebrity skaters: Tessa Virtue (May 17, 1989) and Scott Moir (September 2, 1987).*

Taurus and Libra

Compatibility rating: ***** (5 out of 10)

Both Taurus and Libra are ruled by Venus, the planet representing beauty, good manners, and the finer things in life. Both strive for peace, at virtually any price. But Libra is an air sign— free as the breeze, spontaneous, happy to communicate with people from all walks of life. You, in great contrast, tend to be possessive and rigid. Harmony is crucial for both signs, but it comes naturally to Libra while you make an effort to keep things in balance. Libra loves to socialize, while you prefer the comforts of home. Often, Libra will be ready to go out to the theatre, a sporting event, or a party, while you decide at the last minute to stay home and watch a movie or hockey game. Libra's indecisiveness will frustrate a Taurus companion or friend. In family settings, Libra will often handle the finances, while you provide the comfort. Libra doles out the optimism and you the caution. Because of your shared Venus connection, you strive to make the working environment a harmonious place. Unfortunately, Libra's popularity can irk Taurus, and your rigidity can get on Libra's nerves. So the harmony you both promote may sometimes apply to everyone but the two of you.

Taurus and Scorpio

Compatibility rating: ****** (8 out of 10)**

Taurus and Scorpio are opposite signs, with birthdays half a year apart (more or less). Opposite signs indicate an attraction based on similarities and differences. The Sun sign opposite yours has the same quality (cardinal, fixed, or mutable) as you, but the elements (air, earth, fire, or water) are different. Although opposite signs often share the same goals, each sign has its own reasons for going after those goals and its own methods in reaching them. In your case, it helps that both you and Scorpio are fixed signs—fiercely loyal but possessive. You both enjoy long-term relationships. You're physically compatible, but emotionally Scorpio can overpower Taurus. Scorpio, the most secretive of the signs, will dig like a terrier until it uncovers everyone else's mysteries. It is often successful in the search, but not with Taurus—your middle name is privacy. Scorpio is used to getting what it seeks. But you are not easily persuaded. In fact, Taurus is the most tenacious member of the zodiac, and once your mind is made up not even as powerful a force as Scorpio has a hope of changing it. *Celebrity skaters: Jamie Salé (April 21, 1977) and David Pelletier (November 22, 1974).*

Taurus and Sagittarius

Compatibility rating: **** (4 out of 10)
The Taurus–Sagittarius pairing is among the most challenging in the zodiac. Taurus is rigid and opinionated, Sagittarius easygoing and tolerant. And while Taurus acquires a wealth of knowledge and experiences, and communicates with warmth and humour, in Sagittarius's eyes Taurus lacks an essential ingredient: excitement. Sagittarius is the eternal student of the zodiac and enjoys learning new things. You, in contrast, prefer to become an authority on a few selected topics. As well, Sagittarius is notoriously blunt (although not generally aware of it), and you are ultra-sensitive. For a lasting relationship, each of you needs a more flexible partner. In casual partnerships, the combination can prove more successful. Sagittarius's adventures and travels provide vicarious fun for sedentary Taurus, and you offer a touch of the familiar when Sagittarius stops in for a visit. At work, Sagittarius offers a positive presence, sense of humour, and optimistic outlook. You may find a Sagittarius's work habits a little unorthodox, but the two make a good team. Your rigidity and caution are balanced by Sagittarius's risk-taking and optimism, and neither finds the other a threat.

Taurus and Capricorn

Compatibility rating: ***** (7 out of 10)**

Capricorn and Taurus are both earth signs. You understand Capricorn's chief need (ambition), and Capricorn finds many of your traits (earthiness, loyalty, determination, and appreciation of art and beauty) appealing. Capricorn strives for financial success, and materialistic Taurus is the money sign of the zodiac. In a relationship, you are steadfast and seek the kind of strong connection that Capricorn offers. You want security and know that Capricorn can provide it. And although Capricorn can at times be suspicious, you are willing to put up with this trait in return for Capricorn's earnestness. You and Capricorn are complementary family members. It really doesn't matter who the official breadwinner is—Taurus offers a safe environment, Capricorn looks after the business affairs. At work, Capricorn is disciplined and provides a contrast to your more creative approach. You may find Capricorn to be calculating and reserved. Capricorn may think you're plodding, overly analytical, and preoccupied with aesthetics. But though the approaches differ, each one recognizes, and respects, the other's diligence and sense of humour.

Taurus and Aquarius

Compatibility rating: *** (5 out of 10)**

Taurus and Aquarius are both fixed signs, but your element is earth and Aquarius's is air. Translation: Taurus is stubborn, possessive, determined, and cautious; Aquarius loves freedom, independence, and change. Ideas are important for both of you, but Taurus's are traditional and Aquarius's are innovative. Aquarius is the humanitarian of the zodiac—perennially involved in a good cause. Yet while they love the world, Aquarians can be thoughtless in personal relationships. That attitude is difficult for a Taurus partner to accept. And Taurus, who loves beautiful and unusual things, prefers to lead a conventional life—something that unconventional and downright eccentric Aquarius finds dull and predictable. For a partnership to work, Taurus must be willing and able to live with an independent spirit. At work, Aquarius can excel in many areas—as long as there are challenges. You, in contrast, are content with routine tasks and are highly disciplined, so a professional relationship could prove successful for this pair. *Celebrity couple: Cher (May 20, 1946) and Sonny (February 16, 1935).*

Taurus and Pisces

Compatibility rating: ****** (8 out of 10)**
Taurus is a fixed earth sign, while Pisces is a mutable water sign. You like familiarity, and Pisces prefers change. You are dependable, protective, and affectionate—but insecure. Pisces can be trusting, forgiving, patient, and spiritual—and also insecure. But you share more than a shaky sense of self. Both signs are home-loving, family-oriented, and creative. You are ruled by Venus, the planet of art and beauty. And Pisces is often a gifted artist, sculptor, writer, or poet. Pisces' moods change like the tides, but you understand them. And while Pisceans can be jealous, they are among the most gentle, intuitive, and caring people—another quality that doesn't escape a Taurus partner

or friend. Pisces can be easily influenced, but you provide a healthy measure of stability. Both signs are highly perceptive. Neither gets involved in the politics of the workplace, but you both have a sense of what is going on behind the scenes. This shared awareness provides a bond and gives each of you a boost in self-confidence. Even if they aren't in the same department or on the same team, the two signs are known to form alliances on the job or within an organization. *Poetic couple: Robert Browning (May 7, 1812) and Elizabeth Barrett Browning (March 6, 1806).*

GEMINI
COMPATIBILITY GUIDE

The following descriptions, based on your Sun sign, provide a broad picture of how you relate to members of all twelve signs (including your own) in the different spheres of your life.

Gemini and Aries

Compatibility rating: ******** (8 out of 10)
Gemini and Aries have a great deal in common—both are communicators, neither one stands still for very long, both enjoy adventure. As a couple or a team, you complement and have the potential to bring out the best in each other. You're ruled by Mercury, famous for wit and charm. Aries is an ambitious cardinal sign ruled by action-oriented Mars, planet of excitement. You both prefer crowds to small gatherings. You prefer

to contemplate rather than initiate things, while Aries' motto is "I do." In a romantic, domestic, or professional relationship, each of you provides what the other needs without stealing any thunder from the other. You're both impulsive. As the two of you circulate, you provide much of the entertainment, while Aries makes the decisions. Yet each of you is an independent spirit, and neither sign feels threatened by the other. You thrive on each other's optimism and provide an upbeat mood to family events. In a working relationship you're more than happy to let self-centred Aries enjoy centre stage as long as you can take charge of communications and PR. *Celebrity couple: Douglas Fairbanks (May 23, 1883) and Mary Pickford (April 8, 1892).*

Gemini and Taurus

Compatibility rating: ***** (5 out of 10)

What's going for this pair is that both you and Taurus are peace-loving, like to make new friends, and have a way with words. As well, being neighbours in the zodiac, it is likely you share a number of planetary influences. There's friction in this partnership, however, because you're restless and enjoy flitting about the globe—or at least the neighbourhood. Taurus is inclined to stay closer to home. Of the two, you're chattier and the more original, and you're more inclined to compromise and change. More than that, Taurus has a jealous side and a possessive streak and can easily become resentful of witty Gemini's immense popularity. And while you're adaptable, you're also superficial—a quality that irks Taurus, who wants a partner with both feet planted on the ground. In a family setting, Taurus provides nurturing, a comfort that you always appreciate and often need. But Taurus's stubbornness and your indecisiveness can create a stalemate—and usually some other family member needs to step in and get the ball rolling. At work, both signs are artistic and bring lovely finishing touches to a project. But sometimes substance is sacrificed for style. The best thing is that, when Taurus and Gemini tackle something, there's usually laughter in the room. *Royal couple: Prince Phillip (June 10, 1921) and Queen Elizabeth II (April 21, 1926).*

Gemini and Gemini

Compatibility rating: ******* (7 out of 10)

When two members of the same sign join forces, the connection can bring out the best and the worst in each. In the case of Gemini, there's potential for a lively and enjoyable relationship or a complicated and confusing one. We have two air signs—on the go, rushing about, witty and charming, funny and active . . . and impossible to pin down. Whatever the outcome, a pair of you will provide fascinating dialogue. Ruled by Mercury, you are the great communicator of the zodiac—ever curious, flitting about from event to event, and passing along information, knowledge, and gossip. There's no more entertaining a guest than Gemini. On the downside, little things get under a Gemini's skin—so two of you are likely to be exchanging barbs as well as *bon mots*. But your sign is optimistic, and, while not overly emotional, you're a good listener as well as a good talker. You also have a kind heart. Gemini brightens any family event, and two of you double the entertainment value. You're not consistent, and you're not very good at keeping in touch or returning emails. But if any relative can forgive that character flaw, it is, of course, a fellow Gemini. You also find something interesting and unique in even the most routine work and are popular and well-liked on the job. Some people think that the twins (your symbol) represent a split personality, but that's not the case. They represent multiple talents. And, in the case of a Gemini and Gemini partnership, one should double that number—at least.

Gemini and Cancer

Compatibility rating: ****** (6 out of 10)
Home-loving Cancer is among the most imaginative and affectionate signs but is also moody and unpredictable. Gemini, the zodiac's great communicator, is also unpredictable. So, while you understand each other's changing moods and don't take them as personally as other people may, the combination of two loose cannons makes for a relationship that is, well, unpredictable. Here's the problem: you like new things, new places, and new ideas. Cancer is a cardinal water sign; its shifts are similar to the tides of the sea—changing but according to a pattern. Cancer needs stability and familiarity, while you enjoy zipping about. Cancer likes being surrounded with old friends. You like to deal with new people from all walks of life and corners of the world. Still, a number of important things are going for this combination. You want—make that need—a good listener, and Cancer is one of the best. And because you are zodiac neighbours (Cancer follows Gemini), it's possible that you share planetary influences. For all relationships—romantic, family, work—compromise

is the key. Cancer is more conservative and emotional, and you are idea-oriented. One of you needs to adapt, and the odds are in favour of you being the one. *Celebrity couples: Michael J. Fox (June 9, 1961) and Tracy Pollan (June 22, 1960). Royal couple: Duchess of Windsor (June 19, 1896) and Duke of Windsor (June 23, 1894).*

Gemini and Leo

Compatibility rating: ********* (9 out of 10)

This pairing is, in a number of ways, a match made in the heavens. Leo is ruled by the Sun—big ego, centre of attention, flamboyant, star performer. Not too many signs can handle the king/queen of the jungle without being overshadowed. You're one of the few. On one level, you make a Leo partner look good. On the other, you're never less than your own person. You're secure enough in your own strengths and talents. More than that, both signs are sociable, lively, and generous. And while Leo is dramatic and you like to perform, your audiences are different, so there's little competition between you. In fact, you admire and take pride in each other's talents. If Leo gets too bossy or begins to interfere in your life, you're bound to sulk—but it never lasts long, since you bounce back like a kid on a trampoline. In a work or organizational setting, you admire a Leo boss as fair and hard-working (Leo can be counted on to do the lion's share of the job). The balance is off-kilter when you're the one in charge, but chances are that Leo will still find a way to dominate without Gemini feeling threatened about it.

Gemini and Virgo

Compatibility rating: *** (5 out of 10)**

Both signs are curious but in different ways. You are ever on the lookout, in a quest for knowledge, while Virgo seeks ways to use knowledge for profit. Both signs are ruled by Mercury, which represents intelligence, and both are mutable—versatile and, to an extent, willing to adapt. But Gemini's element is air and Virgo's is earth. So, when Gemini is flying off to explore new ideas, Virgo stays put with both feet planted firmly in the ground. Emotionally, Gemini is a lot cooler than Virgo. At home, you're a collector. Virgo is fanatic and fussy. You each need to adapt, but it's not easy when both partners quickly become irritable as a result of small things. Both of you are courteous. And both of you are expert in dealing with problems involving relatives, co-workers, or the next-door neighbour. Tensions between the two of you are, however, another matter. Virgo has a knack for turning a molehill into the Rockies, and Gemini cares so little about mundane details that the friction between the two signs is inevitable. While Virgo is busy analyzing every last aspect of a problem, you're busily pursuing new ideas and adventures. *Royal couple: Queen Victoria (May 24, 1819) and Prince Albert (August 26, 1819).*

Gemini and Libra

Compatibility rating: ***** (7 out of 10)**

The Gemini–Libra pairing is ideal in many ways. Each of you thrives on new ideas, adventures, and surprises, and if you get together, you keep each other young. You are intellectual equals and you both like to socialize. Communication is a central part of both personalities, with Gemini being the originator of new ideas and Libra happy to refine and edit Gemini's words. There is a potential difficulty in the relationship, however: you are both impractical, and unless independently wealthy (very wealthy), you each benefit from a more decisive partner. Other difficulties may create problems in a romantic, domestic, or professional relationship. Libra, though the diplomat of the zodiac, can sometimes be selfish and quick-tempered. And Libra's indecisiveness can often stifle your need to move on. With such different objectives, a business partnership could prove messy. Still, both signs have so much in common and genuinely like each other that they will make the effort to work out any differences. *Celebrity couple: Paul McCartney (June 18, 1942) and Linda McCartney (September 24, 1941).*

Gemini and Scorpio

Compatibility rating: ** (4 out of 10)**

Scorpio is ruled by two planets—Mars and Pluto—that are responsible for power, magnetism, and sensuality. You're ruled by Mercury—the planet of ideas, intelligence, and communication. You like to flirt, while Scorpio is possessive. You forgive and forget (and then forget what you forgave), while Scorpio will wait—even years—for the perfect opportunity for revenge. Everything light and gentle about your personality is contrasted with Scorpio's intensity. You could, in a word, be crushed. Of course, astrology is based on more than Sun signs; depending on other influences, it's possible for a relationship to work. Here's what your Scorpio partner needs: the influence of a sign such as Libra to enjoy your wit and charm and chatty ways. Based on Sun signs alone, you should remember that Scorpios will always be motivated, intuitive, and, if they can get something in return, willing to help out. And don't forget that they're competitive, resourceful, vindictive, and suspicious. You can accept the first two traits without difficulty, but the last two could create havoc in any kind of relationship. *Celebrity couple: Laurence Olivier (May 22, 1907) and Vivien Leigh (November 5, 1913). Royal couple: Prince Rainier III (May 31, 1923) and Grace Kelly (November 12, 1929).*

Gemini and Sagittarius

Compatibility rating: ******** (8 out of 10)

Gemini and Sagittarius are opposite signs, with birthdays half a year apart (more or less). Opposite signs indicate an attraction based on similarities and differences. The Sun sign opposite yours has the same quality (cardinal, fixed, or mutable) as you, but the elements (air, earth, fire, or water) are different. Although opposite signs often share the same goals, each sign has its own reasons for going after those goals and its own methods in reaching them. In the case of Gemini, a freewheeling air sign, and Sagittarius, an adventurous fire sign, the similarities are based on traits that include intelligence, enthusiasm, and the ability to communicate ideas. Both enjoy an intellectual sparring match. As for the differences, you're modest and a rational thinker. Sagittarius exaggerates (if Sagittarius talks about number of goals scored or amount of money earned, it's safe to cut the figure in half) and is outspoken. Both signs are positive, and although your ego pales in comparison to Sagittarius's, you enjoy each other's company in family and professional settings. Sagittarius shies away from permanent commitment but genuinely enjoys Gemini's friendship. Your styles are definitely different—Sagittarius takes chances that you would never consider—but you share an important objective: you each seek wisdom rather than possessions. *Celebrity couple: Angelina Jolie (June 4, 1975) and Brad Pitt (December 18, 1963).*

Gemini and Capricorn

Compatibility rating: **** (6 out of 10)**
You're a mutable air sign and Capricorn a cardinal earth sign. Capricorn's symbol is the goat and, like that animal, will climb relentlessly to reach its objective. Capricorn is, without doubt, the most ambitious sign of the zodiac. You're not without ambition, but you don't seek out challenges. While it seems you have little in common, you admire Capricorn's determination and business sense. And Capricorn, a pessimist, enjoys your optimism and social skills. You can provide a nice balance to each other, and in the right circumstances your differences dovetail rather than conflict. You have different types of friends (yours are of all ages and backgrounds; Capricorn's are more serious and conservative). Your sense of humour (witty) balances Capricorn's (wry). Regardless of actual age, you're younger than Capricorn and certainly less cautious. But Capricorn is always

calm and not emotional, and that can be a deal-maker in a relationship with someone as independent as you. In a family environment, Capricorn is perceived as rigid, but you provide a softening effect. Working in the shadow of a Capricorn can be daunting. But you have nothing but admiration for Capricorn's work ethic and can be inspired to become more businesslike under Capricorn's influence. *Celebrity couples: Priscilla Presley (May 24, 1945) and Elvis Presley (January 8, 1935); Johnny Depp (June 9, 1963) and Vanessa Paradis (December 22, 1972); Royal couple: Prince William, Duke of Cambridge (June 21, 1982) and Catherine, Duchess of Cambridge (January 9, 1982).*

Gemini and Aquarius

Compatibility rating: ******* (7 out of 10)
There's no question about it—you like to have the last word. And the first. And most of the sentences in between. These two air signs may never set off sparks of passion, but they can certainly strike a pleasant and long-lasting friendship. And in Aquarius, you find your ideal audience—someone genuinely interested in what you have to say and who can help you articulate your message effectively and with style. At the same time, you accept—in fact, encourage—Aquarius's need for independence and enjoy his or her quirks. One of your best traits is that you never try to change anyone, and there are few as appreciative of that as Aquarius. By the same token, Aquarius is never jealous and enjoys your popularity among people from all walks of life. There are times when Aquarius is brutally outspoken. If that ruffles your feathers, you get over it while other

family members remain hot and bothered. At work, Aquarius doesn't suffer in silence and can be critical of other people's work habits and scruples. Most of the time, you quietly agree—and are glad that Aquarius has the kind of nerve that you know you lack. *Celebrity couple: John Ralston Saul (June 19, 1947) and Adrienne Clarkson (February 10, 1939).*

Gemini and Pisces

Compatibility rating: **** (4 out of 10)

Both Gemini and Pisces are mutable signs—restless, easily moulded, and compassionate. And you're both natural communicators. You also have something else in common: you're both "doubles." Your sign is the twins, and Pisces is made up of two fish joined together. In other words, you're both versatile and have a desire to please everyone. A Gemini–Pisces relationship usually starts out promisingly. Initially, you respect Pisces' sensitivity, and Pisces enjoys your free spirit. But before long Pisces becomes clingy, and you're on the move. That doesn't mean things evaporate between you—you're drawn to Pisces' imagination and compassion. But Pisces' pessimism is often stronger than your optimism. Another difference is that Pisces is intuitive and emotional—drawing on hunches. In contrast, you get your information from books or the Internet. Of course, the descriptions given are based on Sun signs alone, and if you share other planetary influences there is a stronger potential for a good relationship. Both of you are selfless. As relatives, you and Pisces often establish a bond because you are both kind and enjoy spoiling others with little gifts. But on the job, given your short attention span and Pisces' hyperactive imagination, the combination of your signs can be unproductive, to say the least.

CANCER COMPATIBILITY GUIDE

The following descriptions, based on your Sun sign, provide a broad picture of how you relate to members of all twelve signs (including your own) in the different spheres of your life.

Cancer and Aries

Compatibility rating: *** (5 out of 10)**

This pairing of two cardinal signs has a strong foundation. You both go after what you want, and neither of you is passive. On the plus side, you complement each other. Aries has an ego the size of the Yukon, and you respect that larger-than-life personality. You, in turn, are the sign of home and hearth, and Aries—although fiercely independent—is family-minded. But there are clear differences in your personalities and philosophies. You're conservative and a creature of habit, while Aries is spontaneous—keen to try something new and take off on a last-minute adventure. The major challenge is that Aries is strong-willed and mystified by your feelings of insecurity and possessive streak. Although nobody is more supportive than Cancer, in this relationship you need to recognize the line between supportive and clingy. In domestic or professional relationships, you are happy to leave the leadership role to Aries—the zodiac's pioneer and trailblazer. But Aries will have to respond to your need for security and safety, and be attentive to your demands to control certain reckless tendencies. *Celebrity couple: Donald Sutherland (July 17, 1935) and Shirley Douglas (April 2, 1934).*

Cancer and Taurus

Compatibility rating: ***** (7 out of 10)**

Venus-ruled Taurus is a fixed earth sign, determined and stable. You're ruled by the Moon and are a cardinal water sign. The two of you have a sufficient number of shared interests and unique qualities to keep the relationship fresh and challenging. There's a sense of comfort in this relationship, as well as a stimulation factor. Leo wants to take over your life, Virgo bores you, and Aries comes on like gangbusters. But Taurus, like you, doesn't favour change, enjoys routines, and seeks commitment. You also share an interest in acquiring objects, and both of you prefer vintage to new. If you get together, you're likely to find yourselves a fix-it-upper rather than a brand-new condo. In a family relationship, Taurus, the nurturer, will always provide a listening ear, and you'll be able to share your insecurities with Taurus. The reverse holds true—to a point. But generally, you're the talker and Taurus the listener. On the job, the two of you do best if Taurus is in charge—even nominally. (Taurus has been known to undermine a Cancer boss's authority.) You're both hard workers, thrifty, and ready to provide reassurance. *Celebrity couple: James Brolin (July 18, 1940) and Barbra Streisand (April*

24, 1942). Celebrity dance team: Ginger Rogers (July 16, 1911) and Fred Astaire (May 10, 1899).

Cancer and Gemini

Compatibility rating: **** (6 out of 10)**

Cancer is the protective sign of the zodiac—eager to provide the comforts of a secure home. Gemini is not domestic but appreciates a warm environment. A child at heart, Gemini brings out your nurturing instincts. You're both imaginative and affectionate. But you need to realize, early on, that Gemini, although kind and gentle, does not always provide the emotional commitment you seek. As a cardinal water sign, your moods change like the tides of the sea. Whether it's because Gemini is tolerant or oblivious, it is one of the few signs that can live easily with your emotions. Still, the two of you need to work out basic differences. Gemini likes new things, places, and ideas, plus the excitement that people from all walks of life can provide. You need stability, familiarity, and the security of being among old friends. If you can meet each other partway (the greater effort will be yours, for sure), you'll find that this relationship has a strong foundation. In all areas, Gemini needs a good listener. You're one of the best. And because you are zodiac neighbours (Cancer follows Gemini), it's possible that you share a number of planetary influences. *Celebrity couples: Tracy Pollan (June 22, 1960) and Michael J. Fox (June 9, 1961). Royal couple: Duke of Windsor (June 23, 1894) and Duchess of Windsor (June 19, 1896).*

Cancer and Cancer

Compatibility rating: **** (6 out of 10)**

When two members of the same sign join forces, the connection can bring out the best and the worst in each. In the case of Cancer and Cancer, there's potential for a lively and enjoyable relationship or a complicated and confusing one. We have two cardinal (action-oriented) water signs ruled by the Moon. You have strong nurturing instincts and are home- and family-oriented creatures. Like the crab, your symbol, you have a crusty exterior with tenderness within your protective shell. You are romantic, possessive, sentimental, intuitive, and sometimes psychic. But you're both shy—so one wonders who's going to make the first move. If or when that move takes place, the partnership will prove among the most loyal in the zodiac. Each of you will be devoted to the home and family. As well, Cancer–Cancer friendships are frequently based on nostalgia—you often live in the past, so a pair will have considerable trouble coming to grips with the modern world. Then there's the possessiveness, which two Cancers living together may cancel out. Working together, a Cancer duo will usually get along if they're of the same vintage or on the same level. But a senior Cancer colleague often resists keeping a junior in the loop, while a junior member of the team will expect to be indulged. Of course, being so intuitive, one Cancer will know what the other is thinking. *Celebrity couple: Dan Aykroyd (July 1, 1952) and Donna Dixon (July 20, 1957).*

Cancer and Leo

Compatibility rating: ***** (5 out of 10)

Your element is water and Leo's is fire, and it doesn't take a mind reader to know how that could play out. But there are some positive things going for this pair. Leo thrives on attention and is happiest when performing. Cancer is affectionate, artistic, and supportive. Both signs are extremely loyal. And though Leo is dynamic and assertive, and Cancer is moody, you complement each other. As well, because you are zodiac neighbours, it's possible that you share planetary influences. Cancer the crab has a protective shell, and Leo will work to coax you out of it. You need someone to understand your mood shifts—to keep a low profile when you get into a funk. It may seem surprising, but Leo can be sentimental, especially around someone as gentle as Cancer. There are stumbling blocks too. Thrifty Cancer is the bargain hunter of the zodiac, while Leo spends lavishly. On the positive side, Leo tends to ignore health issues, but you'll be there to take charge. In a working relationship, you'll provide a conservative balance to Leo's extravagant spirit. Interestingly, although Leo takes on the starring role and you're content to play a supporting part, when the two of you make competing requests or suggestions, you're the more convincing of the two.

Cancer and Virgo

Compatibility rating: ***** (5 out of 10)

Virgo is a mutable earth sign, ruled by Mercury—the zodiac's communicator. You're a cardinal water sign—ruled by the

Moon, which controls your shifting moods. The most important thing you share is tenacity—you're determined and will work to make a relationship a success, once it takes off. But are you drawn to each other? It's neither a sure thing nor a long shot, but what helps is that you're both affectionate and funny. If you join forces, you'll find that you're both house-proud. Another thing you share: a sense of being unappreciated. You could spend an excessive amount of time complaining to each other about why relatives and co-workers don't give you credit for all that you do. That would make for a sombre relationship, but the good thing is that you're both resourceful. You enjoy retreating into the past, while Virgo lives in the present tense. Of the two, you're the more demonstrative and Virgo the cooler sign. You're also the more sociable. If you're planning a joint event, the draft guest lists will vary dramatically. At work, Virgo is an analyst and you're in tune with people and personalities. Neither one of you is power hungry, but you're laid-back while Virgo can be demanding and petty.

Cancer and Libra

Compatibility rating: ***** (7 out of 10)**
Cancer and Libra relate well because they share many interests. Libra's taste is more expensive than yours, but you have a common passion in antiques. As well, both like to rub shoulders with the rich and famous. Cancer does well in the arts. Libra has many artist friends. You're the most patriotic of the signs, and Libra, the zodiac's diplomat, is often drawn to politics. Also, you're both cardinal signs, meaning that you have strong

drives. And neither of you likes conflict. There are differences as well, but they don't seem like deal-breakers. Libra may find you too clingy (you tend to nag), and you may find Libra too independent. Libra is an intellectual sign and enjoys galleries and the theatre, while you're happier to spend an evening at home. In family and work settings, you both try to make the environment as enjoyable as possible. (At work, you're likely to go on lunch breaks together.) Both signs often find themselves working at home, so you and Libra would make good partners in a home business. *Celebrity couple: Pamela Anderson (July 1, 1967) and Tommy Lee (October 3, 1962).*

Cancer and Scorpio

Compatibility rating: **** (6 out of 10)**
Your element is water—Cancer is a fluid, changeable sign. And you're ruled by the Moon, which makes you moody. More accurately, your moods change, and though you can be sullen, you are caring, affectionate, and funny. You and Scorpio are compatible at several levels. You are both water signs, so you both have emotional personalities. You understand each other's needs. As well, you are both possessive, yet not as possessive of each other as you are of other signs. You both seek commitment, and you're both intuitive as well as demanding. You and Scorpio take a long time to make a commitment, but when you finally do, it is for the right reasons. Some of your shared traits complicate a relationship. You both bear grudges and neither of you forgets a personal affront. (You hold the record for time taken to kiss and make up.) If a relationship

or friendship comes to an end, Cancer is reluctant to cut it loose, but Scorpio is ready to get on with things. Scorpio is the more competitive of the pair and also the more persuasive. Determination is what a Scorpio is all about. Cancer is more protective and nurturing. This formula applies to family and work settings as well, where Scorpio will be the driving force and Cancer the refiner and protector. *Celebrity couples: Harrison Ford (July 13, 1942) and Calista Flockhart (November 11, 1964); Tom Hanks (July 9, 1956) and Rita Wilson (October 26, 1956). Royal couples: Camilla Parker Bowles (July 17, 1947) and Prince Charles (November 14, 1948); Princess Diana (July 1, 1961) and Prince Charles (November 14, 1948).*

Cancer and Sagittarius

Compatibility rating: ****** (6 out of 10)
Sagittarius is a mutable fire sign and you're a cardinal water sign. That makes you seem like opposites, but there's a starting point—you're both restless. Your restlessness, however, is internal, while Sagittarius likes to try new things and discover new places. (Your idea of adventure is to experiment with decor.) Sagittarius is intellectually inclined, while you operate on instinct. You also need security and reassurance, while Sagittarius is the epitome of self-confidence. Finally, Sagittarius has a broad circle of acquaintances, and your Facebook page is likely to include a narrower selection of friends. Still, there's definite potential for a satisfying relationship—thanks largely to your partner's upbeat and adaptable nature. Sagittarius will make the effort to enjoy your interests and get to know your

friends. In return, you need to understand that you can't rein in this fiercely independent sign. At the family level, Sagittarius, like you, will take on a caregiving role. In business, Sagittarius climbs quickly up the career ladder but is never ruthless. Intuitive Cancer understands that Sagittarius needs stimulation, and the two are generally supportive of each other. *Celebrity couples: Meryl Streep (June 22, 1949) and Don Gummer (December 12, 1946); Tom Cruise (July 3, 1962) and Katie Holmes (December 18, 1978).*

Cancer and Capricorn

Compatibility rating: ******* (7 out of 10)

Cancer and Capricorn are opposite signs, with birthdays half a year apart (more or less). Opposite signs indicate an attraction based on similarities and differences. The Sun sign opposite yours has the same quality (cardinal, in your case) as you, but the elements (air, earth, fire, or water) are different (yours is water, Capricorn's is earth). Although opposite signs often share the same goals, each sign has its own reasons for going after those goals and its own methods in reaching them. As a starting point, you are both ambitious and reliable. Capricorn is the more seriously driven partner, and you're the more creative. But both signs can be downbeat—Cancer moody, Capricorn gloomy—and your combined pessimism can clear a room. The two are often attracted to each other in your younger years, and for the chemistry to continue you need to learn to accept your different approaches. Capricorn will be cool and calculating, using a blueprint in seeking out financial security. You use intuition, and your goal is emotional security. The two of you need to follow a strict division of labour, with Capricorn handling the long-term planning and you setting the mood. You'll not only have a successful relationship but will host some of the best parties in town. *Celebrity couple: Peter Mansbridge (July 6, 1948) and Cynthia Dale (January 1, 1961).*

Cancer and Aquarius

Compatibility rating: **** (6 out of 10)**
Aquarius is attractive, shy, tolerant, eccentric, and drawn to good causes. For Aquarius, charity begins at home, and that is where the strongest connection with Cancer lies. Both signs are comfortable in their home setting (many members of the two signs work at home), and as a couple you enjoy sprucing up your surroundings and enjoying them with a close circle of friends and family members. For both of you, gratitude is an attitude—neither one of you likes being taken for granted. Happily, you know how to make each other feel special. But there's a basic difference in your outlooks. Aquarius is the more independent, and you're less secure and may get jealous. The happy news is that you're both good listeners and can talk things over. And though some people perceive Aquarius as aloof, it is basically a kind-hearted sign. You're both tolerant of others, especially older people, from whom you can always learn. Relatives tend to perceive you as the family nurturer and Aquarius as the family eccentric, and at gatherings you provide a nice mix of warmth and laughter. At work, Aquarius is the innovator and you're the creative force. You're both idea

people and understand when it's necessary to bend the rules. *Celebrity couple: Natalie Wood (July 20, 1938) and Robert Wagner (February 10, 1930).*

Cancer and Pisces

Compatibility rating: ******** (8 out of 10)

Pisces is a mutable water sign. Like you, Pisces is creative and perceptive. It can also be insecure and moody—to a larger degree than even you. Next to a Pisces, changeable Cancer seems downright stable. But both of you are adaptable, gentle, and patient. Neither sign is particularly practical. You both have a nurturing instinct, but Pisces also needs ego-building. Pisces is the more innovative of the two. A Pisces needs periods of solitude and an encouraging environment, something you're ready—and eager—to provide. Pisces, in turn, likes to give loved ones sentimental tokens of affection and appreciation. They're little things, but they mean the world to you. Another plus is that both signs like animals and are drawn to strays. (If they live together, Cancer and Pisces will need lots of space.) Being intuitive and sensitive, each sign knows when to retreat when the other needs time alone. They provide a calming atmosphere for each other. Neither sign is ambitious, so they don't make the most productive team at work. But you certainly understand each other's charms, talents, and, especially, moods. *Celebrity couple: June Carter (June 23, 1929) and Johnny Cash (February 26, 1932).*

LEO COMPATIBILITY GUIDE

The following descriptions, based on your Sun sign, provide a broad picture of how you relate to members of all twelve signs (including your own) in the different spheres of your life.

Leo and Aries

Compatibility rating: ***** (7 out of 10)**

This match can be exciting: two fire elements, both action-oriented, passionate, and opinionated. In short, there's never a dull moment. But you both need some rest. The trick in this relationship is to work out an arrangement that keeps each partner's ego intact. Let Aries (the zodiac's first sign) initiate things while you enjoy centre stage. There's comfort, too, in knowing that if one larger-than-life personality takes over the other's role, neither will hold a grudge. It's also a challenge to be careful about money—you share a philosophy that one can always earn more. You're a fixed sign, and weigh things carefully, while Aries is the more impulsive partner. You want to dominate, and Aries wants independence. In a parent–child relationship, it doesn't matter which sign is the parent—the kid will learn self-confidence at an early age. If a Leo and Aries find themselves working together, there could be a battle over roles. Just be sure to grant Aries a measure of autonomy, and hope that Aries will never ignore you. *Celebrity couple: Ben Affleck (August 15, 1972) and Jennifer Garner (April 17, 1972).*

Leo and Taurus

Compatibility rating: **** (6 out of 10)**

This is an interesting match of two fixed signs, one extravagant (you), the other thrifty; one quick tempered (you), the other stubborn. And despite these differences, or perhaps because of them, there's a strong attraction between you. You both persevere to reach a goal—whether personal or professional. And while Taurus is an earth sign and you're fire, you are both affectionate and congenial. The difficulty lies in the fact that stubborn Taurus does not usually have an open mind. You, in contrast, are generous and tolerant. Ruled by the Sun, you are a born romantic. For the less passionate Taurus, romance is an acquired trait. Both of you are stylish, so any shared environment will be comfortable as well as snazzy. Neither of you has a restless streak, and you're both content staying close to home and family. But Taurus gets possessive and can resent your need to be the centre of attention. You, in turn, are not as confident as you appear. So if Taurus understands your hidden vulnerability and you share the limelight with Taurus, then a relationship— romantic, domestic, or professional—has a chance of growing and thriving. *Celebrity couple: Mick Jagger (July 26, 1943) and Bianca Jagger (May 2, 1945).*

Leo and Gemini

Compatibility rating: ******* (9 out of 10)**

This is a pairing of fire (Leo) and air (Gemini). You admire Gemini's spirit, Gemini enjoys your flamboyance, and you each like to share your interests and friends. In many ways this is a match made in the heavens. You're ruled by the Sun—big ego, star performer. Gemini is one of the few who can handle the king/queen of the jungle without feeling overshadowed. Gemini enjoys your persona and makes you look good. You, in turn, respect Gemini's verbal gifts. And both of you are comfortable with the other's independence. While you're dramatic and Gemini also likes to perform, your audiences are different. (You like to play to a large house. Gemini mingles at social gatherings.) You do get bossy and may interfere in Gemini's life, but Gemini's sulking doesn't last. On the flip side, Gemini's occasional disappearing acts can annoy you, but you don't hold a grudge for long. In a work environment, Gemini admires a Leo boss as fair and disciplined. The balance is off-kilter when Gemini's in charge, but odds are that you'll find a way to dominate.

Leo and Cancer

Compatibility rating: *** (5 out of 10)**
Although on the surface the two of you don't appear to have much in common (Cancer's element is water and yours is fire), you enjoy each other's company. You're assertive, forthright, and dynamic, while Cancer is shy, emotional, and subtle. Leo brings out the best in others and can coax Cancer out of its protective shell. You need attention, are happiest when performing, and are a good listener. Cancer showers its partner with affection and loves to schmooze. Cancer is protective of others and rather than finding you overbearing will admire—and defend—

your larger-than-life persona. You, in turn, know how to keep a low profile when Cancer gets into a funk. There are roadblocks in this pairing. Cancer is thrifty, while you spend lavishly. Ideally, your influences will rub off on each other. Cancer will also nurture you—you tend to ignore your health. In a working relationship, Cancer is best handling the creative side while you take charge of PR. And because you are zodiac neighbours (Leo follows Cancer), it's possible that you share planetary influences. For all relationships—romantic, family, work—compromise is the key. One of you needs to adapt—and the surprise is that you'll be the one.

Leo and Leo

Compatibility rating: **** (6 out of 10)**
When two members of the same sign join forces, the connection can bring out the best and the worst in each. In the case of Leo, the negatives will be reinforced, but each partner will understand the other's approach, taste, values, and, especially, Lake Superior–sized ego. Whatever the outcome, a Leo–Leo pairing will provide enough drama for the Shaw and Stratford festivals combined, with each Leo vying for the spotlight. Based on the Sun sign alone, it's likely that both Leos will be generous, demand loyalty, and be good providers. Leos are protective, caring, and passionate partners. When sparks between two Leos ignite, fireworks erupt. The key to any relationship with a Leo—especially true when two lions are involved—is to applaud the performance. In domestic and professional circles, Leos, not surprisingly, demand a leadership position. Some sort of shared

arrangement is important in order to satisfy each partner. It's not surprising that many Leos are entrepreneurs. Others have taken to sports (Sidney Crosby, Maurice Richard, and Elizabeth Manley). No matter the field, Leos move quickly to the top of their game. But when two Leos appear in the same production, it's always interesting to see which one gets star billing. *Celebrity couple: Antonio Banderas (August 10, 1960) and Melanie Griffith (August 9, 1957).*

Leo and Virgo

Compatibility rating: ****** (6 out of 10)
Because you're neighbouring signs—Virgo follows Leo—the odds are that you share planetary influences and have common qualities. But judging by Sun signs alone, you are, in many ways, opposites. Leo is impulsive and dramatic, Virgo cautious and cool. Leo is larger than life with a monster ego. Virgo is picky and insecure. Leo is extravagant and Virgo is ultra-cautious. But if you can get past these differences, you can learn from each other. You have a tendency to look after the welfare of loved ones and, in the process, ignore your own aches and pains. Virgo is something of a health fanatic and will supervise your needs. Virgo, who obsesses over trivial details, will learn from you that there's more to life than fussing. A Leo–Virgo friendship could be strained when you're ready to head out and Virgo obsesses over what to wear. Still, while neither of you is patient, both of you are devoted. In a Leo parent–Virgo child relationship, your personality could overwhelm or inspire confidence. Your strength is kindness, so the odds are the latter.

At work, Leo needs to be respected. It's not about control—it's the theatrics. The key is for Leo to acknowledge Virgo's contributions and for Virgo to be heaped with praise. Both scenarios are likely. *Celebrity couples: Jennifer Lopez (July 24, 1969) and Marc Anthony (September 16, 1969); Madonna (August 16, 1958) and Guy Ritchie (September 10, 1968).*

Leo and Libra

Compatibility rating: ********* (9 out of 10)

Libra is a cardinal air sign ruled by Venus, meaning that its role is to initiate relationships. Leo is a fixed fire sign ruled by the Sun and needing to take charge. That shouldn't be a challenge, since you have much in common. Both of you are romantic and affectionate souls, love luxuries, and strive to further yourselves intellectually. You're a natural leader and, once a relationship takes off, will command centre stage. You admire diplomatic Libra, and Libra enjoys your flamboyance. You make an attractive couple—you both like to dress well. Libra is flirtatious and Leo is secure—to a point. (Libra has to massage Leo's ego.) Both like to travel—in style—and these two extravagant signs need a financial adviser to help them keep their spending in check. If there are disputes, you take sides, while Libra mediates. At work, you sign up the clients, and Libra looks after communications. Libra doesn't take criticism well, and Leo can be brusque. (You're fair but not always tactful.) Monotony is your enemy and Libra's too. Together you'll seek out enough variety for a couple of lifetimes.

Leo and Scorpio

Compatibility rating: ***** (5 out of 10)

This can be a challenging match: dominating Leo and controlling Scorpio. Both are fixed signs, both are intense, and neither wants its style cramped. The one encouraging thing is that you both have staying power. So if you do wind up together, you're in for the long haul. And the union will be based on attraction and admiration of your unique qualities. Scorpio can be devious, but does everything with passion and intensity—traits that you understand. And you thrive on flattery and recognition, which Scorpio will provide (but only if your performance merits it). Neither of you will admit to being wrong. Leo is very open, while Scorpio is secretive and curious. Still, Scorpio, like you, has its tender side—and funny side. A famous Scorpio trait is its ability to read others. Leo's life is an open book, so that won't be hard. You both do everything in extremes, and the two of you must set ground rules early on, figuring out who is in charge of what. You're both outspoken and neither plays games. *Political couple: Bill Clinton (August 19, 1946) and Hillary Rodham Clinton (October 26, 1947). Literary couple: Graeme Gibson (August 9, 1934) and Margaret Atwood (November 18, 1939).*

Leo and Sagittarius

Compatibility rating: ****** (6 out of 10)

Leo and Sagittarius are both fire signs. Both display idealism and optimism, and you're equally frank. Sometimes you're frank to a fault, but in the case of a Leo–Sagittarius pairing, each is responsive to criticism, which is seen as a learning tool. The two signs have monster egos but are self-confident enough not to be overwhelmed by the other. Both signs are romantic, but friendship is equally important. Sagittarius needs personal freedom, and you're one of the signs that will encourage it. You also share many interests—you both love to learn and are likely to take on volunteer work in addition to your day jobs. Regal Leo provides the elegance and Sagittarius the intellect. Sagittarius is the more spontaneous of the two. A Sagittarius parent will encourage a Leo kid to be a free spirit, while a Leo parent will understand Sagittarius's need to take flight. Sagittarius excels at business—learning quickly and having the ability to read between the lines. You can be extravagant and take risks, but Sagittarius, ruled by Jupiter, attracts money and has the business acumen to prevent you from giving away the bank.

Leo and Capricorn

Compatibility rating: ******** (8 out of 10)
There's potential for great compatibility between these two signs, more so when they are adults than as youngsters. Capricorn is the most ambitious of the signs, and if Leo has a materialistic side—sometimes, but not always, a trait—this can be a particularly successful union. You share a number of characteristics. Neither one is modest—you both want to be recognized for your achievements. But your reasons differ. For you, success means being able to afford life's many pleasures. For Capricorn, it's the quest—the challenge—that's all-important. While you take chances—with flair and drama—Capricorn is pragmatic

and persevering. You want to show off. Capricorn never reveals more than absolutely necessary. But you're both so focused on your goals that neither is perturbed by the other's motives. There is an important difference in personalities: you're optimistic, and Capricorn can be negative. On a more superficial level, you're both naturally attractive. You both also enjoy good food. If one sign can pump up Capricorn's self-confidence, it is Leo. At the same time, Capricorn the refiner can shape Leo's ideas and then patiently carry them to the finish line. *Presidential couple: Barack Obama (August 4, 1961) and Michelle Obama (January 17, 1964).*

Leo and Aquarius

Compatibility rating: ******* (7 out of 10)
Leo and Aquarius are opposite signs, with birthdays half a year apart (more or less). Opposite signs indicate an attraction based on similarities and differences. The Sun sign opposite yours has the same quality (cardinal, fixed, or mutable) as you, but the elements (air, earth, fire, or water) are different. Although opposite signs often share the same goals, each sign has its own reasons for going after those goals and its own methods in reaching them. Both you and Aquarius are intelligent with logical minds. Leo is noble and generous. Aquarius is eccentric and devoted to causes. Both are fixed signs—determined and lively. You have more structure in your life, while Aquarius is full of surprises. Living together, you provide the flamboyance and Aquarius the imagination. You both enjoy being surrounded by people, although you engage in one-on-one conversations

while Aquarius makes the rounds. You're a natural leader and Aquarius doesn't usually follow, but both signs are secure and can work out their roles in a personal or business relationship. As long as Leo makes the major decisions and Aquarius brings new ideas to the table, there won't be competition for the position of head honcho. But Aquarius sometimes hoards information, and Leo may—unintentionally—take credit for Aquarius's ideas. A Leo parent is likely to encourage an Aquarius child's unique traits, while an Aquarius parent will encourage a Leo kid's sense of drama.

Leo and Pisces

Compatibility rating: ***** (5 out of 10)

Your two signs are definitely attracted to each other—more for differences than similarities. Fixed fire sign Leo, with a fiery personality, comes on strong. That sits well with mutable water sign Pisces, who is more inspired than overwhelmed. You thrive on flattery, and there will be no shortage of it from Pisces. Pisces needs to feel loved and appreciated. And though you don't understand Pisces' moods, you admire the sign's spirituality, creativity, open-mindedness, compassion, and romantic nature. Pisces does best with a partner like Scorpio, who will be drawn to its mysterious nature. You do best with a hard-working partner like Capricorn. Pisces has a lazy side, which can be a turnoff. But it adapts easily to its surroundings, and you like to put your mark on your home—so there will be no disagreements about decor. Nor will there be significant differences about bringing up kids, who can inherit a unique combination of assurance and sensitivity. At work, Pisces will provide imagination, and you'll take charge. In the unlikely situation that Pisces is boss and you're the subordinate, Pisces will probably allow you to take over (or to think you're taking over), while you won't feel challenged by Pisces' more prestigious and better-paying job. *Celebrity couple: Lucille Ball (August 6, 1911) and Desi Arnaz (March 2, 1917).*

VIRGO COMPATIBLITY GUIDE

The following descriptions, based on your Sun sign, provide a broad picture of how you relate to members of all twelve signs (including your own) in the different spheres of your life.

Virgo and Aries

Compatibility rating: **** (4 out of 10)
You're a modest and cautious earth sign. Aries is expansive and reckless fire. You're detailed and thrifty. Aries is interested in the big picture—and is the zodiac's mega-spender. In other words, your attitudes are diametrically opposed. You look within and are extremely critical. Aries is an adventurer and, unless its pride is hurt, "gets over it." You may forgive but never forget. Still, an enjoyable relationship is possible because Virgo can be witty and affectionate and is happy to let action-oriented Aries look after life's larger decisions. You're

sometimes perceived as cool, but that's not a fair assessment. There is genuine warmth to your personality, and Aries can encourage your funny side. A Virgo relative or employee may be underappreciated but is always there to save the day. Unfortunately, Aries can take your skills for granted. Similarly, you feel under siege whenever Aries charges in, usually uninvited. For a relationship—personal or professional—to have any chance of success, Aries has to be careful not to exploit Virgo. You, in turn, need to learn a couple of words from the Aries vocabulary: *spontaneity* and *self-confidence*.

Virgo and Taurus

Compatibility rating: ***** (5 out of 10)
Both you and Taurus are earth signs, making you cautious and neat. You both also need to feel secure. Taurus is laid-back and more demonstrative than you are. Both signs prefer a small group to a large circle of entertaining. Both work hard and are careful with their money—it's not uncommon for the two of you to live beneath your means. As well, you take a traditional approach to courtship and romance and make an affectionate if not particularly passionate couple. The difficulty is that both signs will wait for the right moment to strike—and neither one is inclined to make the first, or second, move. Also, although loving and reliable, Taurus can be jealous. And you have high standards—sometimes impossibly high—and can be hypercritical. Taurus's jealousy and your finicky ways, if not kept in check, can bring down a relationship. In family situations, Taurus will be the warmer partner, while Virgo will tend to practicalities. If an

elder relative is ailing, for example, Taurus will provide warmth and compassion, while you will dole out the medications. Work-wise, you're obsessed with the details that Taurus detests (or ignores), so you complement each other neatly in a business arrangement. *Celebrity couple: Jessica (Sklar) Seinfeld (September 21, 1971) and Jerry Seinfeld (April 29, 1954). Celebrity skaters: Scott Moir (September 2, 1987) and Tessa Virtue (May 17, 1989).*

Virgo and Gemini

Compatibility rating: *** (5 out of 10)**

Both signs are curious but in different ways. Gemini is ever on the lookout in the quest for knowledge, while you seek ways to use knowledge for profit. Both signs are ruled by Mercury, which represents intelligence and communication, and both are mutable—versatile and, to an extent, willing to adapt. But Gemini's element is air, and yours is earth. So when Gemini is flying off to explore new ideas and places, you have both feet planted firmly on the ground. And you have a knack for turning a molehill into the Rockies, while Gemini cares so little about mundane details that friction is inevitable. Emotionally, Gemini is a lot cooler than you. At home, Gemini likes "neat clutter," but you're a fanatic. You each need to adapt, but it's not easy when both partners quickly become tense and irritable—often as a result of small things. Both of you are courteous, so you make an effort to understand each other. And you both enjoy helping out with a relative's, co-worker's, or next-door neighbour's difficulties. With your analytical mind, you can solve the most complicated problems; and the ones that remain can be smoothed by Gemini's charm. *Royal couple: Prince Albert (August 26, 1819) and Queen Victoria (May 24, 1819).*

Virgo and Cancer

Compatibility rating: ***** (5 out of 10)

Both Virgo and Cancer have tenacity. When the pair of you set your eyes on something, you're determined to get it. Not surprisingly, you make an effort to stay in a relationship once it's established. You're both affectionate, and there's an even chance you'll be drawn to each other. If you join forces, you'll discover that you're both house-proud. There's something else you share—you feel underappreciated. So you could spend a lot of time in your lovely home complaining about why relatives and co-workers don't give you credit. If that's the case, the relationship could become sombre. That's unfortunate because you share a great sense of humour and could spend time laughing instead. Ruled by the Moon, water sign Cancer enjoys living in the past. You, an earth sign ruled by Mercury, are more practical and live in the present tense. And Cancer enjoys clutter while you're picky, a difference that could be a deal-breaker. People usually give in to Cancer, but not when it comes to Virgo and order. Another difference is that Cancer enjoys company of all ages and interests, while you prefer a tight circle of friends. At work, you're the analyst, while Cancer is more in tune with people and personalities. Neither of you is hungry for power. Chances are you'll enjoy mutual respect.

Virgo and Leo

Compatibility rating: ****** (6 out of 10)

Because Virgo and Leo are neighbouring signs—Virgo follows Leo—the odds are that you share some planetary influences and have some common qualities. But judging by Sun signs alone, there could be difficulties launching a friendship. Leo is impulsive and dramatic, you're cautious and cool. Leo is larger than life with a monster ego. You're picky and insecure. Leo is extravagant and you're ultra-cautious with money. But if you can get past these differences, you can learn from and become devoted to each other. Leos look after the welfare of loved ones and, in the process, ignore their own aches and pains. Virgo, a health fanatic, will take charge of Leo's needs. In turn, you'll learn from Leo that there's more to life than fussing over details. Leo thinks big. For a realistic relationship to work, Virgo will need to think medium. Leo's strong quality is kindness, so the odds are that Leo will indulge you, especially in a family setting. At work, Leo and Virgo need to respect each other—Leo for taking control of the forest, and you for caring for the trees. *Celebrity couples: Marc Anthony (September 16, 1969) and Jennifer Lopez (July 24, 1969); Guy Ritchie (September 10, 1968) and Madonna (August 16, 1958).*

Virgo and Virgo

Compatibility rating: ******* (7 out of 10)

When two members of the same sign join forces, the connection can bring out the best and the worst in each. In the case of Virgo and Virgo, there's potential for a lively and enjoyable relationship or a complicated and confusing one. We have two mutable earth signs—critical, cool, analytical, calculating, and highly intellectual. Neither of you is spontaneous. Rather, you're perfectionism times two. You greatly appreciate each other's positive qualities, but you reinforce the negative ones. In the case of two Virgos, that can mean running a tight ship but with too many teeny rules. On the brighter side, you share a love of books, music, nature, and teaching. Virgos are environmentalists, and a pair of you will make the planet a better place. In family settings, you have a reputation for making sure everything is carefully planned. Children are fortunate to have a Virgo parent, aunt, or uncle—and a pair would be a treat. You inspire youngsters to do their best, and you indulge them too. At work, you'll be more popular with the boss—whose bacon you often save—than with co-workers. A pair of obsessive Virgos is a force to reckon with. Virgo will come down hard on those who don't pull their own weight. If the culprit (though unlikely) is a fellow Virgo, you can be certain that little mercy will be shown.

Virgo and Libra

Compatibility rating: ***** (5 out of 10)

Because Virgo and Libra are neighbouring signs—Libra follows Virgo—the odds are that you share some planetary influences and have some common qualities. But judging by Sun signs alone, you have a mixed relationship. Libra loves peace and gets along with most everyone, but you're fussy about who qualifies for your friendship circle. You both like to laugh, though you have more of a caustic wit. And you both admire good behaviour. As for the differences: You're ruled by Mercury and are down to earth, while Libra is ruled by Venus and enjoys life's luxuries. Libra is easygoing and romantic—qualities you enjoy. But Libra is also flirtatious—and you have a possessive streak. You're supremely organized, and Libra is spontaneous. Where you plan a trip for months, checking maps and weather reports, Libra enjoys spur-of-the-moment travel and will make the most of any situation. Libra can also make you smile. In turn, you try to organize Libra and can add order to Libra's life (and desk). Virgo is a demanding employer and employee and cuts little slack. Libra is fair-minded and understands that Virgo wants only what's best for the team and has no hidden agenda. *Celebrity couples: Margaret Trudeau (September 10, 1948) and Pierre Elliott Trudeau (October 18, 1919); Jada Pinkett-Smith (September 18, 1971) and Will Smith (September 25, 1968).*

Virgo and Scorpio

Compatibility rating: ***** (7 out of 10)**

Virgo is a mutable earth sign, ruled by Mercury, the planet of communication. Scorpio is a fixed water sign, ruled by passionate, intense Mars (along with Pluto). On the surface, it looks like the two of you have opposite temperaments, but there is definite potential for a Virgo–Scorpio relationship. You're a problem-solver who seeks information, which you can use for profitable purposes. Scorpio is a mystery-solver who also seeks out information, which it can use for a variety of purposes, including nefarious ones. Scorpio's interests differ from yours, but you both take extreme pride in your work. And while you are shy and Scorpio is magnetic, you each have a tender side. Each of you has a way with a zinger, though Scorpio is much blunter. You don't understand Scorpio's need for secrecy, and Scorpio doesn't understand your obsession over detail. Both signs can be possessive and unforgiving. You can only hope your traits don't rub off on each other. There's no one harder to deal with than a Scorpio who aspires to perfection or a Virgo who turns jealous. At work, Scorpio doesn't like to take orders and Virgo doesn't like to give them, so a Scorpio boss and Virgo employee scenario usually works better than the reverse arrangement. *Celebrity couple: Elvis Costello (August 25, 1954) and Diana Krall (November 16, 1964).*

Virgo and Sagittarius

Compatibility rating: **** (6 out of 10)**
Virgo–Sagittarius can be a challenging relationship. Sagittarius is gregarious and wants to be surrounded by upbeat family and friends, but this sign needs time alone too. You, in contrast, are content on your own or in a small and familiar group, and you lean toward pessimism. Another difficulty with this partnership is that you require appreciation, and Sagittarius doesn't see the point in acknowledging every contribution. And there's more—Sagittarius is blunt and outspoken, and you respond poorly to criticism. But don't write off this union. You both have impeccable standards, and neither of you will tolerate a phony. As well, you get a kick out of Sagittarius's outrageous sense of humour, and Sagittarius admires your caring heart and eye for detail. You're both mutable signs, so there's a chance that one

or both of you will bend, even slightly. Yes, Sagittarius can't ignore the way you make a production over tiny flaws, and you can't understand why little—or big—things don't upset Sagittarius. But gradually, whether you live or work together, you'll get to depend on each other. You'll tend to Sagittarius's practical needs, and Sagittarius will tend to your emotional ones. In the process, you'll discover that there's much to learn from each other. *Celebrity couple: Beyoncé Knowles (September 4, 1981) and Jay-Z (December 4, 1969).*

Virgo and Capricorn

Compatibility rating: ***** (7 out of 10)**
Both you and Capricorn are earth signs. You both plan a lot and think logically. Neither is spontaneous, preferring to organize every detail in advance. Your ideas are conventional rather than innovative. If that sounds like the ingredients for a boring relationship, you're not off the mark. But it doesn't have to be dull. In fact, this pairing has a high success rate. The two of you can create a strong foundation for a long-lasting relationship at any level. Both of you will continue to climb—you toward perfection, Capricorn toward success. Both signs lean toward pessimism—or, as you would prefer to call it, realism. You both prefer a small, tight circle of friends, and you both place family first. Capricorn is the strong and silent type, and you're more inventive. Both signs know the value of money, and while neither is a cheapskate, you tend to live below your means. What on paper may appear unexciting will, in fact, be as comfortable as a favourite sweater. For both signs, the head, not the heart, takes

command. A Capricorn relative encourages you to realize your potential. A Virgo relative will understand Capricorn's need to persevere. The relationship may sound businesslike, but it is usually harmonious. *Celebrity couple: Lauren Bacall (September 16, 1924) and Humphrey Bogart (December 25, 1899).*

Virgo and Aquarius

Compatibility rating: *** (5 out of 10)**

These two signs do not, on the surface, have much in common. You're the most routine-oriented of the signs, and Aquarius is, well, the most eccentric. You're obsessed with details. Aquarius is focused on ideas. You're compatible with conservative signs such as Capricorn, while Aquarius does best with independent, innovative types. Aquarius is also a humanitarian and philanthropic, and it may be difficult to get you to loosen the purse strings. Of course, given other influences, you can defy the odds. It helps that both are excellent teachers. In certain areas you complement each other. You have a shrewd business mind and will be happy to assume financial responsibilities, while Aquarius will be pleased to delegate day-to-day business matters. Aquarius needs to find a partner who appreciates, or at least accepts, his or her eccentricities, and you like hanging out with achievers. So it helps, at least, if Aquarius is a successful eccentric. With your eye for detail and business acumen, you prefer a rigid work environment, while Aquarius avoids the routine. For the two to live or work together, you need to share at least one common interest, so start comparing notes. (*Suggestion:* Yoga is a good possibility.)

Virgo and Pisces

Compatibility rating: ******* (9 out of 10)**

Virgo and Pisces are opposite signs, with birthdays half a year apart (more or less). Opposite signs indicate an attraction based on similarities and differences. The Sun sign opposite yours has the same quality (cardinal, fixed, or mutable) as you, but the elements (air, earth, fire, or water) are different. Although opposite signs often share the same goals, each sign has its own reasons for going after those goals and its own methods in reaching them. A Virgo and Pisces match can be ideal on an emotional and practical level. Because you are both mutable signs, you communicate easily. You're an earth sign and Pisces is water, so you're grounded, while Pisces is imaginative and creative. You can benefit handsomely from each other. Pisces needs to acquire your planning abilities, and your life becomes more interesting when you let Pisces' inspiration rub off on you. You can be negative and Pisces moody. It's best for one of you to retreat when the other is downbeat. You're both kind, romantic, and vulnerable, and those qualities form a bond. Pisces will help temper your rigidity, while you'll provide order in Pisces' life. You're complementary in a working relationship as well—you're analytical, and Pisces tries new things. As travel companions you're a successful team, with you researching the destinations and, on arrival, Pisces' imagination leading the way.

LIBRA
COMPATIBILITY GUIDE

The following descriptions, based on your Sun sign, provide a broad picture of how you relate to members of all twelve signs (including your own) in the different spheres of your life.

Libra and Aries

Compatibility rating: ******* (7 out of 10)

Libra and Aries are opposite signs, with birthdays about half a year apart (more or less). Opposite signs indicate an attraction based on similarities and differences. The Sun sign opposite yours has the same quality (cardinal, fixed, or mutable) as you, but the elements (air, earth, fire, or water) are different. Although opposite signs often share the same goals, each sign has its own reasons for going after those goals and its own methods in reaching them. You and Aries are cardinal signs—you both love action. But you're diplomacy personified, and Aries is blunt. Still, if anyone can tackle Aries' aggressiveness, it's you—charming and funny. You also admire Aries' free spirit. Your greatest skill is to weigh all sides of a matter before making a decision—life is a balancing act. Aries appreciates your sense of fairness. You know that, through your different methods, you can reach a common objective, whether in love, in domestic harmony, or in a professional environment. The two of you mostly complement rather than duplicate or cancel out each other. And though you are partnership-oriented and Aries is more independent, neither of you is either passive or possessive. You both like to be around upbeat people and are yourselves confident—as well as materialistic. The one glitch is that Aries can cross the line between take-charge and controlling. Still, it's a compatible union—rambunctious Aries and peace-loving Libra—and one is as determined as the other. *Celebrity couple: Avril Lavigne (September 27, 1984) and Deryck Whibley (March 21, 1980).*

Libra and Taurus

Compatibility rating: ***** (5 out of 10)

The fact that you're both ruled by Venus makes you good partners at many levels. Both signs are peace-loving, mature, tactful, artistic—and materialistic. But a gap exists. Taurus is a fixed sign—set in its ways, possessive, and comfortable among a small and safe group. You're air—spontaneous and eager to communicate with people from all walks of life. Stated another way, you'll become involved in Taurus's interests, but Taurus won't learn about yours. You'll be ready to go to the theatre or a party, while Taurus decides at the last minute to stay home and watch a movie or hockey game. Libras are unpredictable and changeable, qualities that many signs find charming and refreshing. Not Taurus. Your indecisiveness will be a source of frustration. In family settings, you'll provide the optimism, while Taurus offers caution, giving a nice balance. And you're both nurturing souls. Because of the shared Venus connection, you like to keep the working environment harmonious. However, your popularity can tick off Taurus, and Taurus's rigidity can get on your nerves. So the harmony you promote may apply to everyone but the two of you.

Libra and Gemini

Compatibility rating: ***** (7 out of 10)**

The Gemini–Libra pairing is ideal in many ways. Each of you thrives on new ideas, adventures, and surprises, and if you get together, you keep each other young. You're both air signs, and neither of you is jealous or demanding. You are intellectual equals and you both like to socialize. Communication is a central part of both personalities, with Gemini as the originator of new ideas and Libra happy to refine and edit Gemini's words. There are potential conflicts, however. You're both impractical, and unless independently wealthy (very wealthy), you each benefit from a more decisive partner. Libra, though the diplomat of the zodiac, can sometimes be selfish and quick-tempered. And your indecisiveness can often stifle Gemini's need to move on. Your ruling planet is Venus—you need to be surrounded by beautiful (and expensive) things. Gemini, ruled by Mercury, cares about ideas. With such different objectives, a business partnership could prove problematic. Still, both signs have so much in common and genuinely like each other that they will make the effort to work out any differences. *Celebrity couples: Keith Urban (October 26, 1967) and Nicole Kidman (June 20, 1967); Linda McCartney (September 24, 1941) and Paul McCartney (June 18, 1942).*

Libra and Cancer

Compatibility rating: ***** (7 out of 10)**

Cancer and Libra seem to connect well because they share interests. Cancer is the most patriotic of the signs, and you're often drawn to politics. While Cancer enjoys all the comforts of home and Libra is drawn to the more luxurious ones, the two signs have a passion for antiques. As well, you both like rubbing shoulders with the rich and famous. Cancer does well in the arts. You need to be surrounded by beautiful things and have many artist friends. You both have relatively thin skins, but you're both mannerly and not likely to hurt each other. And because you're both cardinal signs, you match each other's strong drive. One difficulty is that you could find Cancer too clingy—you're an intellectual air sign and like doing things on your own. You might also find a Cancer partner to be too homebound, but you have a knack for coaxing people into doing what you want. Interestingly, both signs often find themselves working at home. Cancer and Libra would make good partners in a home business. Both are hard-working and willing to compromise for the common good, although Cancer tends to nag, something you don't handle well. *Celebrity couple: Tommy Lee (October 3, 1962) and Pamela Anderson (July 1, 1967).*

Libra and Leo

Compatibility rating: ********* (9 out of 10)
Fire sign Leo and air sign Libra balance each other. Leo is ruled by the Sun, the centre of the universe. You're ruled by Venus— who provides beauty and romance. You're both optimistic. Leo takes bold strokes, and you follow a subtle approach. Leo is secure enough to allow you your interests, friends, and flirtations, and you're happy to indulge Leo's need to show off and be flattered. You both enjoy luxuries, although Leo's taste is a little gar- ish. As a cardinal sign, you initiate relationships—and you're

drawn to Leo's flamboyance. You also like the fact that you're both goal-oriented, professionally and intellectually. You make an attractive couple and can work a crowd—Leo with magnetism, you with communication skills. You both enjoy travelling and splurging, and that's where the red light goes on. As two extravagant signs, you need a financial adviser. In family relationships, Leo is likely to take sides while you mediate. At work, Leo closes the deals and you look after the public relations. You don't take criticism well, and Leo can be brusque, but this is something you learn to live with. You don't like monotony— and together you seek out enough variety for two lifetimes.

Libra and Virgo

Compatibility rating: ***** (5 out of 10)
Because Libra and Virgo are neighbouring signs—Libra follows Virgo—the odds are that you share some planetary influences and have some common qualities. But judging by Sun signs alone, you have a mixed relationship at best. Both signs like words and both have a good sense of humour, although Virgo's wit is more caustic than yours. As well, you both admire good behaviour and both like to discover new places. As for the differences: Virgo can stir up trouble by being critical and picky, while you personify diplomacy. To some, Virgo appears cool and detached, while you're bubbly, outgoing, and even flirtatious. Virgo is supremely (or annoyingly) organized and needs routines. Libra is more spontaneous. Where Virgo will plan a trip for months, checking maps and weather reports, you enjoy spur-of-the-moment travel. Virgo is opinionated, often in a

negative way, but you provide a boost of optimism. The fact is that you're fundamentally fond of each other, and though it takes work, you're both willing to compromise. Virgo will help organize you—adding some needed order to your life (and desk). As an employer or employee, Virgo is demanding. You're fair-minded and one of the few who understands that Virgo wants what's best for the team and has no hidden motives. *Celebrity couples: Pierre Elliott Trudeau (October 18, 1919) and Margaret Trudeau (September 10, 1948); Will Smith (September 25, 1968) and Jada Pinkett-Smith (September 18, 1971).*

Libra and Libra

Compatibility rating: ****** (6 out of 10)
When two members of the same sign join forces, the connection can bring out the best and the worst in each. In the case of Libra, there's potential for a lively and enjoyable relationship or a complicated and confusing one. We have two air signs—on the go, rushing about, witty, and charming . . . and utterly indecisive and extravagant. Whatever the outcome, a Libra–Libra pairing will provide a fascinating duet—two people who enjoy parties, need stimulation, and avoid tedious work. You're a cardinal sign, so you solve problems by being active. You're ruled by Venus—the planet responsible for art and beauty. Two Libras are thus likely to find themselves living in sumptuous surroundings. Even if you don't have the funds to support your taste, you attempt to provide elegance. Together, a pair of Libras will strive to create a peaceable environment. However, if there are long-term problems—money-, family-, or job-related—you're likely

to find two Libras burying their heads in the sand. Libras insist on loyalty, and a pair under the same roof provides a lesson in harmony. But when one of you reaches a breaking point—it's inevitable—take cover. At work, Libra is "the voice of sanity." You generally work well with others, and you rarely find a Libra–Libra competition. But because Libra needs change and is known to daydream and flirt, it's best to keep them on separate teams. *Celebrity couples: Catherine Zeta-Jones (September 25, 1969) and Michael Douglas (September 25, 1944); Susan Sarandon (October 4, 1946) and Tim Robbins (October 16, 1958).*

Libra and Scorpio

Compatibility rating: ****** (6 out of 10)

There are many differences between these two signs, yet there's no denying an attraction exists between romantic Libra and passionate Scorpio. You're discreet while Scorpio is a snoop. If a friend had a date, you'll ask cautiously about "the weekend," while Scorpio will try to dig up as many details as possible. (Interestingly, it's Libra who usually gets the information.) Libra is flirtatious. Scorpio has a jealous, possessive, and demanding side. Libra is the zodiac's peacemaker. Scorpio is the zodiac's troublemaker. But Scorpio is an exciting sign, as well as a loyal one. And beneath your calm exterior often lies a stormy interior. So you often bring out each other's hidden sides and meet each other halfway. Because Libra and Scorpio are neighbouring signs—Scorpio follows Libra—the odds are that you share some planetary influences and have some common qualities. You're a cardinal (action) sign, ruled by Venus, the planet responsible for love and beauty.

Scorpio is a fixed sign, co-ruled by warlike Mars and powerful Pluto. Your different approaches to almost everything—Scorpio, intense; you, subtle—can be confusing. But curiously, you rarely seem to get in each other's way. Scorpio admires your taste, social skills, and intellect, and you respect the intensity that Scorpio brings to relationships, beliefs, and work.

Libra and Sagittarius

Compatibility rating: ******** (8 out of 10)

This combination has many differences yet manages a high compatibility index. Both signs are sociable, charming, and intelligent—and those qualities provide a strong bond between you. You're a cardinal air sign ruled by Venus, and you need to be surrounded by beautiful (and expensive) objects. Sagittarius is generous and likes to indulge others. Sagittarius also needs a wide berth—lots of space. You're not possessive, but you need companionship—so you'll have to cultivate your own friends. People say you're indecisive, but in a relationship with Sagittarius you're generally the one making the decisions, as well as the plans. There are more things that bother you about Sagittarius than the reverse. Notably, you have difficulty handling criticism, and Sagittarius has no problem dishing it out. However, Sagittarius builds up credits in your ledger book and you're more forgiving than you would be of other signs. (*Note:* This is not the case if you work together.) In fact, Sagittarius can alienate others—friends and associates alike—because of the bluntness factor, but you remain a loyal partner. *Celebrity couple: Randy Bachman (September 27, 1943) and Denise McCann (December 16, 1948).*

Libra and Capricorn

Compatibility rating: ****** (6 out of 10)

You're an artistic sign and need to be surrounded by lovely, luxurious things. You don't obsess about how you'll attain those objects of your desire. Capricorn, in contrast, is the most ambitious of the signs, and the quest for achievement is more important than the actual things that success can bring. Capricorn isn't extravagant the way you are and may not be as generous as you would wish, but you'll find security in a Capricorn. And in you, Capricorn will find adventure, albeit of the vicarious variety. For Capricorn, relationships are not as important as they are for you. Yet the two of you often get along well. Both cardinal signs, you initiate action and excel at communicating with each other. Another thing that leads to chemistry between you is that, superficial as it sounds, appearances are important. You're far more sociable than Capricorn, who isn't antisocial but is rarely the life of the party. You also bring optimism to the relationship. Capricorn isn't gloomy but is introspective. You're the official caregiver in the family, and often, though not always, Capricorn prefers to be the main breadwinner. Both at home and at work, you complement each other neatly. You provide the ideas, and Capricorn shapes them.

Libra and Aquarius

Compatibility rating: ********* (9 out of 10)

This is potentially one of the happiest combinations in the zodiac. In a nutshell, you're both devoted to making the world a better—and more beautiful—place. That world includes your world, of course, and each of you indulges in life's pleasures and luxuries. You complement rather than duplicate each other. Libra thrives on company, and Aquarius needs privacy. Neither of you will cramp the other's style. It's not surprising that both are air signs, Libra being a cardinal one and Aquarius a fixed sign. Libra vacillates but under pressure will take over in a crisis. Aquarius is the more focused of the two and can get irritable if you don't pull your weight—but Aquarius brings out your best, so that is rarely an issue. Although you seek permanence in a relationship, you don't always find it and are content on your own. Aquarius isn't as interested in commitment but enjoys an upbeat partnership. Your relationship isn't always going to set off sparks, but it's comfortable. It's not surprising that Libra and Aquarius frequently form platonic relationships. If one of the signs loses its cool, it's more likely to be Libra, who is sensitive to Aquarius's (and everyone else's) criticisms. But every family has its squabbles, and the ones between these two signs never last long. *Celebrity couple: John Lennon (October 9, 1940) and Yoko Ono (February 18, 1933). Royal couple: Sarah Ferguson, Duchess of York (October 15, 1959), and Prince Andrew (February 19, 1960).*

Libra and Pisces

Compatibility rating: ***** (7 out of 10)**
Libra is ruled by Venus, Pisces by Neptune. The two planets get along nicely, with one encouraging the other and both sharing a spiritual side. You help Pisces to let its imagination wander, and Pisces inspires you to think intuitively. Pisces has a number of Venus-related qualities, so the two of you are romantically in-

clined, sentimental, and giving. The one similarity that may create havoc is that neither sign is practical. Pisces is a mutable water sign—moody and insecure, and needing change. Libra is upbeat, and while you avoid clingy types, you're drawn to Pisces' poetic nature. Of the twelve signs, Pisces is the most easily influenced and will assume many of Libra's traits—everything from your indecisiveness to your love of the arts. Of the two, Libra will take control when the need arises. Both signs are compassionate and will treat each other well, even if they're simply acquaintances. Pisces is the more intuitive of the two, and will figure out your motives, which are sometimes complicated. Neither of you is orderly, and you both like to be surrounded by treasures. One can always locate a Pisces or Libra work station: cluttered with photos, plants, and, most likely, a mountain of unorganized papers.

SCORPIO COMPATIBILITY GUIDE

The following descriptions, based on your Sun sign, provide a broad picture of how you relate to members of all twelve signs (including your own) in the different spheres of your life.

Scorpio and Aries

Compatibility rating: **** (6 out of 10)**
Scorpio is a fixed water sign, and Aries a cardinal fire sign. You're both ruled by warlike Mars (Scorpio is ruled by Pluto as

well). Not surprisingly, you admire each other's strengths. But both of you want to take the initiative—and take control. You are two freedom-loving, independent signs, and compromise isn't in either of your vocabularies. You take control in different ways. Scorpio is possessive, intense, mysterious, and emotional. Aries, the first sign in the zodiac, is the more spirited, resilient, and optimistic. Of course, other planetary influences can soften either personality, so the union has potential. As well, there are traits that you pick up from each other. You may learn to be more spontaneous from Aries, and Aries can learn patience from you. You also respect Aries' passion and drive but purely on an intellectual level. In a relationship, you want it all, and Aries isn't going to hand over the reins. You're usually the family member whom relatives call in time of crisis. But your intense nature is something Aries needs a break from. In a business relationship, your intuition and Aries' forcefulness can be a powerful combination. You have a great business mind, but your secrecy is too much for open-book Aries to handle. *Celebrity couple: David Furnish (October 25, 1962) and Elton John (March 25, 1947).*

Scorpio and Taurus

Compatibility rating: ******** (8 out of 10)
Scorpio and Taurus are opposite signs, with birthdays half a year apart (more or less). Opposite signs indicate an attraction based on similarities and differences. The Sun sign opposite yours has the same quality (cardinal, fixed, or mutable) as you, but the elements (air, earth, fire, or water) are different. Although opposite signs often share the same goals, each sign

has its own reasons for going after those goals and its own methods in reaching them. In your case, it helps that you're both fixed signs—fiercely loyal but also possessive. Both of you enjoy long-term relationships, and you're physically compatible, with strong drives. You're the most secretive of the signs, and you need to uncover everyone else's secrets too. You'll dig like a terrier until you root them out. You're often successful and always determined, but not when it comes to Taurus, whose middle name is privacy. In fact, Taurus is the most tenacious member of the zodiac, and once its mind is made up not even as powerful a force as Scorpio has a hope of changing it. In family and work settings, your intuitive and resourceful nature is generally welcomed. But when controlling Scorpio and stubborn Taurus take on a joint project, it's often a case of push meeting shove. *Celebrity skaters: David Pelletier (November 22, 1974) and Jamie Salé (April 21, 1977).*

Scorpio and Gemini

Compatibility rating: **** (4 out of 10)
Gemini is witty and chatty and gets along with anyone—almost anyone. You may be one of the few who find Gemini's friendly nattering and quick wit to be annoying. As well, your intensity can crush friendly, flirtatious Gemini. You're ruled by Mars (along with Pluto), responsible for power, magnetism, and sensibility. Gemini's planet is Mercury, which inspires ideas, intelligence, and communication. Gemini circles the world in a casual way. You, in contrast, are possessive and demanding. Of course, astrology is based on more than Sun signs; depending

on other influences, it's possible for a relationship between the two of you to work. (If, for example, your Gemini partner's tenth house, which relates to career, is ruled by Capricorn, you may wind up with a partner more driven than you are.) But based on Sun signs alone, you will remain suspicious and mysterious. Don't forget either that you're competitive, resourceful, vindictive, and suspicious. Gemini is fine with the first two traits, but the last two could create havoc in any kind of relationship. *Celebrity couple: Vivien Leigh (November 5, 1913) and Laurence Olivier (May 22, 1907). Royal couple: Grace Kelly (November 12, 1929) and Prince Rainier III (May 31, 1923).*

Scorpio and Cancer

Compatibility rating: **** (6 out of 10)**

Cancer's element is water—it's a fluid and changeable sign. Its quality is cardinal, making it driven. And ruled by the Moon, it's moody. But that's not necessarily a negative thing. Although sullen at times, Cancer is also caring, affectionate, and funny. And for Cancer, the home and all it symbolizes is of greatest significance. You and Cancer are compatible on several levels. First, you're also a water sign, so you understand each other's emotional personalities. You're also both possessive—but in a way that cancels each other out rather than reinforces this trait. You're also both intuitive, demanding, and seek out a permanent relationship. Cancer is more flexible than you. (Who isn't?) But you both bear grudges, and neither of you forgets a slight, no matter how minor. Because of your shared element, you pick up some of each other's tastes. And while you are more eager to venture outside the home, you're each happy in your own little world, wherever that may be. As colleagues, Scorpio is the more passionate and more competitive, but Cancer is no wuss. Scorpio likes to dominate and control, and Cancer is content being creative and inventive. *Celebrity couples: Calista Flockhart (November 11, 1964) and Harrison Ford (July 13, 1942); Rita Wilson (October 26, 1956) and Tom Hanks (July 9, 1956). Royal couples: Prince Charles (November 14, 1948) and Camilla Parker Bowles (July 17, 1947); Prince Charles (November 14, 1948) and Princess Diana (July 1, 1961).*

Scorpio and Leo

Compatibility rating: ***** (5 out of 10)

Both of you are fixed signs (neither is likely to change), and both are intense. Neither you nor Leo likes having your style cramped. The most encouraging thing is that you both have staying power. So if you do get together, you're in for the long haul. It will be an interesting union based on attraction and admiration. You can be devious, but you do everything with passion and intensity—traits that Leo appreciates. And Leo thrives on flattery and applause, something you'll provide . . . if you admire the performance. Neither of you will readily admit to being wrong—and it will take an outsider to break a stalemate. Leo is the more trusting partner; you can be suspicious and nosy. But you have a tender side and a funny side, and even egotistical Leo will find your wit irresistible. Another trait is your ability to read others—and you'll see that beneath Leo's bluster is a heart of gold. The key is for you and Leo to set ground rules; the big question being, Who's the boss? At work, Leo's larger-than-life personality and your intuition make both of you suited to sales. You're both outspoken, but you'll discover you bring out the best in each other. *Political couple: Hillary Rodham Clinton (October 26, 1947) and Bill Clinton (August 19, 1946). Literary couple: Margaret Atwood (November 18, 1939) and Graeme Gibson (August 9, 1934).*

Scorpio and Virgo

Compatibility rating: ******* (7 out of 10)

You're a fixed water sign, ruled by warlike Mars (co-ruled by Pluto), and Virgo is a mutable earth sign—feet planted firmly on the ground and ruled by Mercury, planet of communication. You take a haphazard approach, and Virgo is meticulous. You're emotional and passionate, and Virgo intellectual and cool. But both of you are hard-working, shrewd, and practical. Virgo is a problem-solver—methodical and analytical. You do everything with great passion. And yet you each have a tender side. You're both cynical too. Virgo makes small but pointed digs, while you're blunter. Virgo doesn't understand your mysterious ways but finds you fun to be around. You find it frustrating to wait for Virgo to finalize every detail but relish Virgo's dry wit. As well, nobody wants to cross either sign—both can be unforgiving. At work, Scorpio doesn't like to take orders, and Virgo doesn't like to give them, so a Scorpio boss and Virgo employee scenario usually works better than the reverse arrangement. Neither sign knows the meaning of moderation. *Celebrity couple: Diana Krall (November 16, 1964) and Elvis Costello (August 25, 1954).*

Scorpio and Libra

Compatibility rating: ****** (6 out of 10)

Because Scorpio and Libra are neighbouring signs—Scorpio follows Libra—the odds are that you share some planetary influences and have some common qualities. But judging by Sun signs alone, you are, in many ways, opposites. Libra is discreet, while you're a snoop. If a friend had a date, Libra will ask cautiously about "the weekend," while you'll ferret out as many details as possible. (Interestingly, it's Libra who usually gets the information.) Libra is light-hearted and eager to please. You have a possessive, shrewd, and demanding side. Libra is the zodiac's peacemaker. You're the zodiac's troublemaker. Yet an underlying attraction exists, and you're both committed to a lasting relationship. As well, beneath Libra's calm exterior lies a stormy interior—something you discover quickly. Libra is a cardinal (driven) sign, ruled by Venus, the planet of love, beauty, and sophistication. You're a fixed sign and deeply passionate. A relationship can be explosive unless jealous Scorpio understands that Libra's flirtations are harmless. You are both generous and supportive parents (or uncles or aunts), but Scorpio is more demanding. At work, Libra will excel at communications and you at sales and marketing, and your combined intellect can be a formula for success.

Scorpio and Scorpio

Compatibility rating: ****** (6 out of 10)

When two members of the same sign join forces, the connection can bring out the best and the worst in each. In the case of Scorpio, we have a duplicated fixed sign (energetic, stubborn) and water sign (passionate, intense), so there's potential for a lively and enjoyable relationship, a complicated and emotional one, or something in between. On one level, your suspicion may be reinforced. But so may your passion, commitment, chemistry, and drive—all of which define Scorpio. You also understand each other's insecurities. Scorpio reads people like a book and has built-in relationship radar. For a pair, it translates into either love or the opposite at first sight. Each Scorpio seeks someone who is passionate and driven—and when you find your match, prepare for sufficient power to light up Nunavut on December 21. With that level of motivation, anything is possible. But there are other traits that come with the Scorpio–Scorpio package, notably jealousy and secrecy. Whether they cancel each other out, even partly, or reinforce each other depends on the mix of other planetary influences. In the worst-case scenario, this pairing would be better suited to international espionage than romance. In other areas of your life, two Scorpio relatives or co-workers bring with them a rare mix of determination, magnetism, creativity, and cunning. Their combined investigative powers are extraordinary. So is their memory: an asset or a liability for everyone else, depending on what each Scorpio chooses to remember.

Scorpio and Sagittarius

Compatibility rating: *** (5 out of 10)**

Because Scorpio and Sagittarius are neighbouring signs—Sagittarius follows Scorpio—the odds are that you share some planetary influences and have some common qualities. But judging by Sun signs alone, you are, in many ways, opposites. To begin, you are co-ruled by Mars (militant) and Pluto (intense), and Sagittarius by Jupiter (expansion and luck). Scorpio is a fixed water sign, and Sagittarius a mutable fire sign. You lean toward extremes—you can be magnetic and charming, as well as suspicious and obsessive. Sagittarius shares the first two qualities but not the last. Among the things you have in common: both are driven, both frequently attain success, and both are intellectually oriented (although your interests differ). And it's not in either nature to compromise. But in many ways—notably how you approach life—you are polar opposites. Sagittarius is blunt and outspoken, while you're mannerly. You operate on an intuitive level, and Sagittarius uses logic. In a Scorpio–Sagittarius relationship, your intensity and Sagittarius's restlessness may present too large a gap to bridge. Still, Sagittarius takes chances and Scorpio likes adventure—so you may decide to take a chance with each other. As parents, your approaches differ too. Sagittarius relates to children and will give them lots of latitude, while a Scorpio parent is far more protective. A business pairing—Sagittarius's flamboyance, Scorpio's passion—can be successful, but only if Scorpio is less secretive and Sagittarius less reckless.

Scorpio and Capricorn

Compatibility rating: ****** (6 out of 10)
You are intense and seek power, and Capricorn is the zodiac's most ambitious sign. The result is that, in a relationship, you understand each other's drive and determination. There's definite potential for a financially successful partnership. But

what about getting along on an emotional level? That's a tough call, because Capricorn rarely shows feelings while your first need is emotional security. What's often found in a Scorpio–Capricorn relationship is respect. You're both self-centred, so it's no surprise that the traits you like in each other are ones you admire about yourself: hard-working, demanding, disciplined, competitive. Capricorn is a cardinal (action) earth sign, while you're a fixed water sign. You react to your surroundings while Capricorn zeroes in on a specific task. And where you look for hidden messages in words and actions, Capricorn is far more literal-minded. For you, unlike for Capricorn, life is not a case of "what you see is what you get." You're too mysterious. To achieve something more fulfilling in a relationship, you'll need to convince Capricorn that life is more than a quest. You have the passion to do that. As family members, both signs are dependable. It's up to Scorpio to encourage a Capricorn's curiosity, while Capricorn needs to convince Scorpio that not everything in life is a mystery to be solved.

Scorpio and Aquarius

Compatibility rating: ****** (6 out of 10)

There are certainly things you enjoy about each other and, in fact, Scorpio and Aquarius have the potential to be a highly compatible pair of signs. Scorpio is a water sign ruled by warlike Mars (and Pluto). Aquarius is an air sign ruled by Uranus (independence and originality). You accept—in fact, appreciate— many of Aquarius's eccentricities and admire its humanitarian spirit. You also like that Aquarius is attentive without being smothering. However, you may find Aquarius's independent nature hard to adapt to, and Aquarius won't give up freedom. This is something to resolve because both of you are stubborn—and you're downright demanding. Both signs are very curious and love to investigate the world around them, and both have a good sense of humour, so you're ideal travel companions. As parents, this union offers the best of both worlds. Aquarius encourages children to be curious and independent, and Scorpio is dependable though demanding. Job-wise, you're career-minded from an early age, and your intuition makes you a top problem-solver. Aquarius brings innovation and ideas. Neither of you tolerates laziness, and in many ways you make an ideal team. *Celebrity couple: Demi Moore (November 11, 1962) and Ashton Kutcher (February 7, 1978).*

Scorpio and Pisces

Compatibility rating: ******* (7 out of 10)
Scorpio and Pisces are both water signs, which may explain why you understand each other so well. You're also both possessive. Water signs are intuitive and perceptive—you can both be psychics or psychologists. Pisces brings out Scorpio's positive qualities—tenderness, charisma, and charm. You have a surprising level of strength—it's not always apparent, but Pisces sees it. In a similar way, while others find Pisces emotional and moody, you respond to its creative and gentle ways. Pisces is easy to mould, which is one of the things that attracts you to that sign—you like to mentor, teach, and shape. If the two signs connect, you'll find you depend on each other. You have to be

careful, however, that you don't overwhelm Pisces, since you're ruled by aggressive Mars (and co-ruled by powerful Pluto). Neptune rules Pisces, and Pisces will stand up for its beliefs. Both signs are intuitive and can pick up on even the most subtle vibes. But Scorpio can be unforgiving, while Pisces shows tremendous empathy. Sometimes Pisces takes on other people's problems and concentrates on them rather than on his or her own. Scorpio needs to be sure that a Pisces partner, relative, or co-worker does not lose his or her identity. Encourage Pisces' talents, and share in interests that appeal to you as well, such as meditation and yoga. Remember, too, that Pisces needs stimulation. *Celebrity couples: Richard Burton (November 10, 1925) and Elizabeth Taylor (February 27, 1932); Goldie Hawn (November 21, 1945) and Kurt Russell (March 17, 1951).*

SAGITTARIUS COMPATIBILITY GUIDE

The following descriptions, based on your Sun sign, provide a broad picture of how you relate to members of all twelve signs (including your own) in the different spheres of your life.

Sagittarius and Aries

Compatibility rating: ****** (8 out of 10)**
Both you and Aries are fire signs, but Aries is ruled by warlike Mars and you by Jupiter, who represents expansiveness (and

attracts money). You're both energetic and adventurous, and neither of you likes being tied down. You're also both good listeners. Fiery Sagittarius is mutable, never possessive, and feels secure letting Aries take charge of things. And while both signs are prone to a quick temper, your anger, though intense and sometimes nasty, is short-lived. A potential drawback in this relationship is that both signs lack commitment, so that in a romantic union especially, neither one is in a hurry to bite the bullet. But when a commitment is made, each sign is willing to respect the other's need for independence. In other areas, such as family and career spheres, you and Aries are equally enthusiastic. As a bonus, Aries is usually amused rather than put off by your outspokenness. You're wise in business and can help implement Aries' ideas. Since there is generally no battle over turf—there's no question that Aries will lead the way—the potential for achievement is strong indeed.

Sagittarius and Taurus

Compatibility rating: ** (4 out of 10)**
Sagittarius is ruled by Jupiter, and Taurus by Venus—both expansive planets that represent sociability. Taurus's appearance is attractive, well dressed, projecting an elegant image. You're not pretentious, but you do like people with presence and a strong backbone. The Taurus–Sagittarius pairing can, however, be challenging. Taurus is rigid and opinionated, you're easygoing and tolerant. And while Taurus acquires a wealth of knowledge and experiences, and communicates with warmth and humour, in your eyes Taurus lacks excitement. You're the eternal student

of the zodiac and enjoy learning new things. Taurus, in contrast, prefers to become an authority on a few selected topics. As well, you are notoriously blunt (although not generally aware of it; and your flare-ups are short-lived), while Taurus is ultra-sensitive. For a lasting relationship, each of the two needs a more flexible partner. In less intimate partnerships, the combination can prove more successful. Your adventures and travels provide vicarious fun for sedentary Taurus, and Taurus offers a touch of the familiar when you stop by for a visit. At work, you offer positive energy, a sense of humour, and an optimistic outlook. Taurus may find your work habits a little unorthodox, but the two signs make a good team: Taurus's rigidity and caution are balanced by your risk-taking and optimism, and neither finds the other a threat.

Sagittarius and Gemini

Compatibility rating: ****** (8 out of 10)**
Sagittarius and Gemini are opposite signs, with birthdays half a year apart (more or less). Opposite signs indicate an attraction based on similarities and differences. The Sun sign opposite yours has the same quality (cardinal, fixed, or mutable) as you, but the elements (air, earth, fire, or water) are different. Although opposite signs often share the same goals, each sign has its own reasons for going after those goals and its own methods in reaching them. In the case of Gemini, a freewheeling air sign, and Sagittarius, an adventurous fire sign, the similarities are based on traits that include intelligence, enthusiasm, and the ability to communicate ideas. Both enjoy an intellectual sparring match.

And neither of you is a sentimentalist. As for the differences, Gemini is modest and a rational thinker. You exaggerate (if you talk about number of goals scored or amount of money earned, it's pretty safe for your audience to cut the figure in half) and are outspoken. Still, you admire Gemini's free spirit, and Gemini takes Sagittarius's embellishments with a grain of salt. You use your accumulated knowledge to impress others, and Gemini, who doesn't try to impress anyone, gets points for quick wit (there is no better punster) and charm. Both signs are positive, and although Gemini's ego pales in comparison to Sagittarius's, you enjoy each other's company in family and professional settings. Sagittarius shies away from permanent commitment but genuinely enjoys Gemini's friendship. Your styles are definitely different—Sagittarius takes chances that Gemini would never consider—but you share an important objective. You each seek wisdom rather than possessions. *Celebrity couple: Brad Pitt (December 18, 1963) and Angelina Jolie (June 4, 1975).*

Sagittarius and Cancer

Compatibility rating: ****** (6 out of 10)

Cancer is focused on home and family, not the adventure you cherish. Ruled by the Moon, Cancer's moods change with the tides. You're a mutable fire sign, determined and driven, and as a starting point the two of you are restless. But Cancer's restlessness is more internal. You like to try new things and discover new destinations. Cancer, whose idea of adventure is to decorate the den, is content to enjoy the comforts of home. Another difference is that you're an intellect—the eternal student—continually expanding your knowledge (your ruling planet is Jupiter). Cancer, in contrast, operates on intuition. You're also the epitome of self-confidence, while Cancer needs reassurance. Finally, you enjoy mingling, while Cancer's Facebook page has a far smaller, but more selective, friends list than yours. Despite these differences, there's potential for a satisfying relationship. You each adapt easily and will make an effort to enjoy your partner's different interests. Cancer, like you, is also deeply devoted to family. In business, you excel at almost any profession, as long as there's the chance to learn new things. Intuitive Cancer understands what motivates you—a need for stimulation—and is usually content to play a supporting role. *Celebrity couples: Katie Holmes (December 18, 1978) and Tom Cruise (July 3, 1962); Dan Gummer (December 12, 1946) and Meryl Streep (June 22, 1949).*

Sagittarius and Leo

Compatibility rating: ****** (6 out of 10)
Sagittarius and Leo are both fire signs, idealistic, honest, and frank. Sometimes you're both frank to a fault, but in the case of a Sagittarius–Leo pairing, each likes to learn from constructive criticism. The two signs have egos larger than Saskatchewan, but they are supremely self-confident. Leo is a fixed sign, while yours is mutable, so Leo is not likely to take off on a whim the way you are. You're not always in harmony, but you like each other—friendship, in fact, is as important as romance. You also share many interests—both love to learn, and both will take on volunteer work in addition to their day jobs. Leo is extravagant,

and Sagittarius, ruled by Jupiter, seems to attract money. You're not likely to rebel against Leo's domination, and you definitely won't feel overshadowed. There's one thing for each of you to remember. You need to be sure Leo gets star billing, and Leo has to remember that nobody can cramp Sagittarius's independent style. You excel at business—learning quickly and able to read between the lines. Leo can take risks, and your generosity can be extreme. Both need to be sure the other doesn't give away the bank.

Sagittarius and Virgo

Compatibility rating: **** (6 out of 10)**

Sagittarius–Virgo can be a challenging relationship. You're gregarious and upbeat and want to be surrounded by family and friends, but you need private time too. Virgo, in contrast, is most comfortable in a small and familiar group and leans toward pessimism. Another difficulty with this partnership is that Virgo requires ongoing appreciation, and you don't see the point in acknowledging every contribution. (In fact, you sometimes claim them as your own.) And there's more—you're blunt and outspoken, and Virgo responds poorly to even mild criticism. But don't write off this union. You both have impeccable standards, you're both honest (though you're prone to exaggeration), and neither of you will tolerate a phony. Virgo gets a kick out of your outrageous sense of humour, and you admire Virgo's caring heart and eye for detail. You're both mutable signs, so there's a chance that one or both of you will bend, even slightly. Yes, you can't ignore the way Virgo makes a production over tiny flaws, and Virgo can't fathom why little—or big—things don't upset you. Nor can Virgo accept your restless streak. But gradually, whether you live or work together, you'll become more tolerant of each other. Virgo will help tend to your practical needs (such as banking), and you'll look after Virgo's emotional ones (self-confidence). In the process, you'll discover that there's much to learn from each other. *Celebrity couple: Jay-Z (December 4, 1969) and Beyoncé Knowles (September 4, 1981).*

Sagittarius and Libra

Compatibility rating: ******** (8 out of 10)
Sagittarius–Libra has definite possibilities. Both signs are sociable, charming, intelligent, and romantic. Libra is a cardinal air sign ruled by Venus and needs to be surrounded by beautiful (and expensive) objects. You're a mutable fire sign—flamboyant, fun, funny, and independent. Happily, Libra is not a possessive sign and won't fence you in. In fact, that's the magic ingredient in your relationship. Libra just wants commitment. What you seek is companionship, and if it comes with commitment, you'll pay that price. You enjoy extremes, and Libra strives for balance and a happy medium. And you're decisive, where Libra continually weighs pros against cons. But Libra is, in fact, more decisive than you realize, and guess who often makes the decisions (while you claim credit)? You're both flirtatious, yet you're more accepting of Libra's flirtations than Libra is of yours. One stumbling block is that Libra has difficulty handling the criticism that Sagittarius dishes out. (And Libra is not alone—you can lose friends because of your bluntness.) The key to the relationship is Libra's loyalty and Sagittarius's enthusiasm. Both signs are versatile and suited

to various professions. In a work setting, Libra will always remain the peacemaker. You're both inclined to take chances, which can be an asset as well as a liability. *Celebrity couple: Denise McCann (December 16, 1948) and Randy Bachman (September 27, 1943).*

Sagittarius and Scorpio

Compatibility rating: *** (5 out of 10)**

Because Sagittarius and Scorpio are neighbouring signs—Sagittarius follows Scorpio—the odds are that you share some planetary influences and have some common qualities. But judging by Sun signs alone, you are, in many ways, opposites. To begin, you're ruled by Jupiter (planet of expansion and luck), and Scorpio is coruled by militant Mars and powerful Pluto. You're a mutable fire sign, and Scorpio a fixed water sign. Your glass is half full—you're upbeat and optimistic. Scorpio leans toward extremes—loving and charming one minute, suspicious and vindictive the next. There are common qualities too—some assets, others liabilities. Sagittarius often attains success, as does Scorpio—both signs are motivated and driven. And neither one is eager to compromise. Scorpio seeks the dominant spot in a relationship, and you have an equally healthy ego. You're both loyal, but you don't want to be held back, and Scorpio is highly possessive and not happy to allow you the independence you demand. In other words, Scorpio's intensity and Sagittarius's restlessness may present too wide a gap to fill. The biggest obstacle could be your tendency to take people for granted—something Scorpio can't abide. Still, you take chances and may choose to take one with Scorpio. Relatives are inspired by the combination of your enthusiasm and Scorpio's passion. In a business arrangement, you're both determined, but you'll be the more flamboyant personality and Scorpio the driven (and suspicious) member of the team.

Sagittarius and Sagittarius

Compatibility rating: ****** (6 out of 10)

When two members of the same sign join forces, the connection can bring out the best and the worst in each partner. In the case of Sagittarius, a mutable fire sign, we have two independent people in motion. You're the great adventurer, and the eternal student, of the zodiac. When we're blessed (and it *is* a blessing more than a curse) with a pair, we wind up with two people who appreciate each other's positives and negatives (although a true Sagittarius thinks there are no negatives). We get a double whammy of enthusiasm, intelligence, rebelliousness, restlessness, and self-centredness. Sagittarians are larger than life, outspoken, and generous. Two Sagittarians living together can always count on each other— they are loyal and almost never possessive. They also understand each other's need for independence. But their sarcasm will have a double edge. You're easygoing but have a serious breaking point— and when one Sagittarius finally blows, the response from another will be explosive. In friendship and family circles, one Sagittarius is usually enough. Two will be extraordinarily supportive, but the combined bluntness factor can be overwhelming. At work, Sagittarius is the local know-it-all. Two Sagittarians work well side by side—they're fair-minded and won't tolerate any kind of exploitation. In tandem, they provide a healthy supply of optimism and knowledge but also encourage each other's tendency to take risks.

Sagittarius and Capricorn

Compatibility rating: *** (5 out of 10)**

Because Sagittarius and Capricorn are neighbouring signs—Capricorn follows Sagittarius—the odds are that you share some planetary influences and have some common qualities. But judging by Sun signs alone, you are, in many ways, opposites, with different temperaments. Among your similarities, you're both goal-oriented and determined. But determination operates in different ways. Capricorn is an ambitious planner who'll climb hurdles to reach a goal, no matter how long the journey. You're adventurous, spirited, and spontaneous—determined to learn as much about as many things as possible. The Sagittarius–Capricorn pairing is a match between you, a mutable fire sign ruled by Jupiter (expansion), and a cardinal earth sign ruled by Saturn (restriction and patience). On paper, it's not entirely promising. But your quest for new pursuits and Capricorn's need to restrict and consolidate can prove complementary rather than conflicting since you're both tolerant and generous people. Along the way, Capricorn will absorb your optimism, and some Capricorn patience may rub off on you. The two of you bring mutual respect to the table, and a Sagittarius–Capricorn relationship, if meant to be, will likely develop over time. Within a family, you'll introduce adventure to Capricorn, and Capricorn (who is born mature) will introduce a balancing dose of caution. At work, you'll provide the new ideas that Capricorn will refine. Just remember to pay the occasional compliment—even indirectly.

Sagittarius and Aquarius

Compatibility rating: ****** (8 out of 10)**

Sagittarius and Aquarius share priorities: both seek freedom, independence, and individuality. Not surprisingly, you're quickly drawn to each other. You'll be shocked (but delighted) to find someone even more independent than you. Aquarius, an air sign, likes to make the first move, a role you usually assume but are happy to relinquish. Neither of you can handle moody or needy signs, so there's certainly no problem here. And though you usually do best with the other fire signs, Aries and Leo, Aquarius has enough individuality (translation: eccentricity) to spark and sustain an interest. Some find you too exuberant and blunt. Aquarius enjoys the first trait and matches you on the second. You find it hard to commit to a long-term relationship, and Aquarius is happy if one evolves but is never desperate for it to happen. If there are disagreements, it's over your recklessness, especially in finances, where Aquarius is conservative and prudent. You make a memorable team for family members—especially youngsters. Being with the two of you is like being on holiday. At work, Aquarius brings the more logical mind. You like to experiment—and Aquarius is a willing guinea pig on whom you can test your ideas.

Sagittarius and Pisces

Compatibility rating: *** (5 out of 10)**

The two of you seem on the surface quite different—independent Sagittarius and emotional Pisces. You love your freedom

and are outspoken, while Pisces searches for emotional security and its ego is easily bruised. You're an intellectual sign, on a
perpetual journey to learn new things. Pisces is emotional and
intuitive—interested in psychology and the spiritual world.
Yet there are grounds for hope. Although your temperaments
differ—you're upbeat, and Pisces is often moody—your positive nature can bring almost anyone out of a funk. Still, that
takes work, and you need to decide if it's worth the effort. As
well, Pisces can be possessive but requires time alone, so you
may be able to slip out and enjoy the freedom you seek. You're
both mutable signs. (You *need* change, Pisces is simply restless.)
Pisces is the most easily moulded sign and can pick up your
good habits (optimism) as well as questionable ones (recklessness). You're the most outspoken among the signs, and Pisces
is among the most sensitive and can be easily hurt. There are
many possible scenarios, and frankly this relationship can go
anywhere. In a family or on the job, neither you nor Pisces is
big on rules, but your combined imagination is extraordinary.
You can both go off on a tangent, so it would be helpful to have
a grounded influence on the scene.

CAPRICORN
COMPATIBILITY GUIDE

The following descriptions, based on your Sun sign, provide a broad picture of how you relate to members of all twelve signs (including your own) in the different spheres of your life.

Capricorn and Aries

Compatibility rating: *** (5 out of 10)**

Both Capricorn and Aries are cardinal signs, meaning there's at least a minimum of attraction between you. Capricorn is the great achiever of the zodiac. Aries is also ambitious and a force to be reckoned with. Aries admires that trait in others and feels protective toward a Capricorn partner, relative, or associate. You, in turn, enjoy Aries' outspokenness—you see it as an extension of the honesty you live by. The connection may end there, however, because in outlook the two signs are opposites. You're ruled by Saturn, which represents restriction, while feisty Mars represents Aries. You need security, and Aries wants excitement. Your symbol is the goat and, like that persistent creature, you will climb to the top of a mountain, over hurdles, determined to reach your goal. Aries the ram is eager to arrive at its destination—then move on to newer, greener pastures. You require security and appreciate the value of a loonie. Aries, on the other hand, is the idea person—happy to give away the family fortune and start again. It is the first sign in the zodiac and always on the lookout for a new adventure. There is nothing conservative or conventional about Aries.

As it happens, those are the two adjectives that best sum up your character. *Celebrity couple: René Angélil (January 16, 1942) and Céline Dion (March 30, 1968).*

Capricorn and Taurus

Compatibility rating: ***** (7 out of 10)**

Capricorn and Taurus are both earth signs. You find many of Taurus's traits (earthiness, loyalty, determination, and sense of aesthetics) appealing, and Taurus understands and will encourage your chief need—driving ambition. You seek financial security, and Taurus, who is an excellent saver, is the money sign of the zodiac. There's a definite affinity here, and, in fact, both of you often live below your means. In a relationship, Taurus requires the kind of strong presence that you provide. Your determination and Taurus's stubbornness, on paper, sound like a successful yet dull combination. But you each have a nice sense of humour—Taurus is droll, and you have a dry wit. You both can be a little untrusting. If you don't cancel each other out on that score, the atmosphere will be heavy with suspicion. Tradition is important to both of you, although Taurus may find you emotionally cool and even calculating. As family members, Taurus and Capricorn complement each other. Taurus is nurturing and offers an emotionally safe environment; you provide a financial safety net. At work, Capricorn is disciplined and provides a contrast to Taurus's more creative approach. But though your styles differ, you appreciate each other's diligence.

Capricorn and Gemini

Compatibility rating: ****** (6 out of 10)

You're a cardinal earth sign (grounded), and Gemini is a mutable air sign (likes to circulate). Your symbol is the goat and, like that animal, you will climb relentlessly to reach your objective at the summit. You are, without question, the most ambitious sign of the zodiac. Gemini is not without ambition but doesn't seek out challenges. While it seems you have little in common, Gemini has great admiration (and a need) for your determination and business sense. And you, a pessimist, benefit from Gemini's optimism and social skills. You can provide a nice balance to each other, and in the right circumstances your differences dovetail rather than conflict. Gemini has friends of all ages and backgrounds; yours are more serious and conservative. Gemini's sense of humour (witty) balances yours (wry). Regardless of actual age, Gemini is young and adventurous while you're, well, mature (you were born mature) and cautious. But you're calm, and that can be a plus in a relationship with someone as independent and, yes, flighty as Gemini. If one partner needs to come around, it's more likely that you'll be the one to budge. In a family environment, you're perceived as rigid (your ruling planet, Saturn, reflects rigidity), but Gemini will provide a softening influence. Working in the shadow of a Capricorn can be daunting for anyone, since nobody is as disciplined. Gemini has admiration for your work ethic and will be inspired to become more businesslike under your influence. *Celebrity couples: Elvis Presley (January 8, 1935) and Priscilla Presley (May 24, 1945); Vanessa Paradis (December 22, 1972) and Johnny Depp (June 9, 1963). Royal couple: Catherine, Duchess of Cambridge (January 9, 1982) and Prince William, Duke of Cambridge (June 21, 1982).*

Capricorn and Cancer

Compatibility rating: ******* (7 out of 10)

Capricorn and Cancer are opposite signs, with birthdays half a year apart (more or less). Opposite signs indicate an attraction based on similarities and differences. The Sun sign opposite yours has the same quality (cardinal, fixed, or mutable) as you, but the elements (air, earth, fire, or water) are different. Although opposite signs often share the same goals, each sign has its own reasons for going after those goals and its own methods in reaching them. Both are cardinal (action) signs—ambitious and reliable. Capricorn is the more seriously driven of the two, and Cancer the more creative. What you lack in originality, you make up for in determination, and these two signs complement each other nicely in various types of relationships. But both signs can be downbeat—you gloomy; Cancer moody—and your combined pessimism, if not tempered, can clear a room. Still, each of the two signs has a gentle quality. The two of you are often attracted to each other in your younger years, but for the chemistry to continue you need to learn to accept your differences. You take pride in your home, while Cancer takes comfort in it. You need financial security, but for Cancer emotional security is what it's all about. In your family and professional lives, you need a blueprint, while Cancer acts intuitively. If pragmatic Capricorn looks after the long-term planning and creative Cancer focuses on atmosphere, the two can create memorable projects and events. *Celebrity couple: Cynthia Dale (January 1, 1961) and Peter Mansbridge (July 6, 1948).*

Capricorn and Leo

Compatibility rating: ******** (8 out of 10)

There's considerable potential for compatibility between these two signs. You're a cardinal earth sign, and Leo is a fixed fire sign. You're action-oriented and the most ambitious sign in the zodiac. Leo is the most flamboyant and probably the most egotistical. The two signs share a number of characteristics. On a superficial level, you're both naturally attractive; Leo is regal and you have a noble bearing. You and Leo strive to reach the top, and neither of you is modest—you both expect recognition. You also both like good food. But your motives and approaches differ. For Leo, success means being able to afford life's many pleasures. For you, the quest is everything. You're cool under pressure, and if life is a poker game, you never reveal your hand. Leo is a total show-off. Another important difference is that Leo is optimistic, while you often have a negative outlook. Leo admires your ambition but finds something lacking—a sense of pizzazz. If any sign can plump up your self-confidence, it's Leo, who, after all, is ruled by the Sun. Leo is an innovator, and you're a refiner, so you can help shape Leo's ideas and then bring them to the finish line. For both of you, home and family are priorities that you'll fiercely protect. *Presidential couple: Michelle Obama (January 17, 1964) and Barack Obama (August 4, 1961).*

Capricorn and Virgo

Compatibility rating: ***** (7 out of 10)**

Both you and Virgo are earth signs who plan a lot and think logically. Neither of you is spontaneous, preferring to work out details in advance. And your ideas are generally conventional rather than innovative. To many, it seems that you both lean toward pessimism (though you prefer to call it realism). That sounds like a recipe for a safe relationship, and this pairing has a high success rate. You're both confident and dependable, and you both put family first. Capricorn is the strong, silent type who never lives through a partner. And Virgo prefers reliability to flamboyance. You both know the value of money, and you both have high standards and a strong code of ethics. So what on paper appears to be unexciting is a comfortable arrangement built on respect. For both signs, the head, not the heart, takes charge—and you understand and encourage each other's strengths. Virgo recognizes your need to persevere, and you are one of the few to appreciate Virgo's meticulous attention to detail. This is a harmonious pairing in business too. Virgo will provide a fund of knowledge that you will interpret and refine, and neither cramps the other's style. *Celebrity couple: Humphrey Bogart (December 25, 1899) and Lauren Bacall (September 16, 1924).*

Capricorn and Libra

Compatibility rating: **** (6 out of 10)**

You're both cardinal signs, meaning you're action-oriented. For Capricorn, action and ambition are synonymous. Your quest for success is everything, even more than the prize itself. Libra takes action to achieve harmony. You're ruled by Saturn, a planet associated with consolidation and rigidity. Venus, representing beauty and art, rules Libra. While you're not cheap, you're not extravagant the way that Libra is. And while companionship rates high on Libra's list, for you commitment is what it's all about. There are other differences. You're patient but decisive. Libra is spontaneous but hems and haws over issues. Yet the two signs often get along well because you're both intelligent and have a gentle demeanour. You complement each other—Libra brings optimism to the table, and you're more introspective. It doesn't hurt either that you're a good-looking sign—something that appeals to Libra, who is attracted to beauty. Within a family, you often seek out private time. Libra won't miss a function, and isn't put off if you prefer to stay home. Libra is the hands-on caregiver while you're more comfortable providing financial security. You work well together. Libra provides the ideas, and you know just how to develop them.

Capricorn and Scorpio

Compatibility rating: **** (6 out of 10)**

You're the most ambitious sign, and Scorpio is the most intense. The result is that you understand each other's drive and determination, and there's definite potential for a financially successful partnership. But what about getting along on an emotional level? That's a tough call because you seldom reveal your feelings, and Scorpio is the most secretive sign in the zodiac. What's often found at the basis of a Capricorn–Scorpio relationship is mutual respect. You're both self-centred, so it's no surprise that the traits you like in each other are ones you each see in yourself: hard-working, demanding, disciplined, and competitive. You're a cardinal (action) earth sign, while Scorpio's a fixed water sign. Capricorn zooms in on a specific task, while Scorpio takes in its surroundings and then proceeds on intuition. And where Scorpio looks for hidden messages in words and actions, you are far more literal-minded. Within a family, Capricorn is dependable but not always flexible enough, and Scorpio will mentor youngsters. Scorpio has the passion to make your world more varied and encourage your curiosity. You, in turn, need to convince Scorpio that not everything in life is a mystery to be solved.

Capricorn and Sagittarius

Compatibility rating: ***** (5 out of 10)

Because Capricorn and Sagittarius are neighbouring signs—Capricorn follows Sagittarius—the odds are that you share some planetary influences and have some common qualities. But judging by Sun signs alone, you are, in many ways, opposites with different temperaments. Among your similarities, you're both goal-oriented and determined. But determination operates in different ways. You're an ambitious planner who'll climb hurdles to reach a goal, no matter how long the journey. Sagittarius is adventurous, spirited, and spontaneous—determined to learn as much about as many things as possible. The Capricorn–Sagittarius pairing is a match between you, a cardinal earth sign ruled by Saturn (restriction and patience), and a mutable fire sign ruled by Jupiter (expansiveness). On paper, it's not entirely promising. But your need to consolidate and Sagittarius's quest for new pursuits can prove complementary rather than conflicting, and it helps that you're both broad-minded and generous people. Along the way, Sagittarius will absorb some of your patience, while you'll absorb some of Sagittarius's optimism. The two of you bring mutual respect to the table, and a partnership, if meant to be, will likely develop over time. Within a family, Sagittarius will introduce adventure into your life, while you (it's said that you're born mature) will provide a balancing dose of caution. At work, Sagittarius will provide the new ideas that you'll rework and refine. Just hope that Sagittarius will pay the occasional compliment—even indirectly.

Capricorn and Capricorn

Compatibility rating: ****** (8 out of 10)**
When two members of the same sign join forces, the connection can bring out the best and the worst in each. In the case of Capricorn and Capricorn, you each understand what is important to the other—ambition, challenge, achievement, goals. But you have a tendency to reinforce each other's negative traits, and in the case of your sign, that can lead to a double dose of worrying and poor self-confidence. You're inhibited, so it's often best for Capricorn to pair up with an extrovert or at least someone not as reserved as you. You need a little feistiness in your life, and a fellow Capricorn will often bring out your pessimism. However, one very important thing going for this combination is that you "get" each other, particularly each other's quirky sense of humour (comedian/actor Jim Carrey is a Capricorn). You're well

mannered, orderly, restrained, disciplined, and attractive, and you present yourselves as an appealing couple. You're protective of your children and your beliefs. Still, your personal relationships may be on the less-than-emotional side and business-oriented, and often a Capricorn–Capricorn partnership is based on practicalities. Capricorns are strong leaders (Prime Minister John A. Macdonald, for example) and if pushed will use anyone to advance their cause. Always cautious, you feel you can trust few people. But because you understand the workings of your own mind so well, you're aware of what drives a fellow Capricorn. *Celebrity couples: Jude Law (December 29, 1972) and Sienna Miller (December 28, 1981); Tiger Woods (December 30, 1975) and Elin Nordegren (January 1, 1980).*

Capricorn and Aquarius

Compatibility rating: ******** (8 out of 10)

Because Capricorn and Aquarius are neighbouring signs— Aquarius follows Capricorn—the odds are that you share some planetary influences and have some common qualities. But judging by Sun signs alone, you are, in many ways, opposites. You are conventional, cautious, and traditional, while Aquarius is the most unconventional and among the most independent of the signs. It may sound unlikely, but there are attractions between the two. Although you join for different reasons (you for business, Aquarius for socializing and self-improvement), you're both involved in organizations, which may be where you get to know each other. From the start, your good manners and Aquarius's smart attire will appeal to each other. You'll find that

Aquarius is a good listener, and you'll discover that you're both cool cats: neither flares up, becomes jealous, tries to impress the other, or is judgmental. You're both intellectually inclined and enjoy exchanging ideas. Of course, you'll soon see differences: you're a cardinal earth sign (grounded), and Aquarius is a fixed air sign (less persevering). You're persistent, while Aquarius, a quicker study, tries to set a record at going for the goal. In family relationships or on the job, you'll find Aquarius isn't immersed 24/7 the way you are. But when a crisis erupts, each sign can count on the other to do what it takes. And most important, you'll find someone who measures up to your high ethical standards. *Celebrity couples: Janet Jones (January 10, 1961) and Wayne Gretzky (January 26, 1961).*

Capricorn and Pisces

Compatibility rating: ******* (7 out of 10)
Somehow a Capricorn–Pisces relationship is possible—even favourable—although looking at individual traits it seems unlikely. You're ruled by Saturn, the planet of caution and restriction. Pisces is ruled by spiritual Neptune. You're an earth sign, conservative and mainstream. Pisces is an offbeat and poetic water sign. Pisces is warm and affectionate, while you're cool. The interesting thing is that you each have a capacity to draw out qualities from the other. Pisces will bring its greatest strengths: warmth and imagination; and you'll introduce your strongest quality: a sense of security. You climb (toward your goal) and Pisces swims (navigating around obstacles), so you won't get in each other's way—usually. There are two possible barriers to success. First,

Pisces clings, and you find any kind of hovering a turnoff. As well, when happy, you both withdraw like clams. Still, Pisces desperately needs someone with your business acumen, and you greatly benefit from Pisces' imagination. Neither will let the other down. Pisces will likely widen your focus with a bit of adventure, and you'll encourage Pisces to combine art with ambition.

AQUARIUS COMPATIBILITY GUIDE

The following descriptions, based on your Sun sign, provide a broad picture of how you relate to members of all twelve signs (including your own) in the different spheres of your life.

Aquarius and Aries

Compatibility rating: ******** (8 out of 10)
Aquarius and Aries, if not initially attracted to each other, can easily grow to like each other. The differences are complementary rather than conflicting. You and Aries are one of the zodiac's mutual admiration societies, with Aries the strong, fiery, and independent partner and you the friendly, cool, non-aggressive, and quirky half. Aquarius is inventive, a quality that you—always willing to try something new—admire. In personal relationships, both signs are happy to be alone or together, as the mood dictates. Aries can be egotistical and domineering, and you won't be controlled, so Aries will have to back off and learn

to be comfortable with your independent nature. Aries will also need to allow you the mental stimulation you require. You're a progressive thinker and a great humanitarian, qualities that Aries respects and encourages. A possible stumbling block is created by your emotional coolness, but Aries—as a boss, co-worker, or subordinate—is often oblivious to that trait and is grateful for Aquarius's tenacity. And while some relatives may be embarrassed by their Aquarius cousin's eccentricities, Aries finds these qualities endearing and understands that your heart is always in the right place. *Celebrity couples: Farrah Fawcett (February 2, 1947) and Ryan O'Neal (April 20, 1941); Colleen Howe (February 17, 1933) and Gordie Howe (March 31, 1928).*

Aquarius and Taurus

Compatibility rating: *** (5 out of 10)**
You and Taurus are both fixed signs, but your element is air and Taurus's is earth. In other words, Taurus is bull-headed, possessive, determined, and cautious. You love freedom, inde-pendence, and change. Ideas are important for both of you, but yours are innovative while Taurus's are traditional. (You'll read books on a variety of topics, while Taurus has specific areas of interest.) You're the humanitarian of the zodiac—perennially in-volved in a good cause. Yet while you love the world, you can sometimes be thoughtless in personal relationships. That atti-tude is difficult for a Taurus partner to accept. And Taurus, who loves beautiful and unusual things, prefers to lead a conven-tional life. You also appreciate *objets d'art*, but "conventional" isn't in your vocabulary. Taurus is money-oriented, and though

you have expensive taste you are, first and foremost, idealistic. For a partnership to work, Taurus must be willing and able to live with your independent spirit and often eccentric ways. At work, you can excel in many areas—as long as there are challenges. Taurus, in contrast, is content with routine tasks and is highly disciplined, so a professional relationship could prove successful for this pair. *Celebrity couple: Sonny (February 16, 1935) and Cher (May 20, 1946).*

Aquarius and Gemini

Compatibility rating: ******* (7 out of 10)

There's no question about it—Gemini likes to have the last word, and the first, and most of the sentences in between. This is a promising relationship because you're such an outstanding listener (when there's something worth listening to)—probably the finest in the zodiac family. As two air signs that need to circulate, you may never set off sparks of passion. But you can certainly strike a pleasant and long-lasting friendship. And you're hardly a passive listener either; you bring out the best in Gemini's storytelling. Gemini, in turn, accepts—in fact, encourages—your need for independence and enjoys your eccentricities. One of Gemini's best traits is that it never tries to change anyone. Not that anyone *can* change you, but you're appreciative of the fact. By the same token, you're never jealous, and at gatherings you're perfectly happy to let Gemini flit from person to person. There are times when you're outspoken, but Gemini gets over these things quickly, while other family members would stew. On the job, you don't suffer fools lightly and can be critical of other people's work habits and scruples. You sometimes object to Gemini's habit of making light of serious situations, but you never mind playing the bad cop to Gemini's good one. *Celebrity couple: Adrienne Clarkson (February 10, 1939) and John Ralston Saul (June 19, 1947).*

Aquarius and Cancer

Compatibility rating: **** (6 out of 10)**
You're attractive, shy, tolerant, eccentric, and drawn to good causes. For you, charity may not begin in the home, but it certainly extends to it. And that is where the strongest connection with Cancer lies. Both signs are comfortable in the home environment (many members of the two signs work at home), and as a couple you enjoy sprucing up your surroundings and enjoying them with a close circle of friends and family members. Neither of you likes being taken for granted and, happily, you know how to make each other feel special. But there's a basic difference in your outlooks. You're the more independent, and Cancer the less secure, of the two. Ruled by the Moon, Cancer has a possessive and jealous side. You're ruled by Uranus, the planet of innovation. The good news is that you're both good listeners and can talk things over. And though some people perceive you as aloof, you're essentially a kind-hearted sign. Both you and Cancer are tolerant of others, especially older people—from whom you feel there's always something to learn. Family members tend to perceive you as the family eccentric and Cancer as the nurturing relative. At gatherings the two of you provide a nice mix of warmth and laughter. At work, Aquarius is the innovator, and Cancer is the creative

force. You're both idea people and understand when it's necessary to bend the rules. *Celebrity couple: Robert Wagner (February 10, 1930) and Natalie Wood (July 20, 1938).*

Aquarius and Leo

Compatibility rating: ***** (7 out of 10)**

Aquarius and Leo are opposite signs, with birthdays half a year apart (more or less). Opposite signs indicate an attraction based on similarities and differences. The Sun sign opposite yours has the same quality (cardinal, fixed, or mutable) as you, but the elements (air, earth, fire, or water) are different. Although opposite signs often share the same goals, each sign has its own reasons for going after those goals and its own methods in reaching them. You and Leo are fixed signs (determined and lively), but Leo is fire and you're air. You're both intelligent and have sharp, logical minds. Leo is noble and generous, and you devote yourself to good causes. Where you're full of surprises, Leo leads a more structured life. Leo needs the spotlight, and you're content working behind the scenes. As partners, you provide the imagination and Leo the theatrics. You both enjoy circulating among people, though you generally listen and Leo performs. Leo is a natural leader, but you're no follower. Still, both signs are secure and can work out their roles in a personal or business relationship. There could be some serious disagreement over who makes the major decisions—but no matter who takes charge, you bring the ideas to the table. A Leo parent is likely to encourage an Aquarius child's talents, while an Aquarius parent will encourage Leo children to expand their interests. At work, and everywhere else, Leo's a show-off. But you're happy to let Leo make the presentations, as long as you look after the creative end. Just make sure you get credit.

Aquarius and Virgo

Compatibility rating: *** (5 out of 10)**

These two signs do not, on the surface, appear to have much in common. Virgo is the most routine-oriented of the signs, and you, well, are the most eccentric. Your life is devoted to ideas, while Virgo is obsessed with details. You do best with independent, innovative types (not surprisingly, your best match is with a fellow Aquarius). Your ruling planet, Uranus, emphasizes individuality and unique qualities, and you're sometimes hard to communicate with. Virgo's planet, Mercury, rules communication. You reach out, while Virgo can be introverted. Of course, given other influences, you can defy the odds. It helps that both of you are excellent teachers. In certain areas you complement each other. You'll be pleased to delegate day-to-day business matters to Virgo, who has a shrewd business mind. Most important, though, you need to find a partner who appreciates, or at least accepts, your eccentricities. (And Virgo needs to find someone who understands, or at least ignores, an obsession with details.) For the two of you to live or work together, you need to share at least one common interest, so start comparing notes. (*Suggestion:* yoga, health, and fitness are good possibilities.)

Aquarius and Libra

Compatibility rating: ********* **(9 out of 10)**

This is potentially one of the happiest combinations in the zodiac. In a nutshell, you're both devoted to making the world a better—and more beautiful—place. You both also indulge in life's pleasures and luxuries. You're ruled by Uranus, the planet that emphasizes originality. Libra's ruling planet is Venus, related to the arts. You complement rather than duplicate each other. You need time for solitude, while Libra thrives on company. You're both emotionally secure, and neither cramps the other's style. It's not surprising that both of you are air signs—the communicators and dreamers of the zodiac. You're the more focused of the two signs and get irritable if people don't pull their weight. That's not likely to happen with Libra, who vacillates but is hard-working. You aren't as commitment-oriented as Libra. You each want a partner who continues to keep the relationship fresh. Not surprisingly, the two signs often form platonic friendships. You also form one of the best working partnerships. If one of you loses your cool, it's likely to be Libra, who is sensitive to Aquarius's (and everyone else's) criticisms. But every family has its squabbles, and the ones between these two signs never last long. *Celebrity couple: Yoko Ono (February 18, 1933) and John Lennon (October 9, 1940). Royal couple: Prince Andrew (February 19, 1960) and Sarah Ferguson, Duchess of York (October 15, 1959).*

Aquarius and Scorpio

Compatibility rating: ****** (6 out of 10)

There are certainly things you enjoy about each other, and, in fact, Aquarius and Scorpio have the potential to be a highly compatible couple. To start, you're both strong—and bull-headed. Scorpio is a water sign ruled by warlike Mars (and Pluto). You're an air sign ruled by Uranus (independence and originality). Scorpio will accept—in fact, appreciate—many of your eccentricities and admire your humanitarian and philan-thropic spirit. You, however, will not give up an ounce of your freedom, and suspicious Scorpio can be highly possessive. This issue is important to resolve because both of you are stubborn. Both signs are very curious and love to investigate the world around them, and both have a good sense of humour, so you're ideal travel companions. As parents, this union offers the best of both worlds. You encourage children to be curious and indepen-dent, and Scorpio is dependable and inspiring, though demand-ing. Job-wise, you're a problem-solver and Scorpio is intuitive. You bring ideas and innovation to anything you tackle. Neither you nor Scorpio will tolerate laziness, and in many ways you make an ideal team on the job. *Celebrity couple: Ashton Kutcher (February 7, 1978) and Demi Moore (November 11, 1962).*

Aquarius and Sagittarius

Compatibility rating: ******** (8 out of 10)

Aquarius and Sagittarius share priorities: both seek freedom, independence, and individuality, and both are devoted to good causes. Not surprisingly, you're quickly drawn to each other. You'll be shocked (but delighted) to find someone with as independent a spirit as yours. You're an air sign who likes to make the first move, but you're willing to relinquish the role, so neither of you will be waiting for the other to initiate something. You can't handle moody or needy signs, and neither can Sagittarius. And though Sagittarius usually does best with the other fire signs, Aries and Leo, you possess enough individuality (translation: eccentricity) to spark and sustain an interest. Some find Sagittarius too exuberant and outspoken. You enjoy the first trait and may actually surpass your Sagittarius partner on the second. Sagittarius finds it hard to commit to a long-term relationship, and you're happy if one evolves but hardly desperate for it to happen. If there are disagreements, it's over Sagittarius's recklessness, especially in finances. You're conservative and prudent. You make a memorable team at family gatherings. For youngsters, being with the two of you is like being on holiday. At work, the two of you come up with a surplus of ideas to bounce off each other, but you provide the more logical mind.

Aquarius and Capricorn

Compatibility rating: ******** (8 out of 10)
Because Aquarius and Capricorn are neighbouring signs—Aquarius follows Capricorn—the odds are that you share some planetary influences and have some common qualities. But judging by Sun signs alone, you are, in many ways, opposites. You're ruled by Uranus (eccentric) and Capricorn by Saturn

(rigid). You're the most unpredictable and among the most independent of the signs, while Capricorn is conventional, cautious,
and traditional. It may sound unlikely, but there are attractions
between the two. Although you join for different reasons (you
for socializing and self-improvement; Capricorn for networking), you're both involved in organizations. Capricorn will be
delighted to discover that you're a good listener, and as you get
to know each other, you'll discover that neither is jealous or tries
to impress the other. You're both intellectually inclined and enjoy exchanging ideas. Of course, you'll soon spot differences:
you're an air sign (you circulate effortlessly), and Capricorn is
an earth sign (grounded). Capricorn focuses on a goal and proceeds steadfastly. You're a quicker study—determined to break
a record for reaching your objective. Capricorn is more serious
and likely will pick up some of your sense of fun while teaching
you patience. In family relationships or on the job, you won't be
immersed 24/7 the way Capricorn is. But when a crisis erupts,
each sign can count on the other to do what it takes. *Celebrity
couple: Wayne Gretzky (January 26, 1961) and Janet Jones (January
10, 1961).*

Aquarius and Aquarius

Compatibility rating: ******* (9 out of 10)**
When two members of the same sign join forces, the connec-
tion can bring out the best and the worst in each. In the case of
Aquarius, there's potential for a relationship that's never dull
(Aquarius is the zodiac's eccentric), often fulfilling (Aquarius
is also the zodiac's idealist and one of the most romantic signs),

and occasionally frustrating. Aquarius plus Aquarius bring us two air signs—on the go, rushing about, witty and charming. Aquarius isn't the easiest to live with—except for another Aquarius. An Aquarius is, in many cases, unemotional. But this is one of the most intellectual, well-mannered, and charming signs, and as a couple you make a good initial impression. You're quick studies too—and sometimes believe (often rightly) that the rest of the world is lagging behind. You're also good listeners. A bonus in this relationship is that you have an opportunity to do a little more talking. Even though you are often emotionally detached, you're loyal. Among family members, Aquarians are usually the first to help out in a crisis, and it's not uncommon for Aquarius relatives (even of different generations) to become best friends with each other. At work, you excel in the innovation department because you think outside the box. Not surprisingly, there are an unusually high number of Aquarians at the top of their field, among them Wayne Gretzky and Babe Ruth, Adrienne Clarkson and Oprah Winfrey, Mordecai Richler and James Joyce. The list goes on, and the idea of what two Aquarians could accomplish together boggles the mind. *Celebrity couple: Ellen DeGeneres (January 26, 1958) and Portia de Rossi (January 31, 1973).*

Aquarius and Pisces

Compatibility rating: ****** (6 out of 10)

Because Aquarius and Pisces are neighbouring signs—Pisces follows Aquarius—the odds are that you share some planetary influences and have some common qualities. But judging by Sun signs alone, you are, in many ways, opposites. Still, you're likely to be able to tolerate if not entirely understand your differences, and you certainly make an interesting match. Your element is air, and Pisces' element is water. Both signs like to circulate, but you make an impression, while Pisces is impressionable. The two of you are among the most challenging signs to get along with—you, because of your eccentricities, Pisces because of moodiness. But you are both tolerant and look for the best in others. Pisces enjoys your quirks, and you admire Pisces' creativity. However—a big however—it's not easy for you to live with someone whose emotions change with the tides. Pisces' symbol is two fishes, and it has a choice. It can navigate around obstacles or it can flail and sink. You help your Pisces partner get through troubled waters. You both have high regard for the wisdom of elders and inspire enthusiasm in youngsters. Aquarius understands that Pisces' creativity knows no bounds, and Pisces respects your commitment to humankind. But the two of you benefit from having an action-oriented cardinal sign (Aries, Cancer, Libra, Capricorn) or driven fire sign (Aries, Leo, Sagittarius) on the premises. *Celebrity couple: Paul Newman (January 26, 1925) and Joanne Woodward (February 27, 1930).*

PISCES
COMPATIBILITY GUIDE

The following descriptions, based on your Sun sign, provide a broad picture of how you relate to members of all twelve signs (including your own) in the different spheres of your life.

Pisces and Aries

Compatibility rating: ** (4 out of 10)**

Pisces is a mutable water sign—emotional, sensitive, and often needy. Aries, in contrast, is self-confident and passionate. On a romantic level, this pairing needs an ample supply of TLC. Aries, a cardinal fire sign ruled by Mars, has little patience for Pisces' overindulgences and moods. (It likely has the least patience among the signs.) And you, ruled by Neptune, the spiritual planet, have little understanding of Aries' self-centred disposition and never-ending desire for action. You're highly compassionate, but your great need for security threatens Aries' independent style. You're empathetic and a treasured family member who provides a strong shoulder to lean on. But Aries doesn't always want a shoulder—it requires an audience. In a work setting, you're creative (and some members of your sign have scientific skills) and flexible. But a no-nonsense Aries co-worker may find your need for approval annoying. As for a Pisces boss and an Aries subordinate, that combination is, frankly, rare. But if it exists, generous Pisces will let Aries think he or she is in control—and such an odd coupling may actually work.

Pisces and Taurus

Compatibility rating: ******** (8 out of 10)

You're a mutable water sign, and Taurus is a fixed earth sign. You like change, and Taurus prefers the familiar. You're forgiving, patient, spiritual—and immature. Taurus is dependable, protective, and affectionate—but insecure. But the two signs share more than a shaky sense of self. Both are home-loving, family-oriented, and creative. Taurus is ruled by Venus, the planet of art and beauty. And you're a gifted artist, sculptor, writer, or poet. Your moods change like the tides, but Taurus is perceptive and usually tolerates them. And while you can be jealous, you're nevertheless among the most gentle, intuitive, and caring people—another quality that doesn't escape a Taurus partner or friend. You're easily moulded and easily influenced, but Taurus doesn't try to change you the way other signs do. In fact, Taurus provides a healthy measure of stability. Neither of you gets involved in the politics of the workplace, but you both have an awareness of what's happening behind the scenes. This shared knowledge provides a bond and gives each of you a boost in self-confidence. Even if you aren't in the same department or on the same team, Pisces and Taurus are known to form alliances on the job or in an organization. *Poetic couple: Elizabeth Barrett Browning (March 6, 1806) and Robert Browning (May 7, 1812).*

Pisces and Gemini

Compatibility rating: **** (4 out of 10)

Both Pisces and Gemini are mutable signs—restless, easily influenced, and compassionate. And you're both natural communicators. You also have something else in common: you're both "doubles." Gemini's sign is the twins, and yours is made up of two fish joined together. In other words, you're both versatile and have a desire to please everyone. A Pisces–Gemini relationship usually starts out promisingly. Initially, Gemini respects your kindness and sensitivity, and you enjoy Gemini's free spirit. But before long, you can become clingy, and fidgety Gemini is on the move. That doesn't mean things evaporate between you. But your pessimism is often stronger than Gemini's optimism. Another difference is that you're intuitive and emotional—drawing on hunches. In contrast, Gemini's information comes from books or the Internet. Of course, the descriptions given are based on Sun signs alone, and if you share other planetary influences there is a stronger potential for a good relationship. Both of you are selfless. As relatives, you and Gemini often establish a bond because you both enjoy spoiling others with little gifts. But on the job, given Gemini's short attention span (the size of a gnat) and your hyperactive imagination, the combination can be unproductive, to say the least.

Pisces and Cancer

Compatibility rating: ****** (8 out of 10)**
You're a mutable water sign; Cancer is a cardinal water sign. You're both creative and intuitive. But you're also both insecure and moody (you win that contest). That's not necessarily a liability in a relationship because you each understand the emotional roller coaster that the other is riding. And you both are adaptable,

gentle, and patient. Neither sign, however, is particularly practical. You both have a nurturing instinct, but you, Pisces, need someone who can build your ego. You're the more innovative of the two—artistically gifted. (Cancer is a great supporter of the arts.) You both need periods of solitude and an encouraging environment, something you're each willing to provide. Cancer finds solace at home, and you're happy to disappear elsewhere to recharge your batteries. Another plus is that both signs like animals and are drawn to strays. (If you live together, you and Cancer will need lots of space.) Neither sign is ambitious, so you don't make the most productive team at work. But you certainly understand each other's charms, talents, and, especially, moods. *Celebrity couple: Johnny Cash (February 26, 1932) and June Carter (June 23, 1929).*

Pisces and Leo

Compatibility rating: ***** (5 out of 10)

These two signs are certainly attracted to each other—more for their differences than similarities. Fixed fire sign Leo, with a flamboyant personality, comes on strong (but has a romantic nature). That sits well with mutable water sign Pisces, who is more inspired than overwhelmed by a theatrical persona. Leo thrives on flattery, and there will be no shortage of it from you. You need to feel loved and appreciated, and a Leo partner will admire your spirituality, creativity, open-mindedness, compassion, and romantic nature. But you usually do better with a partner who is drawn to your mysterious nature (Scorpio would qualify). And Leo has a better success rate with a hard-working mate like Capricorn. You have a lazy (or daydreamy) side, which can be a turnoff. On the plus side, you adapt easily to your surroundings and are happy to let Leo take charge of decor. There shouldn't be significant differences about bringing up kids, who can inherit a unique combination of sensitivity and assertiveness. At work, you'll provide imagination, and Leo will lead. In the unlikely situation that you're the boss and Leo the subordinate, let Leo take over (or nominally take over), and there won't be any challenge over your more prestigious and better-paying position. *Celebrity couple: Desi Arnaz (March 2, 1917) and Lucille Ball (August 6, 1911).*

Pisces and Virgo

Compatibility rating: ********* (9 out of 10)
You and Virgo are opposite signs, with birthdays half a year apart (more or less). Opposite signs indicate an attraction based on similarities and differences. The Sun sign opposite yours has the same quality (cardinal, fixed, or mutable) as you, but the elements (air, earth, fire, or water) are different. Although opposite signs often share the same goals, each sign has its own reasons for going after those goals and its own methods in reaching them. A Pisces and Virgo match can be ideal on an emotional and practical level. Because you are both mutable signs, you communicate easily. You're a water sign and Virgo is earth, so you're imaginative and creative while Virgo is more grounded. You can benefit handsomely from each other. You need to pick up some of Virgo's patience and skills at planning, while Virgo's life becomes more interesting when it assumes some

of your spontaneity. You can be moody and Virgo downbeat, and it's a good idea for one of you to retreat when the other gets in a funk—otherwise, you can reinforce each other's negativity. You're both kind, romantic, and vulnerable, and those qualities form a bond. You can help soften Virgo's rigidity, while Virgo will provide order in your life. You're complementary in a working relationship as well—Virgo is analytical and you're experimental. As travel companions you're a successful team. Virgo can research the destination and then, on arrival, your imagination will lead the way.

Pisces and Libra

Compatibility rating: ***** (7 out of 10)**

You're ruled by Neptune and Libra by Venus. The two planets get along nicely, with one encouraging the other and both sharing a spiritual side. You help Libra to think intuitively rather than weighing decisions ad infinitum. And Libra, a patron of the arts, encourages you to let your mind wander as far as it will take you. Pisces has a number of Venus-related qualities, so the two of you are romantically inclined, sentimental, and giving. The one similarity that may create havoc is that neither sign is practical. You're a mutable water sign—moody, insecure, and needing change. Libra is upbeat. Normally, Libra avoids clingy types like the plague, yet you have a poetic nature that attracts a Libra. Of the twelve signs, you are the most easily influenced and will assume many of Libra's traits—notably, diplomacy and a desire to be surrounded by beauty. Of the two, Libra will take control when the need arises. Both signs are compassionate and will treat each other well, even if they're simply acquaintances. You're the more intuitive by far and will be able to read Libra's motives—which are sometimes complex—like a book. Neither of you is orderly, and you both like to be surrounded by your treasures. One can always locate a Pisces or Libra work station: cluttered with photos, plants, and, most likely, a stack of unorganized papers. Side by side, your desks will look like twin peaks.

Pisces and Scorpio

Compatibility rating: ******* (7 out of 10)
You and Scorpio are both water signs, which may explain why you understand each other so well. You're also both possessive. Water signs are intuitive and perceptive, and either of you could be a good psychologist or psychic. You bring out Scorpio's positive qualities—tenderness, charisma, and charm. Scorpio has a surprising level of strength—it's not always apparent, but Pisces sees it. In a similar way, while others find you overly emotional and moody, Scorpio responds first to your creative side and gentle ways. You're easy to mould, and that's one of the things that attracts Scorpio to you. Scorpio loves to mentor, teach, and shape, and Pisces is putty in your hands. If the two of you connect, you'll find you depend on each other. Scorpio (co-ruled by militant Mars and powerful Pluto) has to be careful, however, not to overwhelm Pisces. You, in turn, are ruled by Neptune (creativity and spirituality). Both signs can pick up on even the most subtle vibes. But Scorpio can be unforgiving, while you display tremendous empathy. Sometimes you take on

other people's problems and concentrate on them rather than on your own. You have to be sure that a Scorpio partner, relative, or co-worker does not cause you to lose your identity. Encourage each other's talents and share interests that appeal to both of you. Meditation and yoga are good choices. *Celebrity couples: Elizabeth Taylor (February 27, 1932) and Richard Burton (November 10, 1925); Kurt Russell (March 17, 1951) and Goldie Hawn (November 21, 1945).*

Pisces and Sagittarius

Compatibility rating: ***** (5 out of 10)

The two of you seem, on the surface, quite different—emotional Pisces and independent Sagittarius. You seek out emotional security and your ego is easily bruised. Sagittarius loves freedom and is brash. Sagittarius is also an intellectual sign, while you're ruled by your emotions and intuition. Yet there is reason to be hopeful for this pair. Although your temperaments differ—you're often moody and Sagittarius is mostly upbeat—Sagittarius's positive approach can pull practically anyone out of a funk. You're both mutable as well. (Sagittarius *needs* change; you're simply restless.) Pisces is the most easily moulded sign, and likely you'll acquire some of Sagittarius's optimism. But along the way you could pick up some of your partner's more questionable qualities—notably, recklessness. Sagittarius is the most outspoken among the signs, and Pisces is among the most sensitive and can be easily hurt. There are many possible scenarios, and frankly this relationship can go anywhere. In a family or on the job, neither you nor Sagittarius is big on rules, but your combined imagination is extraordinary. You can both go off on a tangent, so it would be helpful to have a grounded influence on the scene.

Pisces and Capricorn

Compatibility rating: ***** (7 out of 10)**
Somehow a Pisces–Capricorn relationship is possible—even favourable—although looking at individual traits it seems improbable. You're ruled by spiritual Neptune. Saturn, planet of caution and restriction, rules Capricorn. As a water sign, you're unconventional. Capricorn, an earth sign, is conservative and mainstream. Emotionally, you're warm and affectionate, while Capricorn is cool. The interesting thing is that you each have a capacity to draw out qualities from the other. You will bring to the partnership your greatest strengths of warmth and imagination. Capricorn will introduce its strongest quality—a sense of security and reassurance. Capricorn climbs toward its goal while you swim toward yours, so you won't get in each other's way. There are two obstacles to success. First, you cling, and Capricorn finds any kind of hovering a turnoff. As well, when happy, you both withdraw like clams. Still, you desperately need someone with business acumen, and Capricorn greatly benefits from a spiritual and imaginative influence. In families or at work, neither will let the other down. You will likely inject a bit of life into Capricorn's world, and Capricorn will instill in you some ambition to combine with your creativity.

Pisces and Aquarius

Compatibility rating: **** (6 out of 10)**

Because Pisces and Aquarius are neighbouring signs—Pisces follows Aquarius—the odds are that you share some planetary influences and have some common qualities. But judging by Sun signs alone, you are, in many ways, opposites. Still, you're likely to be able to tolerate if not entirely understand your differences, and you certainly make an interesting match. You're the last two signs of the zodiac and absorb a number of the qualities of the preceding ten signs. Both signs like to circulate, but Aquarius makes an impression, while you're impressionable. The two of you are among the most challenging signs to get along with—you because of your moodiness, and Aquarius because of its eccentric personality. But you're both tolerant and look for the best in others. Frankly, Aquarius is the one who'll need to do most of the compromising: it's not easy to live with someone whose emotions change with the tides. Your symbol is two fishes, and you have a choice. You can navigate through troubled waters or you can flail and sink. It helps if you have someone to guide you over the obstacles, and Aquarius is one of the few signs that understands your journey. Another thing in your favour is that you both have high regard for the wisdom of elders and inspire enthusiasm in youngsters. At work, Aquarius has little patience for your lazy side, and you don't appreciate Aquarius's cool manner. It helps if there's an action-oriented cardinal sign (Aries, Cancer, Libra, Capricorn) on the premises. *Celebrity couple: Joanne Woodward (February 27, 1930) and Paul Newman (January 26, 1925).*

Pisces and Pisces

Compatibility rating: **** (6 out of 10)**

When two members of the same sign join forces, the connection can bring out the best and the worst in each. In the case of Pisces, there's potential for a lively and enjoyable relationship or a complicated and confusing one. We have two water signs—emotional, demonstrative, easily influenced—which reinforce each other's strengths and weaknesses. Depending on your other influences (especially the Moon), you have very high or low odds for compatibility. If anyone knows that Pisces is never dull, never insensitive, and often moody, it's a fellow Pisces. Because of your negativity, in theory it's best to match up with one of the zodiac's optimists. But a Pisces–Pisces union has hidden potential. Pisces are highly creative souls, and they can encourage each other's talents. They are also caring and understanding. Two Pisces will further inspire each other to better the world. And while their phobias may depress the rest of us, they are perceptive and know what is happening in the Pisces psyche. In domestic situations, you are open to new ways of thinking, and your creative ideas add life to family events. Pisces are daydreamers, easily distracted and inclined to believe what they hear. Even if their work involves the kind of creativity at which they excel, it's often smart to include no more than two Pisces on a team.

PART THREE

PERSONAL
WEEKLY
HOROSCOPES
FOR 2013

his part of the book includes forecasts for each zodiac sign. By becoming more familiar with the basics of astrology (See The Basics of Astrology, page 1) and the attributes of your sign (see Snapshots of Your Zodiac Sign, page 17) , you can better understand how to deal with the events, trends, and moods that are projected.

A yearly overview precedes the weekly forecasts for each sign. But how does 2013 shape up in a general way—both on an individual and a global scale?

Let's begin by reviewing what happened and *didn't* happen in 2012. Much of the world's economy remained in turmoil, the Queen celebrated her Diamond Jubilee, London hosted the Olympic Games, and advances in technology continued at an extraordinary pace. As for what didn't occur: no Canadian team made it to the Stanley Cup finals, once again the Toronto Maple Leafs did not qualify for the post-season, and, despite those events—not to mention some hysteria as the Mayan calendar reached the end of its cycle—the world survived. Hopefully, on a personal level, we were able to take advantage of the year's planetary movements.

In looking at what's in store in 2013, we won't review every planetary activity but will consider some highlights through the year.

As 2013 begins, Jupiter remains in Gemini. It will stay there until June 26, when it moves into Cancer. Jupiter, the largest planet, is identified with growth, expansion, and beneficial influences. It is commonly called the planet of good luck, although it really brings opportunities. While Jupiter is in Gemini, we are likely to see huge strides take place in communications-related technology—computers, phones, and yet-to-be-imagined gadgets. We may also witness new ventures and missions to the Moon, Venus, and Mars. After Jupiter moves into Cancer, where it will remain through the rest of the year, we are likely to find enormous strength and comfort in family and home. Our most significant accomplishments may happen within our postal code. We can also expect to see influences related to the fields of real estate and medicine.

Neptune, named for the god of the sea, moved into water sign Pisces last year and will remain there until 2025. Because Neptune is Pisces' "host" planet, its placement is especially meaningful for Canada. Water is the country's greatest and most important natural resource, and with Neptune now finding its footing in Pisces, Canada is likely to assume a prominent role on the world stage. Ice of course is a form of water. The World Figure Skating Championships will be held in London, Ontario, this year, and once again, Canadian men's skater Patrick Chan and ice dancers Tessa Virtue and Scott Moir (both born in London) are likely to win gold. The 2013 hockey season, meanwhile, marks the twentieth anniversary of the Montreal Canadiens' championship victory over the Los Angeles Kings—the last time a Canadian team hoisted the Stanley Cup. Given the positioning of the planets this year, the drought may well end in 2013.

The positions of the other "outer" planets remain unchanged. Saturn, the planet of consolidation and hard work, is still in Scorpio, the sign associated with secrecy, intensity, intuition, and real estate. On a personal scale, instead of branching out, we may find it helpful to concentrate on a few select areas of interest. Uranus, connected to nonconformity and discovery, remains in Aries, the planet of action, leadership, and innovation. Aries has an affinity to singers (Céline Dion, Elton John, Jann Arden, and Susan Boyle are all born under this sign), and it's highly possible that a major discovery will be made in this area. As well, the election of a leader of the Canadian Liberal Party is slated for 2013, and we may see a surprising choice. Finally, Pluto remains in Capricorn. Pluto is associated with our attitudes, and Capricorn is the sign of ambition. In other words, this is a good year to explore the way we approach our work and to try a change in perspective.

When a planet is retrograde, it appears to be travelling backwards through the zodiac (but this is actually an optical illusion). During this time, the planet's influence is felt in a more internal way. We need to pay attention to several retrogrades this year.

Mercury is retrograde three times in 2013: February 23–March 17, June 26–July 20, and October 21–November 10. Mercury rules communication and transportation, and things such as travel, speaking, negotiating, and the mail (including email) can be disrupted during these periods. We can expect delays, challenges, and frustrations. We need to back up our computer files and allow extra time for short- and long-distance trips. Most importantly, we should try to organize our thoughts rather than attempt something new. At the end of the year (December 21), Venus turns retrograde for about 40 days. During this time, old friends will re-enter our lives. This will also be a time of learning in general and, specifically, for understanding who our true friends are.

Overall, 2013 is a year for experiencing growth on several levels, including intellectual and financial. With Jupiter's strong influence, we can enjoy long-distance travel but also experience greater contentment in our home and support from our families. We can also aim to simplify our lives, study something in an in-depth rather than a superficial way, and reconnect with old friends. Surprise opportunities open up, not just on an individual plane but on a global one. We also have a special opportunity to make a contribution to the environment.

Throughout the year, there is an emphasis on creativity, and we should continue to look for new and imaginative ways to break down barriers. The movement of the planets can help us unlock doors and open our eyes.

What's Ahead for Aries

March 21–April 20

Pioneering Aries can look forward to a year with several themes: communication (on both a professional and a personal level), travel (also related to work and pleasure), and property. As the year begins, the world comes to you— expect visitors and correspondence from south of the border and abroad. Real estate is highlighted starting at the end of June; whether thinking about selling your property or not, this is a good time to upgrade and renovate your home. Starting early in the summer, you'll feel like you're being tested. There are professional challenges and personal conflicts. However, you see this brief but intense time as a learning experience, and by August, you sense that relationships are on firmer ground and that your reputation is intact. You also begin to experience a greater sense of belonging. Starting around September, you feel more of an equal in a group and realize that people are no longer shutting you out of their inner circle. Around this time, you meet some offbeat individuals who help expand your interests. Overall, you enjoy increased finances, not from inheritances or lotteries, but as a result of hard work and innovative thinking. In other words, you make your own luck. Also on tap this year are opportunities to excel in a sport and experiences that help make you a more confident public speaker. Your sign rules the head and the face. Protect your skin from the elements and, since you're prone to headaches, be sure to eat regularly (yes, you sometimes forget) and get sufficient rest and recreation.

January

Your keywords for the month ahead: progress, reconciliation, hidden opportunity.

Key Days
Romance: Jan. 3, 10, 21, 29
Friends and family: Jan. 1, 11, 26, 27
Career and status: Jan. 4, 7, 16, 29
Finance: Jan. 8, 17, 24, 30

Week of the 1st–6th

Right now, you need to focus on a difficult work situation that's complicated by an indecisive individual. Reread holiday cards, looking for hidden messages, and settle a small but highly annoying family dispute.

Week of the 7th–13th

A project or activity benefits from your strengths. It's up to you to find it, and don't look in the usual places. Make a point of spending time with people you met over the holidays; you'll enjoy getting to know another side of them. Relatives surprise you with their generosity.

Week of the 14th–20th

Don't rush to complete a project. You'll find it benefits from fine-tuning and attention to presentation. You begin to understand why a friend or relative has been remote and can now take steps to mend the relationship. Outline goals for the coming months and then set your priorities.

Week of the 21st–27th

People bring baggage with them—and we're not talking backpacks and suitcases. It seems that the individuals you deal with have decided to unload on you. The full moon on Saturday brings with it several opportunities. This is a good time to branch out into new areas and to patch up an old friendship.

Week of the 28th–31st

Enjoy your privacy while you can as the month comes to a close. Read a favourite book, go for a long winter walk, and take time to gather your thoughts and reshape your goals. The next weeks

will see you hosting unexpected visitors and finding it difficult
to enjoy the solitary time that you cherish.

February

Your keywords for the month ahead: consolidation,
creativity, innovation.

Key Days
Romance: Feb. 8, 14, 22, 26
Friends and family: Feb. 3, 11, 19, 23
Career and status: Feb. 7, 18, 26, 27
Finance: Feb. 4, 10, 20, 25

Week of the 1st–10th
This period is marked by extremes. You feel warm toward some
people but have little patience for others. Not surprisingly, co-
workers and relatives approach you with caution. You learn of a
possible future windfall, but this isn't the time to spend lavishly.

Week of the 11th–17th
This could prove an expensive week. You have an eye for the
kind of objects you won't find in the local dollar store. You're a
superb judge of character and have a sixth sense about whom
to trust and when someone is protesting a little too much. On
Thursday or Friday, an influential person backs your ideas.

Week of the 18th–24th
You're feeling more at home in new surroundings and are able
to express your innermost thoughts. This is a good week to clear

out clutter, resume a favourite creative activity, and entertain close friends. You tend to be overly modest but should play up your strengths when meeting new people.

Week of the 25th–28th

You're concerned about two things this week: your ability to manage a complicated project, and the well-being of someone you're beginning to care about. Draw on past experiences for both situations. As for visitors, you can expected the unexpected—so keep your fridge well stocked.

March

Your keywords for the month ahead: communication, renovation, transition.

Key Days

Romance: March 3, 8, 16, 28
Friends and family: March 6, 14, 22, 26
Career and status: March 5, 13, 20, 28
Finance: March 2, 15, 25, 28

Week of the 1st–10th

Choose your words carefully, especially during the first five days, remembering that "less" is often "more." A relationship picks up speed as it moves to a new level. Be sure you're comfortable with the direction it's taking, as well as the pace.

Week of the 11th–17th

Your sign is associated with initiative and leadership, but now you're happy to take a back-seat role and let others make the decisions. Lines of communication finally open up and you get through to the right people. The weekend is a favourable time for upgrading equipment and going to auctions.

Week of the 18th–24th
The week has its positive and frustrating moments. Things look more promising regarding a property-related matter, but you can also expect scheduling problems, including last-minute cancellations. You'll be thanked for knocking a very large chip off a co-worker's shoulder.

Week of the 25th–31st
Stay clear of manipulative people. A few of them are poking their heads into your business; duck whenever they're near. This is a good week to dabble in different recreational activities and decide which ones you like best. Everyone is keeping an eye on your financial situation—and you should be doing the same.

April

Your keywords for the month ahead: transformation, introspection, intuition.

Key Days
Romance: April 1, 10, 19, 28
Friends and family: April 5, 6, 17, 26
Career and status: April 3, 11, 23, 29
Finance: April 6, 15, 22, 30

Week of the 1st–7th

You're more open-minded right now, thanks to the influence of someone you connected with late last year. Make mental notes of small signs of change in your community or work environment. They may not mean much now but will eventually prove significant.

Week of the 8th–14th

Some of your best ideas arrive at unexpected moments—keep a notebook handy so you can jot them down. Be sure you're comfortable with all the terms of written contracts or verbal agreements. Someone you know casually is taking a more serious interest in you.

Week of the 15th–21st

Details are key this week. Put maximum effort into the smallest jobs, and give attention to even minor health issues. Follow your hunches, especially in financial dealings. You begin to see changes in your attitude toward material things. Weekend plans take shape as they go along.

Week of the 22nd–30th

Motivation is strong and right now you're driven by a sense of adventure. You can put creative touches to even the most mundane activity or project. Co-workers or neighbours may try to keep you out of the loop so watch out for indications of change and ask plenty of questions.

May

Your keywords for the month ahead: ambition, changeability, new beginnings.

Key Days
Romance: May 4, 11, 20, 25
Friends and family: May 5, 18, 20, 30
Career and status: May 2, 7, 16, 27
Finance: May 4, 9, 17, 29

Week of the 1st–5th
Your work ethic, which continues to develop, is noticed by an influential person. A friend's reputation is on the line as a result of rumours making the rounds. You're in a position to stem them but need to act promptly.

Week of the 6th–12th
You'll be dealing with legal documents or verbal agreements and need to be comfortable with all the terms. If you've been trying to publish something—even a letter to the editor—this is a good week for sending out submissions. Be cautious on the weekend, when it's easy to be drawn into someone else's argument.

Week of the 13th–19th
Pay attention to subtle changes in your work environment. Being prepared will give you an advantage. You meet someone from another province or country with whom you agree on movies, books, and wine. A relative's recent shift in attitude suddenly

makes sense. Keep trying to patch things up, but don't expect results for at least a week.

Week of the 20th–26th
You're in a quandary over a friendship that sometimes feels like it's unravelling. Remember, part of the problem may be your own stubbornness. The full moon of the 24th marks the start of a brief but intense period of self-confidence and ambition. Set your standards now, and set them high.

Week of the 27th–31st
You'll be dealing with people who are set in their ways, but don't let that stop you from experimenting with new ideas. It's a good week for expanding your knowledge. You may decide to learn more about health or anatomy. A temporary assignment can turn into a permanent one.

June

Your keywords for the month ahead: affection, new authority, restored balance.

Key Days
Romance: June 3, 11, 16, 26
Friends and family: June 5, 15, 23, 28
Career and status: June 4, 12, 21, 26
Finance: June 10, 14, 22, 30

Week of the 1st–9th

Your usually reliable memory may be playing tricks, so check your calendar for birthdays and deadlines. There's a lot of drama this week—much of it enjoyable. And you're the recipient of someone's generosity.

Week of the 10th–16th

The first few days see you correcting other people's mistakes. When you finally resume your own work, you'll discover it's more meaningful than ever. Martin Short, a famous Aries, said that "no one is any one thing." That's certainly the case this week, when you seem to be wearing two or more hats.

Week of the 17th–23rd

Discuss changes in your professional life with a trusted friend, but don't talk about personal issues with a colleague. The week favours modernization, and it's a good time to update your technical skills. But there's also a theme of nostalgia as you connect with friends or places from your past.

Week of the 24th–30th

You have two ears and one mouth, and the key is to use them proportionately. You need to strike a balance between your personal and professional lives. Your partner is keen to pamper you, but you're juggling new responsibilities. The good news is that you can make everyone happy—especially yourself.

July

Your keywords for the month ahead: charisma, competition, tradition.

Key Days
Romance: July 5, 11, 21, 28
Friends and family: July 1, 14, 23, 30
Career and status: July 8, 19, 25, 29
Finance: July 6, 17, 20, 28

Week of the 1st–7th
This week finds you in an introspective mood. You're also more focused and decisive than you've been. You have a special gift for drawing information out of people, but use it prudently. You could learn more than you want to—or really need—to know.

Week of the 8th–14th
The new moon on Monday seems to affect you. You can be too sensitive for your own good, feeling hard done by or slighted over a trivial matter. Although you may not be aware of it, your status actually soars this week. You also have a chance to pick up something valuable, so check out weekend garage sales.

Week of the 15th–21st
Keep up with changing trends. You may not agree with them all, but you need to be aware of what's current. Routine jobs prove more time-consuming than usual but it's important to complete what you begin. Make the most of your opportunity on the weekend to see the world through someone else's eyes.

Week of the 22nd–31st

There's a potentially great match waiting for you this week. You're interested in someone with whom you share an odd combination of interests (hockey and poetry perhaps, or euchre and fine art). You can be overwhelmed with guests. For your sake—and theirs—you need to block out some time for yourself.

August

Your keywords for the month ahead: stability, artistry, authority.

Key Days

Romance: Aug. 1, 10, 19, 26
Friends and family: Aug. 3, 13, 19, 28
Career and status: Aug. 6, 14, 22, 27
Finance: Aug. 5, 14, 23, 30

Week of the 1st–4th

Loyalties are divided but you really don't need to make a choice. Information about a family member explains a longstanding mystery. Look your best on the weekend—the impression you make is important and can lead to enhanced status.

Week of the 5th–11th

This is an excellent inventory week. You're your own best critic, and this is an ideal time to review your strengths and weaknesses. It's also a good time to advance theories, but think twice before acting on hunches. Transitions are indicated as you begin to think about changes in your career or your home environment.

Week of the 12th–18th
You mingle well with people of all ages, except, perhaps, your own. Friends, relatives, and acquaintances find you non-threatening, non-judgmental, and compassionate. Even if you're not planning an out-of-country trip, it's a good time to be sure all your travel documents are in order.

Week of the 19th–25th
A new relationship shows signs of growing pains, but you're patient. News from an out-of-town relative may lead to a trip. Follow up on medical tests, applications, and unanswered calls. Evaluate and review all important documents, especially legal ones. Be sure not to take anyone's generosity for granted on the weekend.

Week of the 26th–31st
Some of your happiest moments this week take place close to nature and with a partner. Bird-watching and kayaking may be of special appeal, and you may want to spend time in a provincial or national park. A finance-related announcement may sound too good to be true, but some of the information you hear is worth pursuing.

September

Your keywords for the month ahead: eloquence, vivaciousness, tenacity.

Key Days
Romance: Sept. 4, 11, 18, 26
Friends and family: Sept. 7, 15, 20, 29
Career and status: Sept. 5, 16, 24, 30
Finance: Sept. 6, 14, 22, 28

Week of the 1st–8th
Your partner may be travelling this week, or a relative may be able to share a domestic responsibility. Take advantage of the situation and catch up on health, fitness, and getting together with those friends you've been neglecting.

Week of the 9th–15th
No one's sure what you're saying, but it sounds good. You should use your persuasiveness in the best possible way. Be sure to process information before acting on it. Your platonic friend may want to move the relationship up a notch or two. Be more methodical in your health habits and avoid eating on the run.

Week of the 16th–22nd
Follow your intuition. As long as they're not too far outside the box, your hunches pay off this week. One of your professional accomplishments is worthy of recognition. But don't expect kudos, or a bonus—just lots more work as a sign of appreciation.

Week of the 23rd–30th
You could find yourself dealing with incompetent people early in the week, but concentrate on meeting your own goals. Plans that seemed in disarray are quickly falling into place. Despite

age or other differences, you find that you share some unusual interests with a new acquaintance.

October

Your keywords for the month ahead: decisiveness, compromise, networking.

Key Days
Romance: Oct. 3, 12, 19, 30
Friends and family: Oct. 5, 16, 26, 30
Career and status: Oct. 1, 9, 22, 28
Finance: Oct. 2, 10, 21, 29

Week of the 1st–6th
Assorted pieces of information land on your desk. You'll be happily surprised when you discover a common theme. You could become entangled in a messy family situation if you insist on taking sides. Let others work things out for a change.

Week of the 7th–13th
You don't mind someone telling you what to do. It's telling you *how* to do it that's causing tension right now. You can be very entertaining this week. You may not wind up on *Canada's Got Talent*, but your audience is expanding. Remember too that you're ruled by Mars, a planet that inspires initiative.

Week of the 14th–20th
Brush up on your history—your knowledge of family events

can prove helpful later in the year. Ideas for acquiring cash are promising but need more refinement. If you're eager to see a movie or try a new restaurant and can't find anyone to join you, don't let that stop you. You'll have a surprisingly fun time alone.

Week of the 21st–27th

Stay clear of family politics. If you learn anything private, put it in the vault and don't let anyone have the key. You're seeing someone in a new and much more positive light. Late this week you tend to put a lot of unnecessary pressure on yourself. Look for an outlet for bottled-up stress. Something creative or athletic can do the trick.

Week of the 28th–31st

Louisa May Alcott said it takes two flints to make a fire, and this week sees you meeting that other flint. Emotions will ride high, and there's passion in the picture as well. But be cautious not to leap to conclusions. Something you observe or overhear at the end of the month can work to your benefit early next year.

November

Your keywords for the month ahead: new directions, old friendships, renewal, expansion.

Key Days

Romance: Nov. 2, 11, 26, 30
Friends and family: Nov. 5, 9, 23, 26
Career and status: Nov. 4, 12, 21, 28
Finance: Nov. 1, 13, 20, 27

Week of the 1st–10th

You'll be facing a new challenge with which a friend from another province or country can help you cope. The new moon on the 3rd marks the start of a period in which you're more subtle and introspective than usual.

Week of the 11th–17th

It's a good week for expanding your interests and even trying something outside your comfort zone. At the same time, you encourage a young friend to try a new approach. Negotiations that seemed to go nowhere are back on track, and by the end of the week you may actually seal the deal.

Week of the 18th–24th

You're surrounded by people with exceptional manners and refined tastes. Surprisingly, this isn't as dull a week as it sounds. You take on an assignment that interests you and enjoy new activities. And some of those cultured types you're involved with turn out to be more fun than expected.

Week of the 25th–30th

A stalled plan or sluggish relationship gains momentum. Someone's behaviour has been upsetting you, and it's time to tell the offender what the problem is. Diplomacy is key, however. You can make an important connection this week, so don't find excuses to miss out on any possible networking opportunity.

December

Your keywords for the month ahead: expansion, transformation, revelation.

Key Days
Romance: Dec. 5, 9, 18, 27
Friends and family: Dec. 7, 17, 24, 29
Career and status: Dec. 2, 10, 23, 27
Finance: Dec. 11, 19, 23, 31

Week of the 1st–8th
You continue to experiment with ideas, and a friend's suggestions may inspire you. You're rarely fooled, but someone's trying to pull the wool over your eyes. You have a lot of people to
answer to this week. This is not the time to back down.

Week of the 9th–15th
Whether it's a relationship or a job, "firsts" are always difficult.
There's a first of some kind happening this week. This is also
a good time to make end-of-the-year resolutions—your willpower and drive are strong. Follow up on a friend's or relative's
health if you learn that there may be a problem.

Week of the 16th–22nd
You have the opportunity to make things happen, especially
around the winter solstice on the 21st, but you tend to procrastinate. Momentum in a relationship starts to gather, but don't
force anything. The end of the week is a good time to read the

business pages. Knowledge gained now can come in handy in the new year.

Week of the 23rd–31st

You've been struggling to find the right words to express your feelings to someone you care about. Now, as the year draws to a close, you know just what to say. You're also able to help a friend out of a funk. Someone you'll meet will be impressed by your knowledge of Canadian history and politics.

What's Ahead for Taurus

April 21–May 21

For Taurus, this is a key year in several important areas. For the first half of the year, expansive Jupiter is in your second house of personal wealth. You have an opportunity to extend your income. Perhaps you get a promotion (it won't come to you—you need to seek it out); maybe you change jobs. Your attitude toward possessions will also change, and you may begin to collect antiques or art as an investment. In the second half of the year, the emphasis is on both communication and hobbies. You take a new interest in language and understand the power and the beauty of words. Another hobby may lead to a friendship with someone from a different background. This hobby could be either mindless or stimulating; what matters is the friendship that springs from it. As the year progresses, you'll feel more comfortable expressing your opinions and, as a result, you may find yourself in a political role. During the summer months, possibly as a result of travel, you'll spend more time with relatives and even discover some new cousins, aunts, or uncles. Just as your expanded family will prove a mixed blessing—some members will be delightful, others irritating—several pieces of good news will be countered with disappointments. You could be inheriting obligations that take up some of your precious private time, but around September or October, you see a spike in your net worth. Real estate is in the spotlight around October or November. Whether you're buying, selling, or just gathering information, it's better to deal with an objective professional than a friend. At the tail end of 2013, when you take inventory of the preceding twelve months, you'll realize that you've become more independent. You still need to be more disciplined about your health, and may find it best to combine fitness with an activity you actually like, such as gardening, or just working out while listening to your favourite music.

January

Your keywords for the month ahead: discovery, diversification, ambition.

Key Days
Romance: Jan. 2, 13, 21, 29
Friends and family: Jan. 4, 16, 24, 31
Career and status: Jan. 7, 15, 23, 30
Finance: Jan. 8, 16, 25, 31

Week of the 1st–6th

An old friendship or an old interest is revived as the year begins. This is also a good week for expanding your interests and taking on a speaking assignment. Two cautions: be wary about overindulging yourself and careful about lending money.

Week of the 7th–13th

You'll be interacting with people you met late in 2012 and will increasingly enjoy their company. Be careful about impulsive tendencies early in the year. Plot your moves carefully and avoid making snap decisions. You excel at communications and can finally get a difficult point across to a family member or co-worker.

Week of the 14th–20th

Perceptive Taurus's knack for reading people has seldom been so on-target. You understand what motivates others and can tell if anyone has a hidden agenda or two. Deals and more deals— that's the theme of the week. Bring along a magnifying glass to read the fine print.

Week of the 21st–27th

You may be playing a lead or supporting role, but the week favours large-scale projects. A picture really can paint a thousand words, and your visual presentations, combined with a late-week surge of energy, prove a success. Your partner or a relative may seem hesitant and distracted; it's best to allow space and keep a low profile.

Week of the 28th–31st

You turn your attention to a new area of interest. Although a change is good, be cautious not to leave an important job half-done. Bargaining skills are sharp, and something valuable may catch your eye. However, watch out for people trying to draw information from you, especially during the last few days of the month.

February

Your keywords for the month ahead: gratitude, compassion, eccentricity.

Key Days
Romance: Feb. 2, 15, 22, 27
Friends and family: Feb. 5, 10, 19, 26
Career and status: Feb. 4, 13, 20, 25
Finance: Feb. 3, 12, 21, 28

Week of the 1st–10th
These ten days are a productive time. You're tweaking one job and then, around the new moon of the 10th, starting a large project. As well, you're organizing a community event—a role that puts you in contact with a politician or other person in a high position.

Week of the 11th–17th
You're interested in an environmental issue and can now do some important research in this area. It's the kind of week when you're given two days of work and one day to do it in. Friends or relatives may be put off because you're seeing some moments in the sun while they remain in the shade.

Week of the 18th–24th

A recently completed job earns you a rave review. You could sit back on your laurels and gloat, but you have little time. This is an excellent week to discover interesting travel destinations, get to know someone in a field that's new to you, or turn into an escape artist and disappear for a romantic getaway.

Week of the 25th–28th

The week offers several lessons—the most important one being the value of a backup plan. Take a page from a friend's book and consider a more conservative approach to finance and a more light-hearted one to relationships. Someone in a senior position comes to you for advice and guidance.

March

Your keywords for the month ahead: detours, adventures, renewed relationships.

Key Days

Romance: March 6, 15, 21, 27
Friends and family: March 3, 14, 24, 30
Career and status: March 4, 13, 25, 29
Finance: March 2, 11, 22, 28

Week of the 1st–10th

You're asked to work on a team project and can make an important contribution. Two friends or relatives may be fighting for your approval and it's best to let them battle it out. You have a knack for finding bargains, treasures, and odd personalities.

Week of the 11th–17th

People are hard to pin down as you try to organize an event, but persistence pays off. Venus, your ruling planet, is associated with shared pleasure and tranquility. Expect more of the former than the latter this week. Roles are reversed on the weekend as you and your partner start switching responsibilities.

Week of the 18th–24th

Wrinkles are ironed out and, by the spring equinox on Wednesday, your plans finally take shape. Watch out for someone at work or in the neighbourhood who tries to intimidate you. Focus on your strengths and don't try to compete. Be cautious on the weekend, when you're drawn to luxury items or decadent foods.

Week of the 25th–31st

The full moon on Wednesday starts a cycle that emphasizes responsibility. You're paying more attention to your finances—especially shared ones—and it's a good time to draw up a budget. On the holiday weekend a relative tries to force an issue that you figured had already ended. Don't fall into a trap.

April

Your keywords for the month ahead: finishing touches, fence-mending, re-evaluation.

Key Days
Romance: April 3, 15, 21, 28
Friends and family: April 7, 14, 20, 25

Career and status: April 8, 16, 23, 29
Finance: April 4, 12, 22, 30

Week of the 1st–7th

Right now, you need to rely less on others and more on yourself. It's a good time to bite the bullet and get in touch with someone you've been thinking about. Watch out for an overprotective relative who's starting to cramp your style and your space.

Week of the 8th–14th

Spontaneity is the key, and you'll be ad libbing your way through the week. An on-again, off-again project is back on the boards and you can actually finish it and move on to something new. If you're making a major purchase, continue to weigh the pros and cons and seek opinions from an objective source.

Week of the 15th–21st

Don't rely on your usually excellent memory. Early in the week you're prone to mixing up names or forgetting appointments. You're waiting for an important decision. The weekend has the suspense of a seventh hockey game, but you need to hang in a bit longer. Just remember, you're supposed to be patient and persistent.

Week of the 22nd–30th

A long-awaited decision arrives by Tuesday, and on Wednesday or Thursday you move from a supporting role and take charge of a project. Relatives, meanwhile, are more open to your ideas and appreciative of your help. You get mixed messages on the weekend and wonder if a friend is ready to make a commitment.

May

Your keywords for the month ahead: letting go, healing, prestige.

Key Days
Romance: May 4, 15, 24, 29
Friends and family: May 7, 19, 26, 30
Career and status: May 6, 14, 23, 29
Finance: May 2, 11, 22, 28

Week of the 1st–5th
Two of your favourite people are at odds with each other, but you'd be smart not to take sides. This is a good week for attracting top individuals to your team, planning a summer break, or turning a hobby into a source of extra cash.

Week of the 6th–12th
Recent feelings of solitude are replaced by an urge to circulate. You're so upbeat, in fact, that you're in great demand. You're also eager to make a commitment, but test the waters before signing on to anything long-term. Stay clear of people who are meddling in your private life—they seem to be everywhere on the weekend.

Week of the 13th–19th
You thrive on stimulation and will be getting more than your share. Expect changes in your schedule. You may be pressured into making a commitment but think it through before agreeing to something you could regret. Changes are indicated in your

social circle, and the weekend may mark the start of a platonic friendship.

Week of the 20th–26th

Balance is your key, and a more even approach helps you face life's challenges head on. Be alert for opportunities to take on a job that can boost your image and improve your cash flow. The weekend finds you in a sentimental mood. If you're seeking romance, it may be closer to home than you think.

Week of the 27th–31st

You're dealing with someone who's ego is so huge that the Canadian Rockies look puny by comparison. On Tuesday or Friday you receive a gift that on the surface may not seem like much, but is in fact meaningful. A potential new friendship is on the horizon—perhaps you're introduced to a friend of a friend on the weekend.

June

Your keywords for the month ahead: assertiveness, sentimentality, spontaneity.

Key Days

Romance: June 5, 12, 24, 29
Friends and family: June 6, 17, 25, 30
Career and status: June 10, 17, 21, 28
Finance: June 2, 9, 16, 25

Week of the 1st–9th

You could be feeling too independent and should allow—even encourage—your friends to be supportive. You're willing to go out on a limb for someone, but don't promise more than you can deliver. Communication is a strong point, and you may want to start a blog.

Week of the 10th–16th

Think twice before volunteering—or more accurately, being volunteered—for a position, especially if paperwork isn't your favourite thing. You're able to make people feel comfortable and your powers of persuasion are strong. If you need to draw out information, this is the week to do so.

Week of the 17th–23rd

Ingenuity and improvisation are your strengths. You can entertain on a shoestring or fill in for someone on a moment's notice. The summer solstice on Friday marks the start of a period of renewed self-confidence. This is a good time to raise your profile, circulate, and broaden your interests.

Week of the 24th–30th

Watch out for a tendency to think you can do a better job than others. You probably can, but it's not so wise to share the sentiment with others. Indulge someone you're fond of—a small gesture means a lot. Stay clear of controversial subjects—it's easy to alienate an ally toward the end of the week.

July

Your keywords for the month ahead: disruption,
reconnection, expansion.

Key Days
Romance: July 1, 9, 21, 29
Friends and family: July 4, 14, 24, 30
Career and status: July 5, 12, 19, 24
Finance: July 2, 8, 20, 28

Week of the 1st–7th
As the second half of the year gets under way, make moderation
your theme. Avoid extremes in diet, and don't go overboard
making commitments. Momentum picks up in a new relationship. Bargaining power is strong on the weekend since you're
coming from a position of strength.

Week of the 8th–14th
The emphasis is on self-improvement. While your recent criticism has been directed at others, this week look inward. Meanwhile, continue to monitor changes in the workplace that could
affect you at some future point. Details are critical. Double check
your writing and especially your numbers.

Week of the 15th–21st
Several surprising changes occur early this week. Invest time
in making preparations. Once the foundation is in place, your
plans will take shape. A new relationship blossoms toward the

weekend and you're delighted to find someone who enjoys your sense of humour almost as much as you do.

Week of the 22nd–31st

Your entrepreneurial side is prominent as you think about starting a sideline that involves a creative interest. The last thing you need is more family tension, but expect a bit more stress before things ease up. Around the weekend you'll finally figure out why a friend has become distant. The next move is yours, should you wish to make it.

August

Your keywords for the month ahead: conflict, rebuilding, investment.

Key Days

Romance: Aug. 3, 11, 21, 27
Friends and family: Aug. 5, 14, 25, 31
Career and status: Aug. 7, 15, 23, 29
Finance: Aug. 3, 12, 22, 28

Week of the 1st–4th

The next few days have a whirlwind effect. But though the time flies by, be sure to reflect on a relationship that needs to get back on track. Don't hesitate to ask higher-ups for clarification, and focus on the big picture at least as much as on the details.

Week of the 5th–11th

With the new moon on Tuesday, you shift into high gear. You're in demand, are super-alert and, like a sponge, take in everything you see. Toward the weekend, your partner may be uncharacteristically intense and even blunt. At the same time, you're a little impulsive. It's a good idea to reread emails.

Week of the 12th–18th

There's a lot on your plate, and information overload is the current theme. So it's hardly surprising that you're subject to the occasional brain fade. It's an understatement to say that you and a co-worker or neighbour don't see eye to eye. On the other hand, you and your partner express feelings easily.

Week of the 19th–25th

People refuse to take a hint—even a polite hint—so don't attempt to be subtle. Relatives are surprisingly generous, and they're not even playing the guilt card when they loosen the purse strings. Spend more time coaching youngsters this week, and consider taking on a joint project with someone you respect.

Week of the 26th–31st

The last few days of the month are unusually eventful. You could be hosting out-of-town guests, travelling south of the border, or planning a trip abroad. A difficult relative is less abrasive and family tensions diminish. Behind-the-scenes activities can lead to a promotion by the end of the year.

September

Your keywords for the month ahead: individuality, sentimentality, overconfidence.

Key Days

Romance: Sept. 2, 11, 21, 29

Friends and family: Sept. 4, 13, 22, 28

Career and status: Sept. 5, 10, 18, 26

Finance: Sept. 6, 15, 17, 30

Week of the 1st–8th

You're signed on for the kind of job at which you excel, but plan on some unexpected twists. Spontaneity isn't your current strong point. Two words that should not be in your current vocabulary are "wing it." You're starting to feel more settled in a relationship.

Week of the 9th–15th

You've been wearing several hats, and now it's time to remove a couple and concentrate on what you do best. Watch out for a tendency to absent-mindedness early in the week—it's easy to mix up appointments or forget an important day. Your partner is less distracted and begins to show more tenderness.

Week of the 16th–22nd

Put health and wellness at the top of the current agenda. Your ruling planet, Venus, is associated with art, beauty, and harmony—and you're batting two out of three right now. It's a good week to explore galleries and enjoy the late summer scenery. But a family function on the weekend can be fraught with friction.

Week of the 23rd–30th

Through early autumn, you become more self-reliant. This week you escape from the usual grind and find a collaborator for a joint project. The choice may seem unusual to the rest of the world, but proves inspired. A family feud continues to mushroom, but along with the drama are some good laughs.

October

Your keywords for the month ahead: taking charge, making over, advance planning.

Key Days

Romance: Oct. 4, 11, 22, 28
Friends and family: Oct. 5, 14, 23, 30
Career and status: Oct. 3, 9, 18, 29
Finance: Oct. 2, 10, 19, 25

Week of the 1st–6th

You call it gossip, but a friend says it's information exchange. Regardless of the term, stay clear of it this week—it's unreliable and potentially destructive. A new acquaintance hangs on to your every word, while a relative follows you around like a shadow.

Week of the 7th–13th

Be watchful of someone trying to upstage you early in the week. Advancement is in the picture, so your actions—and, especially, reactions—are important. Your partner may seem detached, so it's essential to provide gentle encouragement. Moderation is important, especially in health- and fitness-related areas.

Week of the 14th–20th

It's not too soon to begin holiday planning, especially since your home will be action central. The full moon on Friday marks the start of a take-charge period. Between now and early December, you'll be in decision mode. Be cautious not to divulge private information or secrets.

Week of the 21st–27th

After a few setbacks, you enjoy professional growth and can make some modest financial gains. But don't take things for granted. Question any decisions or suggestions that don't feel right. Make a point of protecting your privacy, not only from strangers but also from trusted—and curious—friends and family.

Week of the 28th–31st

Your sign's symbol is the bull, an animal that symbolizes strength. Inner strength helps you through a week that mixes family arguments and a workmate who tries to upstage you. You also learn something that can work to your financial advantage. And though some relatives are confrontational, others back you up in important ways.

November

Your keywords for the month ahead: ingenuity, discretion, expansiveness.

Key Days
Romance: Nov. 1, 12, 21, 30
Friends and family: Nov. 8, 17, 24, 29
Career and status: Nov. 5, 14, 21, 27
Finance: Nov. 4, 11, 20, 26

Week of the 1st–10th
Right now, you're dealing with a delicate matter and need to be utterly discreet. Expect to receive a rave review for work done earlier in the year. This week, however, you can try too hard and be too easily influenced by others.

Week of the 11th–17th
You can be easily disillusioned, but look on the bright side. If you're offered a supporting role rather than a star turn, use it as a learning experience. And if a project unexpectedly stalls, take a proactive approach and come up with your next bright idea. Relieve stress by taking a more active role in your health and fitness.

Week of the 18th–24th
You seem to reach a fork in the road and need to decide which direction to take. Don't look for outside help. The assorted advice will only confuse things. Someone very high up is admiring your work ethic. You'll ultimately be rewarded for loyalty, but don't expect any instant praise.

Week of the 25th–30th

You finally understand why someone has been so preoccupied with money—but think carefully before offering financial help. By the end of the month you should receive what can best be described as an indirect apology. You know you deserve more than that, but accept it graciously and then move on.

December

Your keywords for the month ahead: introspection, sentimentality, reconciliation.

Key Days

Romance: Dec. 7, 15, 23, 28
Friends and family: Dec. 2, 8, 25, 30
Career and status: Dec. 1, 11, 23, 29
Finance: Dec. 5, 13, 21, 27

Week of the 1st–8th

Whether it's writing, decorating, or speaking before a group, you add a flourish to whatever you take on. As the year begins to wrap up, take inventory of your strong and weak points. It's not too early to map out goals for 2014.

Week of the 9th–15th

Someone is about to come back into your life, but in a different role. You'll both be glad you reconnected. Community or career activities appear to slow down around Friday the 13th but in fact, it's only a temporary lull. Your sense of justice prevails on the weekend when you stand up to a bully.

Week of the 16th–22nd

Your home is the centre of activity, and guests bring with them various types of baggage. The week will be more about "them" than about "you." Shared arrangements are more equitable, and you can now start to do some serious financial planning.

Week of the 23rd–31st

Convincing everyone of your point of view is a challenge during the holidays, and it's best to settle for just a few converts. More people than expected are likely to show up for an event, but you're a master at fancy footwork. Tie up as many loose ends as you can before saying goodbye to 2013.

What's Ahead for Gemini

May 22–June 21

This is a year for establishing yourself in more than one field. That doesn't seem like a challenge for Gemini. After all, your attention span is limited, and you often enjoy dabbling. But multi-tasking, not dabbling, is what 2013 is about. The first six months are especially significant for your sign, since Jupiter, planet of abundance and expansion, is in your first house. That's the house of "me"—of self, temperament, appearance, and attitude. You'll project a confident air, which in turn will attract several exceptional opportunities as well as influential people. The key is in selecting the right ones for you, and the choices won't be obvious. At the end of June, Jupiter moves into Cancer. That's more potential good news, since Cancer, your second house, rules money that you earn yourself. You may not be earning more money, but you'll come up with ideas to stretch what you have. As much as the year is about expansion, it is also about limitation and consolidation, and the theme of the last six months is caution and conservation. Around August and September, you'll realize that many of the people you deal with, including those in high places, are nonconformist, eccentric, or plain weird. Transformation dominates the year's last quarter. Your materialistic side will give way to more spiritual tendencies. That doesn't mean you'll move to an ashram. Simply, you'll feel more in touch with nature and the planet you call home. Some subtly disruptive events in November make it difficult to plan ahead, but the very end of the year favours romantic commitment—with the emphasis on commitment. Be less impatient, not only for your mental well-being but also for your physical health. You don't want to distract yourself and strain your shoulder or injure your hand, two parts of the body ruled by your sign.

January

Your keywords for the month ahead: education, innovation, change in direction.

Key Days
Romance: Jan. 5, 11, 24, 30
Friends and family: Jan. 4, 12, 19, 27
Career and status: Jan. 3, 10, 17, 31
Finance: Jan. 6, 15, 22, 29

Week of the 1st–6th
The year starts off with an eccentric cast of characters, with you as the centre of attention. You're also inclined to overdo things. Cut back a bit on the commitments but not on your flamboyant style. Changes that you observe provide a hint of what's in store for 2013.

Week of the 7th–13th
You receive recognition for something you accomplished in 2012. A family member may belatedly acknowledge your contribution, or a colleague may give overdue credit where merited. Right now, it's up to you to unify a group of people—relatives, neighbours, or colleagues—and work together toward a common goal.

Week of the 14th–20th
Innovation and independence are the twin themes. The week accents your entrepreneurial personality, and you could find yourself planning a sideline. The first few days emphasize solitude while the weekend favours large gatherings. Make the best of both worlds as you get in touch with yourself and then connect with new friends.

Week of the 21st–27th
A sense of perspective is crucial this week. You need to choose

battles carefully. Time is tight—you'll be working to a deadline and can meet it only if you delegate other work and avoid distractions. On the weekend, you and a family member can reach an understanding on a touchy matter—but only if you agree to disagree.

Week of the 28th–31st
It's a catch-up week. Send out belated cards, overdue apologies, and unanswered emails—and make new year's resolutions before the month officially ends. It's tricky, but resist impulse spending. In fact, this is an excellent time to review expenses and see where you can cut corners.

February

Your keywords for the month ahead: drama, resolution, decisiveness.

Key Days
Romance: Feb. 1, 14, 13, 27
Friends and family: Feb. 6, 12, 19, 25
Career and status: Feb. 5, 12, 21, 28
Finance: Feb. 4, 9, 17, 26

Week of the 1st–10th
Right now, you're eager to explore new areas of interest. "You can observe a lot just by watching," Yogi Berra once said. What you absorb this week—notably people's attitudes and changing trends at work—can prove valuable over the next month and a half.

Week of the 11th–17th

Let others dominate in conversations. You make your best impression through a few well-chosen words. Your excellent memory comes to the rescue toward the middle of the week, when you retrieve some key information. Enjoy a modest financial gain through a combination of good timing and commitment to a project.

Week of the 18th–24th

Determination plus creativity gets you through an emotionally charged week. If people try to intimidate you, they don't stand a chance. You're assertive and spontaneous—an unusual but highly effective combination. Relatives may seem whiny but you need to be patient and willing to understand their legitimate needs.

Week of the 25th–28th

Canada may have cancelled its one-cent coin, but "a penny saved is a penny earned" still applies. Budget carefully now and you'll be grateful when travel or another opportunity unexpectedly presents itself later in the year. Be on your toes on the weekend— you can be easily distracted and perhaps accident prone.

March

Your keywords for the month ahead: conflict, intuition, porfessionalism.

Key Days
Romance: March 4, 19, 25, 27
Friends and family: March 6, 16, 23, 31

Career and status: March 3, 14, 21, 28
Finance: March 5, 11, 21, 25

Week of the 1st–10th

Right now, you should check documents with special care. Don't speed read anything—even routine emails. You need to be less casual and more creative about collecting debts. Resist a tendency to overextend yourself on the weekend.

Week of the 11th–17th

A family-related situation starts eating at you, and it's probably in your own interest to forgive, forget, and then forget what you forgave. This is a good week for reflecting on trends over the past two months and setting out short-term goals. The weekend can be romantic if you provide the right atmosphere.

Week of the 18th–24th

You've shied away from unpleasant situations, but this week you're ready to face them head on. You're feisty and forthright. And though some of your opinions won't be popular, the people you deal with will respect your honesty and integrity. Just don't be too heroic when it comes to your health. Dress cautiously and seek out the best professional opinions.

Week of the 25th–31st

You generally prefer working alone, but this week a team approach is best. Avoid taking shortcuts, even if this means putting in extra hours. You may be surprised when you're asked to make a commitment. Pay attention to tips that you hear late in the month—they can be helpful over the next weeks.

April

Your keywords for the month ahead: inner strength, negotiation, trend-setting.

Key Days
Romance: April 5, 14, 23, 28
Friends and family: April 1, 6, 15, 25
Career and status: April 2, 10, 16, 26
Finance: April 7, 12, 19, 24

Week of the 1st–7th
People admire your scruples and respect your opinion. You're everyone's top advice columnist, but you need to be cautious with your time and catch up on things you've been neglecting. An icy relationship begins to thaw.

Week of the 8th–14th
Your exuberance and warmth inspire young relatives to continue a family tradition. It's time to move money matters from the back to the front burner and confront someone about an unpaid bill. Avoid run-of-the-mill routines and make an effort to expand your interests. Be cautious over the weekend when someone tries to trick you into spilling the beans.

Week of the 15th–21st
The week is divided into two chunks. The first four days see you bargaining. You can expect a lot of give and take, but mostly the former. On Friday–Sunday, you're bursting with bright ideas. A

last-minute cancellation or delay gives you extra time to catch up on a difficult project. Make the most of it. You'll soon be juggling several jobs.

Week of the 22nd–30th

You can make things happen this week, and it's no surprise that you approach responsibilities with an upbeat attitude. You need to emphasize pleasant surroundings. For example, don't eat on the run. And, as much as possible, avoid confrontational people. If trying to earn spare cash, be receptive to ideas pitched on the weekend.

May

Your keywords for the month ahead: ingenuity, organization, self-improvement.

Key Days

Romance: May 3, 10, 19, 26
Friends and family: May 4, 11, 22, 27
Career and status: May 7, 16, 23, 30
Finance: May 2, 11, 15, 28

Week of the 1st–5th

You encourage and strengthen ties with people in high places. Keep informed of job-related happenings and don't shy away from asking hard questions. A chaotic family situation benefits from your tough but honest stance.

Week of the 6th–12th

The new moon on Thursday restores your usual upbeat mood. You're able to deal with stress when you come out of your shell. A friend's generosity may embarrass you, but be gracious. It's a good week to make plans for a getaway, but choose your travel companions with great care.

Week of the 13th–19th

Your advice is valued by people you admire. Take some of it yourself, particularly your suggestions on how to juggle multiple responsibilities. Midweek offers you a good opportunity to correct mistakes—even very old ones. Professional networking on Friday or Saturday can lead to friendship.

Week of the 20th–26th

Avoid overanalyzing situations. You could be so involved in weighing pros and cons that you miss the obvious. This is a good week to write letters—the old-fashioned variety. They can bridge even the widest gaps. On the weekend, go after what is rightfully yours without being overly polite or genteel.

Week of the 27th–31st

It's somewhat out of character but this week you actually enjoy following a routine. Make your motto "small is beautiful"—small pleasures bring you the greatest enjoyment. Behind the scenes, someone is observing your willingness to go the extra mile, your ability to adapt, and your gift for bringing people together.

June

Your keywords for the month ahead: new directions, home improvement, partnership.

Key Days
Romance: June 4, 15, 23, 28
Friends and family: June 2, 11, 23, 30
Career and status: June 10, 18, 24, 29
Finance: June 1, 13, 20, 27

Week of the 1st–9th
You seem to be able to concentrate better and may be able to take a brief holiday from your responsibilities. You could find yourself in an unfamiliar environment, so keep a GPS handy. Be careful lifting heavy objects on the weekend.

Week of the 10th–16th
Your greatest strengths include the ability to communicate, and Mercury, the planet that rules your sign, is associated with the intellect. This is an excellent week for expanding your knowledge and taking—or teaching—a class. As well, you connect with someone whose politics or philosophy is very different from your own.

Week of the 17th–23rd
Planning ahead is important thanks to an upcoming summer packed with distractions. Change direction toward the end of the month and opt for a more understated look and approach. You get

wind of useful information and must decide how to act on it. Take caution on the weekend not to be tricked into revealing secrets.

Week of the 24th–30th
A goal is unexpectedly within reach. You'll be shifting priorities as you advance toward it. The end of the month is a good time to bring up some of the things that have been bothering you about a relative's tactics. You support unpopular beliefs, back an underdog, and communicate best with a few well-chosen words.

July

Your keywords for the month ahead: starting from scratch, finishing touches.

Key Days
Romance: July 2, 11, 20, 27
Friends and family: July 5, 16, 22, 30
Career and status: July 3, 12, 20, 25
Finance: July 5, 18, 21, 27

Week of the 1st–7th
Short-distance travel can lead to a new interest or new friendship. Generally, you're feeling more outgoing and less vulnerable. Your recent support for an unpopular position (or person) is validated, but this is not a week for gloating.

Week of the 8th–14th
You're being evaluated, but don't change your behaviour or ap-

proach in an obvious way. You're also asked to sign a document, but check it carefully before putting pen to paper. Seek out a calm retreat and avoid stressful situations and stressed-out people. A family member continues to earn your respect and admiration.

Week of the 15th–21st
A longstanding commitment is coming to a conclusion and you can begin to concentrate on new areas. Health strategies should be at the top of that list. The week also sees you meeting—and perhaps entertaining—people from other countries or provinces. You also discover an opportunity for earning extra cash.

Week of the 22nd–31st
You've learned so much from your recent mistakes that you're almost tempted to make a few more. Don't let yourself be surrounded by downbeat people—you need to be highly motivated. A controversial issue surfaces during this period, and the bottom line is that you need to deal with it by the end of the month.

August

Your keywords for the month ahead: investigation, revelation, clarification.

Key Days
Romance: Aug. 6, 18, 25, 30
Friends and family: Aug. 3, 13, 19, 26
Career and status: Aug. 6, 15, 26, 29
Finance: Aug. 8, 17, 25, 31

Week of the 1st–4th

Nostalgia is a theme of the week as you return to a beloved haunt, rediscover a book, or take some old love letters out of hiding. Given your mellow mood, it's not surprising that a bumpy romantic road suddenly seems to be smoother.

Week of the 5th–11th

This is a good week for detective work, and you can investigate everything from your family roots to a late-summer travel destination. You're up for a mental challenge, so spend time with someone who's at least your intellectual equal. Check the fine print of agreements, but don't forget to read the bold type too.

Week of the 12th–18th

Your attention span is limited and your mind seems to be in half-a-dozen different places. You like initiating things, but then lose interest. If you can, focus on small, fun projects. You're drawn to the visual arts, including sketching and photography. This is a good week to figure out creative ways to stretch your money.

Week of the 19th–25th

People take liberties with the truth, so accept little at face value. You may need to take sides in an argument and could find yourself in a difficult position toward the middle of the week. If you feel stuck in a rut, consider something physical and team oriented rather than an intellectual or solo pursuit.

Week of the 26th–31st

You know how to make your presence felt. Whether away or at home, you now find yourself the focus of attention. Emotions run high when an overbearing relative takes charge of a family-related situation. Elsewhere—at work, or in a community project—you're invited to take on a major responsibility.

September

Your keywords for the month ahead: getting down to the wire, being up to the minute.

Key Days
Romance: Sept. 5, 12, 25, 29
Friends and family: Sept. 6, 12, 23, 30
Career and status: Sept. 4, 12, 24, 27
Finance: Sept. 3, 12, 20, 26

Week of the 1st–8th
Following a recent slump, you're making a professional comeback. Still, beware of occasional traps, particularly around the new moon on Thursday. Seek answers, especially those involving personal finances, and keep on top of trends in your field.

Week of the 9th–15th
Prepare to go into battle for a cause you believe in. A difficult work-related situation remains at an impasse and you may have to make a tough choice by Friday the 13th. Tongues are wagging over a delicate family situation, but you'd be very smart to remain neutral and say nothing.

Week of the 16th–22nd

Avoid taking sides between two battling friends. You could easily wind up on the casualty list of one of them—or both. Long-distance communications bring unexpected news. You could be deceived about someone—check stories and references carefully. Expect a financial news-brightener on the weekend.

Week of the 23rd–30th

This is the right time to design an "achievement" path. Set out what you want to accomplish over the next few months. Early in the week one person is trying to start a fight, but don't take the bait and exchange words. Meanwhile, another person—a friend—tries to patch things up on the weekend.

October

Your keywords for the month ahead: going the extra mile, setting an example.

Key Days
Romance: Oct. 2, 11, 20, 29
Friends and family: Oct. 7, 15, 23, 31
Career and status: Oct. 1, 10, 22, 30
Finance: Oct. 4, 11, 21, 26

Week of the 1st–6th

You can make a huge impact through a combination of diligence and kindness. You're working on all cylinders yet manage to make it look easy. Several stories are coming together and you can now make sense of a family situation.

Week of the 7th–13th
The key this week is to get to the root of a problem and hear all points of view—even far-out ones. Make a mental note of the random bits of information you pick up on Monday through Wednesday. They prove surprisingly useful through the rest of the week. Romance is moving to steadier ground.

Week of the 14th–20th
Expect one of the most surprising weeks in recent memory. People are inconsistent and unpredictable. Monday or Tuesday finds you tangling with an ally, while on Wednesday–Thursday you get along famously with a rival. You see you've made progress, but realize that the road to success remains under construction.

Week of the 21st–27th
Calm replaces chaos, and, though a relationship continues to go through growing pains, it feels more promising. Someone you deal with daily approaches you with a pointed question. The way you respond is as important as the answer itself. A recent collaboration proves a success.

Week of the 28th–31st
After being faced with overwhelming choices, you need to make a decision that can affect how the rest of the year will play out. There's a ripple effect to the week. You pass along a bit of news

on Monday or Tuesday, and by Wednesday everyone seems to knows what's going on in your life.

November

Your keywords for the month ahead: invention, energy, support.

Key Days

Romance: Nov. 8, 16, 25, 28
Friends and family: Nov. 4, 11, 21, 27
Career and status: Nov. 5, 13, 22, 29
Finance: Nov. 2, 10, 19, 26

Week of the 1st–10th

This is a mobile week as you explore new places, some of them close to home. Your creative thinking can help solve a dilemma. You're primed to take on a new position—it's not a leadership role, but you'll be calling a lot of the shots.

Week of the 11th–17th

You're preoccupied with other people—helping a friend out of a funk and refereeing a family feud. If, as a result, you fall behind in your own work, know that the full moon on the 17th marks the start of a period of renewed energy. If making a major purchase before the holidays, do lots of research now. You don't want to wind up with a lemon.

Week of the 18th-24th

You have a strong discipline toward work and your ideas are imaginative, but a current lack of diplomacy can land you in hot water. So bite your tongue before criticizing a colleague—or, for that matter, a relative. As the year starts to wind down you'll enjoy a new platonic relationship.

Week of the 25th-30th

Close but no cigar seems to be the story of your recent efforts to reach a goal. This week, if you continue to hone your diplomatic skills, the prize can be yours. Your ruling planet, Mercury, is associated with observation, curiosity, and flexibility. Start emphasizing these traits now and the rest of the year can be satisfying and fun.

December

Your keywords for the month ahead: acquisition, compromise, investigation.

Key Days
Romance: Dec. 2, 7, 24, 30
Friends and family: Dec. 1, 11, 19, 25
Career and status: Dec. 4, 13, 20, 27
Finance: Dec. 6, 15, 22, 28

Week of the 1st-8th

Something that's been eluding you for much of the year—a commitment perhaps—is finally within reach. You're able to draw a friend out of a melancholy mood. There are last-minute changes on the weekend, so be sure to have a backup plan.

Week of the 9th–15th
Early this week, you find the right words, and the right occasion, to ask for a favour. You could be a little too rigid in your work and may benefit from gently bending the rules. Allow your partner more space and greater input. In the process, you'll realize how valued your own opinions are.

Week of the 16th–22nd
You're on the path to a more harmonious relationship because there is less stress in your partner's life. Two notes of caution: early in the week, you lean toward excess in health and diet areas; and around or on the weekend, you can reveal a secret not by what you say, but by the way you react.

Week of the 23rd–31st
People sometimes say you read too much into things, but this week you have a definite sixth sense about what's really going on at work and down the street. Charisma is your current secret weapon, though it won't get you through every situation. You need to be sensitive to diet and health as the year draws to an end.

What's Ahead for Cancer

June 22–July 22

Kindness is its own reward, and this is what you've always believed. This year, as always, you provide compassion and solace. You also share secrets, reap financial rewards, face challenges and temptations, and—probably most significantly—discover how to ask for what you deserve. Through the first six months, Jupiter is in your twelfth house of emotions, charities, and mysteries. Your kindness will be directed not only to those close to you, but also to people you don't know. You could become involved in an overseas project, and through this work may come to meet someone who shares your values but, in other ways (age, background, politics) is your complete opposite. Through the second half of the year, when Jupiter is in your first house (the house of "I" and "appearances"), you'll assume a more upbeat demeanour and become less private about your good works. You're likely to become an outspoken advocate for what you believe in. But be cautious—you'll also lean toward exaggeration. Saturn's appearance in your chart will help you make money and boost your career throughout the year, but you'll also be tested and, come September and October, you may find yourself dealing with difficult colleagues and clients. You have the potential to strengthen your resolve as a result of these challenges and, finally, learn to fight not only for the downtrodden, but for yourself as well. Several roadblocks appear during the fall months, delaying the completion of a long-term project. Near the end of the year, you cross paths with someone you thought was no longer part of your life. You now have the strength to deal with the inner conflict that results. Continue to monitor your health. While you have no trouble committing yourself to a fitness program, it's time to try something more fun. Your sign rules the stomach, so perhaps belly-dancing would provide the perfect workout.

January

Your keywords for the month ahead: actions speak louder than words.

Key Days
Romance: Jan. 3, 9, 20, 26
Friends and family: Jan. 5, 10, 17, 28
Career and status: Jan. 8, 15, 24, 29
Finance: Jan. 9, 18, 25, 30

Week of the 1st–6th
Your energy level is high and proves contagious. As the year gets off to an active start, you're the driving member of a team. You can relate to people from diverse backgrounds, but you feel most comfortable among unpretentious types.

Week of the 7th–13th
Your usual charm can misfire. You need to rely more on hard facts than on a smooth presentation. A pair of people you deal with regularly seem to go out of their way to irritate you early

in the week. One of your important resolutions involves money, and you should invest time setting a financial foundation for the year ahead.

Week of the 14th–20th
A financial or professional goal is within reach now that a key barrier has been removed. It's important to raise your standards as you advance to the finish line. Don't mince words. You need to be sure you're getting your point across. If you soften the message too much, it will lose its effect.

Week of the 21st–27th
You hear news about an old friend and need to decide whether you wish to renew the relationship. Around the full moon on Saturday, you're drawn to people who are cultured and refined. If something has disappeared, this is the week to find it. It will be like looking for hay in a haystack.

Week of the 28th–31st
You're on something of a winning streak, and people agree with your ideas to a shockingly large extent. This is a good week for writing a first draft, introducing friends to your relatives, and arranging small-scale gatherings. Be sure that back-to-back weekend engagements don't leave you exhausted.

February

Your keywords for the month ahead: assessment, re-evaluation, new directions.

Key Days
Romance: Feb. 8, 14, 22, 26
Friends and family: Feb. 2, 8, 16, 23
Career and status: Feb. 2, 14, 22, 27
Finance: Feb. 3, 12, 20, 25

Week of the 1st–10th
You need all the allies you can gather, so avoid a tendency to find fault over insignificant things. Reflect on past successes as you continue to make resolutions and set goals. This is a good week to educate yourself on finance-related subjects.

Week of the 11th–17th
You're unfazed by the vain people you're dealing with—in fact, they actually amuse you. But the work piling up on your desk is another matter. The task at hand is too big a project for one person, and it's time to delegate some of the chores. A family member shows greater tolerance, largely thanks to your influence.

Week of the 18th–24th
You may experience friction with a more adventurous sign, such as Sagittarius or Leo. But in a reversal, you're the one who wants to go out and explore, while your partner feels like cocooning. A project may be put on hold but is likely to soon come back to life, so don't toss out important papers or delete files.

Week of the 25th–28th
Dig deeper into your memory bank and you'll find the answer you've been searching for. You gain a greater understanding of a grumpy or eccentric neighbour or other acquaintance. Be de-

cisive on Tuesday–Wednesday, when it's easy to be swayed by a charismatic co-worker. Remember to keep family members in the loop.

March

Your keywords for the month ahead: curiosity, confidence, commitment.

Key Days
Romance: March 7, 13, 21, 27
Friends and family: March 3, 13, 23, 29
Career and status: March 6, 14, 21, 30
Finance: March 5, 11, 18, 26

Week of the 1st–10th
This is a good week for putting together top-ten lists of places to see, changes to make, and people to connect with. You'll be witnessing some interesting events, so keep your camera and journal handy. Think twice before declining an invitation or a job offer.

Week of the 11th–17th
You're emerging from a period of introspection. The transition is anything but gradual as you immediately plunge into a social world populated by a mix of interesting characters. The middle of the week involves some kind of competition. You think it's a walk in the park but the results can go either way—so be prepared and well rested.

Week of the 18th–24th

You meet someone in a casual setting—on a train perhaps—who provides useful information and fascinating company. Stay in touch with your home base no matter where you are, and check for important updates. Scientific interests are likely to appeal to you on or after Wednesday's spring equinox.

Week of the 25th–31st

Withdraw from an ongoing family dispute before you're completely pulled into it. Your time is better spent nurturing and protecting those you care about. The spotlight is on creative activities, and this is an excellent time to freshen your home environment and give your appearance a more youthful look.

April

Your keywords for the month ahead: flexibility, discovery, spontaneity.

Key Days

Romance: April 6, 12, 20, 30
Friends and family: April 4, 13, 25, 29
Career and status: April 1, 9, 18, 26
Finance: April 5, 11, 22, 28

Week of the 1st–7th

This is an excellent week for asking questions. They won't all be answered, but you're setting things in motion for the next three months. Take a health-and-fitness inventory. Be willing to adapt and ready to accept last-minute invitations.

Week of the 8th–14th

You're feeling more decisive, and Tuesday–Thursday may see you making a pair of important announcements. Relatives begin to cramp your style. You feel like quoting George Burns, who said that happiness is having a large, loving, caring, close-knit family—in another city.

Week of the 15th–21st

Aiming high is the theme of the week, especially after you're introduced to someone who shares your work ethic. Family activities are lively, to say the least, especially when you get wind of someone's secret plans. Listen carefully and read between the lines—you can pick up important information.

Week of the 22nd–30th

If you wait for the right moment to express your feelings, you could be waiting till the end of May. Speak from your heart, then act when the moment feels right. Avoid misunderstandings about money by writing down all shared expenses. You can afford to dress more dramatically—even flamboyantly—starting on Thursday.

May

Your keywords for the month ahead: motivation, collaboration, spirituality.

Key Days
Romance: May 4, 11, 20, 25
Friends and family: May 5, 18, 20, 30

Career and status: May 2, 7, 16, 27
Finance: May 4, 9, 17, 29

Week of the 1st–5th
Your workload piles up and it's important to decrease your stress level. This may be the time to recruit help, and you don't have to look very far. A "light bulb moment" happens on the weekend and you suddenly know how to handle a tricky relationship.

Week of the 6th–12th
You're getting to know someone with whom you can share your private thoughts. You have several opportunities to play up your strengths at work and can put the finishing touches on a piece of creative writing. On the weekend, you appear to be too thrifty, too protective, or too hesitant.

Week of the 13th–19th
You're not diplomatic when it comes to handing out criticism, but people listen—and respond—when you evaluate their work. This is a good week to join forces on a creative project. Youngsters respond well to your encouragement. Be more security conscious, especially on the weekend.

Week of the 20th–26th
You meet someone who has the potential to be an important ally. Don't hesitate to be candid—your outspokenness will win you points. Personal relationships are another matter. Relatives are vulnerable—and even a small disagreement can grow out of proportion. Finicky people try your patience on the weekend.

Week of the 27th–31st
You're persistent and mysterious this week. Part of your current allure is that people aren't sure how to read you. The end of May starts a period of transition, with relocation or a change of direction on the horizon. Avoid a tendency to procrastinate, especially if you're making travel plans.

June

Your keywords for the month ahead: idealism, generosity, transition.

Key Days
Romance: June 3, 11, 16, 26
Friends and family: June 5, 15, 23, 28
Career and status: June 4, 12, 21, 26
Finance: June 10, 14, 22, 30

Week of the 1st–9th
The week marks the start of a short period of expansion. You could be travelling or assuming new responsibilities, and a temporary job can turn into a permanent gig. You project an aura of confidence but can be slightly gullible on the weekend.

Week of the 10th–16th
Someone in your everyday environment can be driving you up a wall. Your best response is no response. You're feeling less restricted and are better able to realize your potential. A hobby or

creative interest can lead to a second source of income. Travel delays are possible late in the week.

Week of the 17th–23rd
You have two chief concerns—an increased workload and a stalled relationship. Your best tactic is to take a mental break and mingle with people who are fun to be with. By the summer solstice on the 21st you'll be able to take a more systematic approach to your work. You'll also have some new ideas for getting romance back on track.

Week of the 24th–30th
It's a good time to showcase your skills before a receptive audience. It seems that a pet project is back to square one, but you'll soon learn that's really not the case. Although you're known for thrift, you can go on an uncharacteristic binge. You might want to hide your credit cards on the weekend.

July

Your keywords for the month ahead: articulation, inclusiveness, lack of pretention.

Key Days
Romance: July 3, 14, 19, 30
Friends and family: July 4, 17, 25, 30
Career and status: July 5, 11, 23, 31
Finance: July 2, 11, 23, 29

Week of the 1st–7th

You face a fork in the road as the year reaches its midway point. Reflect on the past six months and you'll understand the direction you need to take. Modest financial gains are indicated but you need to put a halt to someone else's spending.

Week of the 8th–14th

Your friendship circle begins to expand, but think carefully when choosing a travel companion. Stay clear of conflict early in the week—you can easily be drawn into someone else's battle. Take a tougher position over shared finances and responsibilities. Enjoy some small luxuries on the weekend.

Week of the 15th–21st

Your craftsmanship, attention to detail, and self-discipline catch the eye of someone who can boost your career. Personal matters, however, come to an impasse, and you'd be wise not to force any issues, especially on Wednesday and Thursday. Keep your eyes and ears open for choice information.

Week of the 22nd–31st

If you're planning to make a presentation or compete in a sport, this is a good week for dry runs. Someone's remarks may initially offend you, but you need to put them in the proper context. The plans you dream up may be over the top and unrealistic, but there are some excellent elements that are worth preserving.

August

Your keywords for the month ahead: adventure, victory, relief.

Key Days
Romance: Aug. 2, 11, 18, 27
Friends and family: Aug. 5, 11, 22, 30
Career and status: Aug. 7, 16, 26, 29
Finance: Aug. 7, 16, 24, 31

Week of the 1st–4th
Barriers come down and you can safely say what you want. Someone you take for granted becomes more special in your life. There's a fine line between being empathetic and meddling too much in someone else's business. Be careful not to cross this line on the weekend.

Week of the 5th–11th
There's an indication of a reconciliation, and the next move is up to you. The week is marked by intellectual growth as you consider joining a book club or signing up for a course in the fall. Projects involving home improvement get the go-ahead and benefit from the input of someone reliable.

Week of the 12th–18th
It may be out of character, but your partner is not in a mood to chat. Don't force the issue—you'll understand what's involved by the end of the week. You finally find your footing and are feeling much more comfortable in a job that initially overwhelmed you. A financial news-brightener arrives by the weekend.

Week of the 19th–25th

Take inventory of your talents and decide how you can make the most of them this week. The full moon on Tuesday restores harmony to the domestic scene. On the job front, however, you may need to actively deal with a confrontational individual. If you can, plan a romantic weekend.

Week of the 26th–31st

Confession may be good for the soul, but be super cautious about what you reveal this week—and to whom. Communication snags mean that important messages may not have arrived, so follow up on unanswered correspondence and calls. Arrange fall courses and other activities while there are still some openings.

September

Your keywords for the month ahead: resolution, calm, perspective.

Key Days

Romance: Sept. 1, 12, 20, 28
Friends and family: Sept. 7, 13, 21, 30
Career and status: Sept. 5, 10, 19, 27
Finance: Sept. 7, 14, 19, 29

Week of the 1st–8th

After a frustrating delay, emails are answered and messages returned. This is in fact an excellent week for tying up loose ends. It's also good to let off steam before the fall season begins. Clear the air, then make plans and decisions.

Week of the 9th–15th

You help friends or relatives boost their confidence. Along the way you realize how intuitive you are. The week emphasizes a change for the better in career or personal relationships, but on Friday the 13th try not to lose your temper over a trivial matter. Expect changes to your schedule, including a late cancellation.

Week of the 16th–22nd

Someone you deal with in your everyday environment—a neighbour, perhaps, or a co-worker—seems to be getting up on the wrong side of the bed. There could be a power struggle on Tuesday or Wednesday. Friday finds you becoming more self-reliant, and you'll hear good financial news on the weekend.

Week of the 23rd–30th

You and a loved one enjoy animated discussions. You may not agree on every point, but agreeing to disagree keeps the relationship on its toes. News from far away can help shape next year's travel plans. Information related to health begins to trickle in. Press for more detailed answers.

October

Your keywords for the month ahead: contemplation, investigation, negotiation.

Key Days
Romance: Oct. 1, 10, 21, 28
Friends and family: Oct. 6, 12, 19, 25

Career and status: Oct. 8, 17, 23, 29
Finance: Oct. 4, 11, 21, 26

Week of the 1st–6th
The week has the feeling of a TV series finale. Several stories are tied up, and you can expect a twist or two. Your words have a powerful impact, so choose them carefully. You can afford to take a tough stand in a weekend transaction.

Week of the 7th–13th
You tend to take things a little too seriously and should aim for a lighter touch. This is a good week for improving both your mind and your body. A platonic friendship gradually shifts to a new level. This is the time to steer it in the direction you'd like it to take.

Week of the 14th–20th
You're dealing with a backseat driver—not literally, but someone is dishing out plenty of unwanted advice. Be less subtle and get to the point about how you feel. The full moon on Friday encourages new friendships and interests as well as a reconciliation.

Week of the 21st–27th
You feel like you're walking a tightrope. Two people, or two jobs, are competing for your attention. Follow your instincts and you'll be able to pull off a balancing act. This is a good time for clearing out clutter and finding a good home for your treasures. Surround yourself with upbeat types on the weekend.

Week of the 28th–31st

You're ruled by the Moon, which is connected to motivation. You're highly driven this week and can accomplish an impressive volume of work. Stay away from fads—you can be easily tempted to buy something you don't really need. You learn a surprising fact about someone you deal with in your everyday environment.

November

Your keywords for the month ahead: empathy, resilience, persistence.

Key Days

Romance: Nov. 3, 12, 21, 27
Friends and family: Nov. 5, 11, 22, 30
Career and status: Nov. 4, 13, 19, 26
Finance: Nov. 2, 14, 22, 28

Week of the 1st–10th

Right now, you're concerned about three things: a friend or relative's mood shifts, the purchase of a big-ticket item, and the motives of a co-worker. In all areas, the key is to put things in perspective. An outstanding debt arrives by the 10th.

Week of the 11th–17th

You figure out how to deal with a self-serving person who's determined to push your buttons. On the other hand, you may not be sufficiently cautious about whom you take into your confidence. Look for opportunities to express yourself creatively and allow time for serious planning in the areas of health and finance.

Week of the 18th–24th
Reach out for comfort and you'll find lots of support. Your role at work continues to change, and your unorthodox style makes an impression on the right people. Your track record improves as you win one or a pair of arguments. Ambience is important. If hosting an event—intimate or large-scale—special touches make the difference.

Week of the 25th–30th
You express yourself clearly, but your fuse can be short. Watch out for a late-month tendency to be critical and even argumentative. You do well in front of a large audience, and this is a good week for performing or trying out for a role. You're adept at negotiating and may be able to pick up some excellent bargains.

December

Your keywords for the month ahead: pragmatism, detachment, understatement.

Key Days
Romance: Dec. 6, 15, 24, 31
Friends and family: Dec. 7, 13, 18, 27
Career and status: Dec. 2, 12, 19, 30
Finance: Dec. 4, 10, 16, 29

Week of the 1st–8th

If you were on the stage this week, the reviews would say you're poised, confident, and sharp. It's an appropriate time for making requests. This is definitely a good week to make an impression, but not in an in-your-face way.

Week of the 9th–15th

Whether swimming in a small or a large pond, you're the big fish. People seek you out for guidance on everything from spiritual to financial matters. You connect with someone who shares your offbeat sense of humour. A personal relationship continues on its roller coaster ride, and the week finishes with a question mark.

Week of the 16th–22nd

As the year ends, you reflect on the past twelve months. Don't obsess over the "could haves" and "should haves," but look at common themes as you contemplate 2014. The winter solstice on Saturday sees a shift in your thinking as you begin a journey along a more spiritual path.

Week of the 23rd–31st

You meet someone who complements you in many ways. Although you each react differently to situations, you can learn from the other's approach. Your business sense is sharp, and you can make preliminary financial plans for the coming year. You become more protective of others, yet also more independent.

What's Ahead for Leo

July 23–August 22

Dynamic Leo will be less of a solo artist this year. Starting as early as February, you'll find yourself involved in teams, clubs, and associations. You'll widen your circle of friends and motivate young and older people. As you assume less of an authoritarian role (even though you may nominally remain a leader or boss), you'll find greater stability in your professional and personal life. Between April and July, many events seem to happen randomly, but expect a pattern to emerge by late summer. The Sun, your ruling planet, represents theatricality, so it's not surprising that you'll be auditioning for the stage sometime this fall. It's likely that you'll excel more in a dramatic than a comedic role. Remember that from late June till the end of the year, Jupiter, the planet of expansion, is in Cancer, your twelfth house of attitudes and intuition. Expect to experience a greater understanding not only of yourself, but also of your close relatives and the people you live with. Meanwhile, Uranus, which represents discovery, is in your ninth house of long-distance travel, language, and politics. This year, you'll be involved in at least two of these areas. Politics, especially, suits your sign and you can make a contribution at any level. Your financial picture is brightest after September, but you're also self-indulgent at that time. You need to be cautious lest you spend what you've worked so hard to earn. Sports come naturally to your sign and, consistent with the year's theme, involve partnership or team activities. You could find yourself enjoying anything from tango lessons to curling. Just remember that Leo rules the heart, the upper back, and the spine. And while fitness is connected with your sign, so is excess—so avoid going into overdrive.

January

Your keywords for the month ahead: ambition, assertiveness, independence.

Key Days
Romance: Jan. 6, 15, 20, 26
Friends and family: Jan. 1, 9, 20, 27
Career and status: Jan. 7, 12, 22, 29
Finance: Jan. 3, 16, 23, 31

Week of the 1st–6th
Shared responsibility is a topic that needs to be discussed early in the year. Watch out for a tendency to take on the lion's share of nearly every job. You may think you can juggle several tasks but, in fact, an exciting challenge is about to take up most of your time.

Week of the 7th–13th
Expect less friction in a professional arrangement, but stay informed of changes in a personal relationship. Your partner is more outspoken and critical than usual. Much of the emphasis this week is on the familiar—proven tactics (including subtlety), a conservative dress style, and the reappearance of a long-lost friend.

Week of the 14th–20th

The emphasis is on the offbeat. You meet quirky, unpredictable individuals and experiment with new styles. You're also prepared to speak out against an injustice and express your private feelings in an assertive yet diplomatic way. Your energy level is high, and it's a good week to try a new hobby or sport.

Week of the 21st–27th

You have a gift for putting people at ease. Devote time to a labour of love. There is lots of goodwill out there this week, so don't hesitate to ask for favours, particularly around the time of Saturday's full moon. A family instigator drops out of the picture and there's more harmony in your domestic setting.

Week of the 28th–31st

Tradition becomes very important to you as the month draws to an end. You may even be bringing out the family heirlooms. You need to pin down elusive people, especially if they're involved in your health or finances. Some people enjoy your droll sense of humour, while others aren't sure how to react.

February

Your keywords for the month ahead: persistence, perfectionism, caution.

Key Days
Romance: Feb. 6, 15, 23, 27
Friends and family: Feb. 7, 16, 23, 26

Career and status: Feb. 5, 13, 22, 28
Finance: Feb. 3, 10, 16, 25

Week of the 1st–10th
The Sun, your ruling planet, is related to energy and achievement. Right now, however, it's important to unwind and slow down a little. Look forward to becoming close to somebody who shares your qualities of openness and integrity.

Week of the 11th–17th
You need to emphasize calm surroundings. Avoid touchy topics too, particularly with someone who's itching to get your goat. People express their gratitude in surprising but sincere ways. How you interact with others is important. Overall it's a good week to set out goals, even those that don't seem like sure things.

Week of the 18th–24th
This is a good week for patching things up and encouraging youngsters. It's easy to brush off someone's poor behaviour, but make a point of expressing your true feelings. Appearance is important, and it's time to update your look. Focus on the future this weekend, and weigh short-term goals and benefits against long-term ones.

Week of the 25th–28th
It's a good time to try out strategies, especially in the realm of romance. You need to be more assertive early in the week, when you find it hard to say no. You understand the causes of a family dispute, but now need to grasp the bigger picture. A movie, book, or play can help guide you as you make an important decision.

March

Your keywords for the month ahead: diversification, individuality, practicality.

Key Days
Romance: March 8, 16, 22, 29
Friends and family: March 2, 10, 23, 31
Career and status: March 7, 12, 22, 29
Finance: March 5, 13, 21, 27

Week of the 1st–10th
You're reunited with a friend, classmate, or co-worker. It's also a week for pitching ideas. Even if you're not in sales and advertising, you shine in these areas. Be wary of people trying to take advantage of your time or appropriating your ideas.

Week of the 11th–17th
Follow up on unanswered messages and questions early in the week. You're interested in doing things on a grand scale, but check your schedule—and budget—before getting in too deep. It's important not to put all your eggs in one basket. Diversification is key, especially throughout the weekend.

Week of the 18th–24th
So many people are picking your brain this week that you're thinking about writing an advice column. But ideas about your own relationships—and about compromise—continue to evolve. Interestingly, although you're most compatible with Gemini, Libra, and Capricorn, you take an interest in poetic Pisces.

Week of the 25th–31st

You start the week with a desire for change. You don't need to look for it—it will find you. Time alone will help you understand the nature of a relationship or a job. Your domestic life becomes calmer when an intrusive individual moves on. Keep refining your ideas for a business venture.

April

Your keywords for the month ahead: achievement, intuition, nonconformity.

Key Days

Romance: April 7, 18, 21, 28
Friends and family: April 4, 17, 20, 28
Career and status: April 10, 16, 23, 29
Finance: April 3, 16, 25, 30

Week of the 1st–7th

You have the ability to read between the lines and see outside the box. The one problem is that you can miss the obvious. Spending time with high achievers can raise your own standards and inspire a period of personal growth.

Week of the 8th–14th

Your goals are more spiritual, and on or around Wednesday's new moon you understand how strong your inner resources are. You and a friend or associate need to work closely together, so it's important to clear the air over unresolved issues. Business and pleasure mix well, and you may want to bring your partner along on a work-related trip.

Week of the 15th–21st

Take a break from stressful situations by enjoying comfort foods (butter tarts? pea soup?) and a favourite novel. Acquaintances and co-workers are more welcoming and ready to include you in events and groups. You may also be surprised to learn who'd like you as a travel companion.

Week of the 22nd–30th

You're becoming more extroverted, so it's no surprise you're more in demand socially. Toward the end of the month you butt heads with someone who shares your level of professionalism but has an entirely different style. Don't hesitate to make a snap decision—it reactivates a stalled operation.

May

Your keywords for the month ahead: transitions, sharing, tenacity.

Key Days

Romance: May 6, 15, 23, 28
Friends and family: May 4, 16, 18, 25
Career and status: May 1, 8, 21, 29
Finance: May 7, 12, 22, 27

Week of the 1st–5th

Shifts in your everyday environment happen so gradually that you're hardly aware of changes. By the end of the week you realize that something—perhaps a work arrangement—is different. Your social life looks brighter.

Week of the 6th–12th

It's better to do jobs the tried-and-true way. Shortcuts prove unreliable, and old-fashioned methods provide satisfaction. Make an added effort to surround yourself with cheerful people, since you can be a bit downbeat this week. On Thursday–Friday, you could be taking on a role of authority.

Week of the 13th–19th

You enjoy prestige for your contribution to your community or workplace. Your reward? More work, of course. Romance is highlighted through much of the week as you and your partner are very much on the same wavelength. The May two-four weekend begins with a mix-up and includes a surprise announcement.

Week of the 20th–26th

Persistent or stubborn? Aggressive or enthusiastic? People react to your approach in different ways, but the main thing is that you get the results you want. You're also about to rebel against family members who aren't pulling their weight. Have one last talk before getting into battle gear.

Week of the 27th–31st

Win some, lose some—that's the story of the week, but by the 31st the wins outweigh the losses. Try to approach a stressful situation in a new way, and spend time cultivating a new friendship. Enjoy a change of scene, either alone or with your favourite travel companion.

June

Your keywords for the month ahead: modernization, initiation, reflection.

Key Days
Romance: June 3, 18, 23, 27
Friends and family: June 5, 14, 26, 30
Career and status: June 10, 17, 21, 28
Finance: June 1, 14, 19, 25

Week of the 1st–9th
You're the captain of your own ship—working alone a good deal and making unilateral decisions. But you still interact with people, and in the process you find a new hero. Someone you've been estranged from is hoping to get back together.

Week of the 10th–16th
It's taken a while, but you've started updating your ideas and attitudes and modernizing your surroundings. A relationship becomes more comfortable once you become less critical and finicky. This is a good week to continue—or even to start—a family tradition.

Week of the 17th–23rd
People can be opinionated, petty, and self-centred. You'd be wise to listen to the opinions, ignore the pettiness, and laugh at

the full-blown egos. You're on something of a winning streak—ideas are accepted, your partner begins to loosen up, and financial news is encouraging.

Week of the 24th–30th
Plans change by the hour and lines of communication get tangled. Monitor situations closely and be sure to get updates. Watch out for a tendency to go to extremes—especially where your health is involved. Stay clear of feuding relatives, but be more direct with co-workers and neighbours.

July

Your keywords for the month ahead: persistence, partnership, decisiveness.

Key Days
Romance: July 5, 11, 21, 28
Friends and family: July 1, 14, 23, 30
Career and status: July 8, 19, 25, 29
Finance: July 6, 17, 20, 28

Week of the 1st–7th
There are peaks and valleys in a relationship, but the week finishes on a high note as you and your partner rediscover what you like most about each other. Continue to explore new territory at work. Chilly feelings toward a relative start to thaw.

Week of the 8th–14th

Bold colours suit your mood. Your energy level is high, and you're ready to activate a major project. Watch for a tendency to take risks with your health—don't leave things to chance. News arriving from another town or province will affect your plans over the next month. Nature revitalizes you, so consider a weekend trip to the country.

Week of the 15th–21st

Draw up a game plan that balances your home and work life. People are being less than direct. You need to draw out information, read body language, and even resort to trickery. On the other hand, friends can use some TLC, so don't hold back when it comes to expressing your affection.

Week of the 22nd–31st

Start the week by creating a brief to-do list, then work your way through it. Co-workers may not be friendlier, but they start to respect your work ethic. Intuition is a good guide to a relationship. Follow your instinct rather than a friend's well-meaning suggestions. Someone you're estranged from is thinking of you.

August

Your keywords for the month ahead: disruption, resourcefulness, structure.

Key Days
Romance: Aug. 9, 17, 25, 31
Friends and family: Aug. 3, 10, 22, 28
Career and status: Aug. 8, 15, 22, 30
Finance: Aug. 7, 13, 23, 29

Week of the 1st–4th
Take a pragmatic attitude to a week packed with interruptions and last-minute changes. Your managerial skills can help bring order to a disorganized setting. You're highly disciplined now and are able to follow diet and fitness plans.

Week of the 5th–11th
You seem to step back into another time. For a short but welcome period, people act more civilly and the recent hectic pace slows down. A story you hear or read has an emotional impact. Think twice before trying to "improve" your work. It's probably fine just as it is.

Week of the 12th–18th
Relatives are less combative and a higher-up more approachable. Your workload lightens by the middle of the week and you're able to devote more time to some of the people you've been neglecting. Compare prices if investing a significant amount of money in your home.

Week of the 19th–25th
The week offers an interesting lineup. You're asked to take part in a new venture, a buyer is interested in something you've been wanting to unload, and a friend seeks you out for advice.

Schedules change frequently, so keep track of your responsibilities and your deadlines.

Week of the 26th–31st

The period marks the end of a drought in at least one aspect of your life. You love an audience, and this week you get to perform. Not every review will be a rave, however, and you need to be more receptive to criticism. This is a good time to assume a supervisory position and to raise funds for others.

September

Your keywords for the month ahead: endurance, circulation, willpower.

Key Days

Romance: Sept. 5, 13, 21, 27
Friends and family: Sept. 7, 14, 20, 25
Career and status: Sept. 4, 10, 19, 27
Finance: Sept. 3, 10, 19, 24

Week of the 1st–8th

Right now, make it a priority to stay fit and healthy—you'll feel rejuvenated by the end of the week. Your leadership qualities are strong and you gain the edge in a competitive situation. Don't rest on your laurels. Continue to polish your skills.

Week of the 9th–15th

This is a good week to network and make connections. Someone in a high position appreciates your persistence. It's also a good time to spruce up your wardrobe, opting for a style as bold as your personality. The information you pick up on the weekend will prove invaluable by the end of the month.

Week of the 16th–22nd

Your role is to initiate action, and diplomacy is key. You'll need to step in before tensions reach a tipping point. You're also skilled at making people feel welcome, and this weekend your home is everyone's favourite meeting place. With the fall equinox on Sunday, your interests begin to broaden and your thinking becomes less rigid.

Week of the 23rd–30th

You discover what it means to be between a rock and a hard place. Option B is just as tricky as Option A. Keep searching, and by the end of the week you're likely to find there's an Option C. You have a knack for articulating your opinions. It's an excellent time to write a letter to the editor—or even to your Member of Parliament.

October

Your keywords for the month ahead: letting go, new beginnings.

Key Days
Romance: Oct. 3, 11, 23, 30
Friends and family: Oct. 5, 18, 23, 29

Career and status: Oct. 9, 18, 23, 31
Finance: Oct. 4, 11, 19, 26

Week of the 1st–6th

As the last quarter of the year begins, you start something on a large scale. Stay focused, and keep in mind that you work best as part of a team. Thanks to a trusted confidant, you're able to come to come to terms with a one-sided relationship.

Week of the 7th–13th

Long-distance news is a current theme. You receive useful information from someone in another province or country. Shared agreements are featured, and you need to be comfortable about all the terms—even minor ones. On the weekend, you see someone in a new and vastly improved light.

Week of the 14th–20th

You find your rhythm—and you're resourceful, energetic, sentimental. On Thanksgiving Day, resist the temptation to speak your mind. There is an emphasis on group activities, and you may be joining a club or a team. Friday's full moon marks the start of a romantic period.

Week of the 21st–27th

The best advice? Don't give advice. Someone wants to unload—and you're the lucky person. You don't know the whole story, so listen and provide quiet support. Take a more active interest in your health, tie up loose ends well in advance of the holiday season, and be more assertive about collecting debts.

Week of the 28th–31st

You and your partner are ready to exchange ideas about where a relationship is heading. You can initiate the discussion, but don't take it over. Remember that the Sun, which rules your sign, is connected to ego. Continue to refine your business-related ideas—they're bright, but you're not quite ready to present them.

November

Your keywords for the month ahead: invigoration, ambitions, frankness.

Key Days

Romance: Nov. 7, 14, 18, 22
Friends and family: Nov. 4, 11, 21, 26
Career and status: Nov. 2, 12, 20, 28
Finance: Nov. 5, 16, 24, 30

Week of the 1st–10th

Don't take it personally if a friend is too stressed to see you. It's better to provide quiet support than to make a big deal of a perceived slight. Your energy level picks up and you can achieve a lot. Still, curb your enthusiasm and don't go overboard making commitments.

Week of the 11th–17th

As the year winds down, you should look for patterns at work or in your relationship and figure out your next move. You're making an important contribution to your community. You develop a higher profile and may even consider running for politics. At home, however, continue to massage your partner's ego.

Week of the 18th–24th
The Sun rules your sign, and the bigger the challenge the happier you are. But this week, tension is eased when you assume a supporting role. You'll have time to expand your interests. Perhaps you'll learn a new language or maybe even take tango lessons.

Week of the 25th–30th
You're connecting with people you've met before, and this time around you'll like them much more. You don't realize how great your influence is on others until you see people mimicking your style. Put long-term planning on the week's agenda. Enjoy hearing a juicy secret on the weekend.

December

Your keywords for the month ahead: drive, unpredictability, imagination.

Key Days
Romance: Dec. 7, 17, 24, 30
Friends and family: Dec. 5, 14, 20, 31
Career and status: Dec. 3, 12, 18, 27
Finance: Dec. 1, 8, 16, 28

Week of the 1st–8th
Conflicts are best dealt with if you're rested, so sleep on the

problem and by midweek you should have a plan. Your top priority is to promote your ideas before someone else pre-empts you. Look after unanswered calls and emails before the weekend.

Week of the 9th–15th

A co-worker's or neighbour's attitude raises suspicions. Don't make rash moves, but continue to monitor the warning signals. Avoid heated exchanges, especially on Friday the 13th. Property matters demand attention. Be careful that someone isn't taking advantage of your generosity.

Week of the 16th–22nd

Don't be passive, especially when it comes to your health. Someone you deal with is itching to restart a conflict, but don't take the bait. You thrive in an atmosphere of high pressure and won't be disappointed during the last three days. A person you've mentored shows greater maturity and leadership skills.

Week of the 23rd–31st

You get a taste of the year ahead as the week offers a glimpse of new ideas and interests. Trust your instincts and replenish your energy. Last-minute shopping finds you looking for gifts that are personal rather than practical. Variety is a theme in a week filled with quirky people and eclectic menus.

What's Ahead for Virgo

August 23–September 23

The theme of expansion continues, and this year you take one of your interests (a foreign language, perhaps, or a hobby or volunteer activity) to a higher level and become something of an expert in it. January starts with a financial question mark. You'll find answers through careful research, not by following your hunches or going to unreliable sources. Saturn, the planet that helps us make choices, is in your third house, Scorpio, which rules over personal commitments. Your decisions about relationships will evolve throughout the year. By November or December, you'll understand where a partnership is headed and know the direction to take as one year ends and another is about to start. Between April and June, you'll discover something important about yourself. Not coincidentally, you'll reach a new level in your profession or education. The fall months include a mix of peaks and valleys. You may receive a promotion or other recognition by September, and you'll be overjoyed with your renewed connection with a relative. However, a series of pesky cancellations or delays will be frustrating. Look forward to some spontaneous travel this year; you may be visiting a coastal province or other seaside destination. Your natural curiosity will be satisfied later in the year, when you collect facts from different sources that are both valuable and fascinating. Your sign likes to stay fit, but you need to watch your diet carefully. Keep in mind that Virgo rules the digestive system, and you may be vulnerable to certain stress-related conditions. Look for a tension buster like yoga or meditation. As well, make an effort to achieve greater balance in your life by learning from others to become more tolerant and, especially, more adaptable.

January

Your keywords for the month ahead: discipline, productivity, precision.

Key Days
Romance: Jan. 4, 11, 16, 27
Friends and family: Jan. 5, 12, 20, 30
Career and status: Jan. 4, 14, 22, 31
Finance: Jan. 7, 16, 24, 29

Week of the 1st–6th
Your protective nature is emphasized. You may be mentoring a young friend or relative, or looking after a pet. Life is a comedy of errors on the weekend. Wires are crossed and messages misinterpreted. Although you're lucky right now, don't leave too much to chance.

Week of the 7th–13th
You can get into a rut by being too rigid. Just remember that Mercury, your ruling planet, is associated with flexibility. Start off the year by taking on a humanitarian cause, such as fighting for the rights of the elderly. As well as being a kind thing, your work in this area can lead to a personal success.

Week of the 14th–20th

Aim to be more selective in several areas. Choose your work projects carefully, and don't feel the need to be best friends with everyone you meet this week. This is a good time to start a creative project, especially the kind that you can pick up whenever the mood strikes.

Week of the 21st–27th

This week seems like a slow-motion scene in a movie. But there's much to see, enjoy, and absorb along the way. Your significant other may be surprisingly stingy while a relative is unexpectedly generous. You meet someone on the weekend who can give your career a boost.

Week of the 28th–31st

Your best skill right now is sizing up people and knowing what their next moves will be. Pay particular attention to details. On a scale of one to ten, a relationship moves from seven to seven-and-a-half. Don't force anything. Just be happy that things are now heading in the right direction.

February

Your keywords for the month ahead: reflection, perception, coordination.

Key Days:
Romance: Feb. 4, 15, 24, 28
Friends and family: Feb. 2, 10, 18, 24

Career and status: Feb. 5, 11, 21, 26
Finance: Feb. 1, 9, 20, 27

Week of the 1st–10th

Be less resistant to change, work to eliminate fears, and learn to laugh at yourself. You're on the final stretch of a difficult project and can't afford to be careless. Slow and steady is the pattern of a relationship that continues to evolve.

Week of the 11th–17th

You're becoming less of a traditionalist and, by Valentine's Day, you're ready to try a new approach. You manage to be both highly affectionate and super-productive. Don't take the bait when a relative tries to make your life complicated. A late-week financial offer sounds promising, but be sure there isn't a catch.

Week of the 18th–24th

This is a period of expansion and you're able to surmount obstacles that previously would have stopped you. On a personal level, your partner makes a big deal over something you consider trivial, but try to keep things in perspective. A major task this week is to encourage someone you believe in.

Week of the 25th–28th

Keep an eye on finances this week—check your bank statement carefully, and look for ways to save your loonies. Expect communication mix-ups early in the week. By Friday, however, you get your message through clearly. Whether you're entertaining on a large scale or a small one, be sure to check your guest list—and the seating arrangement.

March

Your keywords for the month ahead: self-promotion, assertiveness, expansion.

Key Days
Romance: March 1, 9, 19, 28
Friends and family: March 4, 15, 20, 31
Career and status: March 5, 12, 21, 27
Finance: March 3, 11, 20, 29

Week of the 1st–10th
Virgo is an excellent teacher. This week, youngsters are influenced by your example—especially the way you stand up for your beliefs. Diversification is an important theme, and a new interest can lead to a new friendship.

Week of the 11th–17th
The week is divided into two parts. The first few days see you reviewing financial options. From Thursday on you're planning everything from trips (look for sales) to reunions. A project you've been angling for gets the green light. Make sure the powers-that-be know you're interested and up to the job.

Week of the 18th–24th

On Tuesday or Wednesday, you're "voluntold" to take charge of a group activity such as organizing a trip. Be sure to work out the financial details in advance and think twice before laying out any of your own money. The spring equinox on the 20th marks the start of a period of renewed self-esteem.

Week of the 25th–31st

You stumble on information that initially seems inconsequential but ultimately proves valuable. The full moon on Wednesday marks the start of a period of reconciliation. Make peace with someone at work and the environment will soon improve. Even if travel is not on the horizon, check now that your documents are current.

April

Your keywords for the month ahead: cautious optimism, upgrades.

Key Days

Romance: April 5, 14, 20, 26
Friends and family: April 3, 11, 21, 30
Career and status: April 4, 10, 25, 29
Finance: April 2, 16, 23, 28

Week of the 1st–7th

You're in a more buoyant mood, thanks to the presence of up-beat friends. A rival steps out of the picture but it's too soon to sign a truce. Look after business-related issues before the weekend. Saturday and Sunday should be safe for introducing a sensitive subject.

Week of the 8th–14th
You know how to handle the rebellious people you deal with this week. But you have trouble getting through to a more placid type of individual. It's a good time to plan a business or pleasure trip. Bring along a consultant if you plan to acquire any kind of technical gadget.

Week of the 15th–21st
You find it easier to express your love and loyalty. It's a good week for renovations and acquisitions. Avoid sensitive topics later in the week—not just the usual ones, politics and religion—but those that involve family issues. Try to respond to criticism in a more mature manner.

Week of the 22nd–30th
Your powers of persuasion are strong, but use them carefully and selectively. Nostalgia is an ongoing theme. You could experiment with an old-fashioned look, but don't retreat too far back into the past. Make your presence known over the weekend and do some serious networking.

May

Your keywords for the month ahead: empathy, candour, caution.

Key Days
Romance: May 2, 15, 24, 29
Friends and family: May 1, 19, 28, 30
Career and status: May 6, 14, 23, 29
Finance: May 4, 13, 24, 28

Week of the 1st–5th
The emphasis is more on the routine than on the new. It's a good week for enjoying comfort foods, being around familiar faces and showcasing your strongest skills. You share in a friend's achievements, happy to know you played a role in them.

Week of the 6th–12th
Your home is an inviting place and, sure enough, an assortment of people start inviting themselves to it. The new moon on Thursday puts you in a more decisive frame of mind. Avoid flip-flopping over work-related issues and cut to the chase. Spontaneity is the key if you're planning a weekend getaway.

Week of the 13th–19th
The week has an international flavour, and you're likely to bond with someone from another country. People understand your frustrations, and this is a good week to gain support and recruit help. Don't be passive when dealing with medical or legal professionals. Ask direct questions and speak your mind.

Week of the 20th–26th
May two-four, the official launch of summer, finds you volunteering for a family-related assignment. Be sure you really know what you're getting into. Following the holiday weekend,

you're introduced to someone you'd been hoping to meet—and quickly discover that the admiration is mutual.

Week of the 27th–31st
You show great motivation and can channel your energy into a positive direction. In fact, it's possible to end the month with a pair of triumphs—professional and personal. You learn about a friend's difficulties through a third person. Approach the situation with honesty and sensitivity.

June

Your keywords for the month ahead: foresight, skepticism, objectivity.

Key Days
Romance: June 7, 16, 22, 29
Friends and family: June 4, 9, 17, 26
Career and status: June 5, 14, 19, 28
Finance: June 2, 11, 23, 30

Week of the 1st–9th
Look for missing pieces of information. For example, maps may need updating. This is a good week for planning or attending large-scale events. Be careful not to take too casual an approach to your health and continue to probe till you're satisfied with the answers.

Week of the 10th–16th
There's a new kid on the block or in the office. Chances are you

have a lot in common—including your strong opinions about someone you deal with daily. Take plans off the drawing board on Monday or Tuesday and put them into action on Wednesday. Opportunities to earn extra cash are closer than you may think.

Week of the 17th–23rd
This week sees you confronting issues that you've been ignoring for a long while. Being a perfectionist can be both your strength and your weakness. This week it's your strength. Your attention to detail can lead to a commendation. On the weekend, watch out for a tendency to take financial risks or to spend foolishly.

Week of the 24th–30th
It goes against your nature, but you need to delegate more responsibility, especially where a family obligation is involved. It seems that people change their moods like the weather—blazing one day, torrential the next. Thankfully, your temperament is consistent and helps get you through an action-packed week.

July

Your keywords for the month ahead: recruitment, upgrades, reconnection.

Key Days
Romance: July 7, 16, 21, 30
Friends and family: July 1, 8, 21, 28
Career and status: July 8, 15, 25, 30
Finance: July 5, 10, 17, 24

Week of the 1st–7th

Presentation is your secret weapon. Your ideas shine, but you need to promote them in an eye-catching way. Midweek turns into a comedy of errors thanks to a series of miscommunications. Double check your calendar, and be sure your emails are reaching the right recipients.

Week of the 8th–14th

You receive a last-minute invitation or offer. Your pride may tell you not to accept, but if you decline you may miss out on something quite special. Shared finances need a thorough review, no matter what your relationship with your partner is like. Overall, it's an excellent week to raise standards as well as expectations.

Week of the 15th–21st

It's taken a long time to receive credit or appreciation, but it finally arrives. Surrounding yourself with exuberant people will help elevate your spirits. Expect to run into an influential person who can help guide your career. Your timing isn't so impeccable in family matters and you might find yourself in the midst of a weekend feud.

Week of the 22nd–31st

You tend to be too critical of others and too demanding of yourself. A family-related responsibility continues to weigh you down. Ask for assistance, but make sure no strings are attached. Taking time out to enjoy a hobby or a cultural event can be healing.

August

Your keywords for the month ahead: intuition, imagination, diplomacy.

Key Days
Romance: Aug. 1, 10, 18, 26
Friends and family: Aug. 3, 11, 19, 28
Career and status: Aug. 6, 14, 22, 27
Finance: Aug. 5, 14, 19, 28

Week of the 1st–4th
Opposites attract like metal to a magnet. Enjoy spending time with someone whose career or interests differ from your own. This is also a good week to update your look and spruce up your wardrobe. Business ideas are bright but need some tweaking.

Week of the 5th–11th
You've been rooting for the underdog, and this week your support pays off. You're ready to make a big commitment to a work or community project. Your partner may seem withdrawn, but you need to provide space and gentle encouragement. A weekend competition proves both challenging and fun.

Week of the 12th–18th
You have a sixth sense about what is going on behind the scenes and how it can affect you. Early in the week you meet someone who proves a good match on an intellectual level and shares

your strong work ethic. Resist the urge to splurge—an unexpected windfall will be offset by a surprise expense.

Week of the 19th–25th
Brevity is your friend. Use a few choice words to express your thoughts. Much of the week has a sentimental feeling, and things you recently squabbled about seem unimportant. Respect a friend's privacy, especially after Thursday, being sure not to step over any invisible boundary lines.

Week of the 26th–31st
Learning about the past—both your personal history and Canada's—can prove helpful in future weeks. The last days of the month may seem uneventful, but behind-the-scenes happenings can lead to a busy September. Your partner can be oversensitive as well as extravagant. It's up to you to keep things in balance.

September

Your keywords for the month ahead: reconciliation, creativity, finishing touches.

Key Days
Romance: Sept. 3, 12, 22, 30
Friends and family: Sept. 7, 13, 21, 26
Career and status: Sept. 4, 9, 17, 27
Finance: Sept. 5, 14, 21, 29

Week of the 1st–8th

You'll be gathering a lot of news, and your task—not an easy one—is to separate fact from fiction. Good financial influences make this a strong week for planning. You're also able to pin down an elusive friend or colleague.

Week of the 9th–15th

People think of you as reserved, but this week you sport an uncharacteristic flamboyance. You make your presence known and, as a result, people want to be seen with you. But there's someone in your everyday environment who's trying to provoke a fight. The good news is that you've rarely had so many allies eager to defend you.

Week of the 16th–22nd

The full moon on Thursday heralds the start of an extended period that accents creativity, with an emphasis on painting, photography, and other visual arts. Self-confidence and ambition are also highlighted. Although a major goal remains out of reach, you have a clearer vision and realize what you still need to accomplish.

Week of the 23rd–30th

Your usual objectivity is put to the test, and you can be too critical of someone's weaknesses. Education is highlighted, but mainly at an informal level—you study a new subject for its own enjoyment. Gradual shifts take place within your everyday environment, with several arrivals and departures on the horizon.

October

Your keywords for the month ahead: insight, responsibility, appreciation.

Key Days
Romance: Oct. 2, 11, 19, 26
Friends and family: Oct. 5, 16, 24, 31
Career and status: Oct. 9, 16, 24, 29
Finance: Oct. 4, 10, 21, 27

Week of the 1st–6th
As October begins, you explore new territory and begin to assert your independence. Your dealings with the public are unusually rewarding at this time. Agreements, especially partnership arrangements, require a prompt, impartial, and thorough review.

Week of the 7th–13th
You're like a hockey team that rallies late in the game. The week starts off quietly, but momentum builds and by Friday your output is impressive. You learn something about a friend that explains a recent change in your relationship, and you can gradually begin rebuilding bridges.

Week of the 14th–20th
There's little doubt this week that Virgo is both shrewd and observant. You make some clever choices and don't miss a thing that's going on behind the scenes. Property matters demand special attention toward the end of the week, and on the weekend you rediscover a once-favourite hobby.

Week of the 21st–27th

It's easy to get into difficulties by divulging too much information. Discretion is key. Finances are bright, provided you avoid taking gambles—you tend toward risks on the weekend. People only seem to contradict each other. They're actually saying the same thing, but in different ways.

Week of the 28th–31st

You're preoccupied with a couple of issues as the month draws to a close: the direction a relationship is taking and the thoughtless remarks of someone you work with. In both situations, share your concerns directly with the person involved. Self-doubt can turn into self-confidence, but you need to be upfront.

November

Your keywords for the month ahead: forgiveness, logic, protection.

Key Days:
Romance: Nov. 2, 11, 23, 27
Friends and family: Nov. 3, 12, 19, 30
Career and status: Nov. 4, 14, 20, 26
Finance: Nov. 5, 13, 23, 28

Week of the 1st–10th

The new moon on the 3rd marks the start of a period of drive and determination. You're on the verge of making a personal or professional commitment. Your altruistic nature inspires you to reach out and help someone you like, but be careful that your intentions aren't misinterpreted.

Week of the 11th–17th
Aim to resolve family conflicts well before the holidays get under way. Some of the people you deal with regularly can be moody or unpredictable. Although Mercury, your ruling planet, is associated with movement, this week you seem to do your best work—and meet the most interesting individuals—close to home.

Week of the 18th–24th
There's a song about brushing yourself off and starting all over again—and that's how you feel this week. You're ready for a makeover and eager to forgive others—and especially yourself. You're also good at nurturing older friends and relatives and encouraging younger ones to be more independent.

Week of the 25th–30th
You won't win a popularity contest this week by defending the actions of a relative or a co-worker, but that won't (and shouldn't) stop you. You have an eye for detail and will discover some important facts that can work to your advantage early in 2014. Meanwhile, continue to review and refine your goals.

December

Your keywords for the month ahead: tactics, adventure, foresight.

Key Days

Romance: Dec. 5, 9, 18, 27

Friends and family: Dec. 7, 17, 24, 29

Career and status: Dec. 2, 10, 23, 27

Finance: Dec. 11, 19, 23, 31

Week of the 1st–8th

Use your considerable energy to reactivate interests that you pursued earlier in the year. You continue to regain your self-confidence. Expect some last-minute changes late in the week. Continue to negotiate shared expenses and responsibilities.

Week of the 9th–15th

You have a knack for drawing out information. When you learn something from a trusted individual, a load will be lifted off your shoulders. Sports are a theme, with an emphasis on competitive events. You may not be the strongest team member, but few surpass your tactical approach.

Week of the 16th–22nd

You're an advocate for others, but sometimes you neglect your own health. This week, take a proactive approach—not only to your own well-being, but also to your finances. Late in the week, your partner or a close friend makes a surprise announcement. You'll soon be updating your technology, and this is a good time to do research.

Week of the 23rd–31st

You see things differently than you did through much of the past year. You realize, for example, that someone is a friend rather than a rival, and you understand a relative's change in attitude. Being receptive to suggestions and new ideas will help you launch 2014 on a highly positive note.

What's Ahead for Libra

September 24–October 23

You may feel confined and even isolated early in the year, but in fact you're the object of various activities taking place behind the scenes. It's as if this is a play, and the first couple of scenes are being set up in advance of your big entrance. This entrance takes place around April, when you find yourself ready to sign on for a major project. You're not so sure about the person you'll be working for, but the chance to spread your wings is highly appealing. After late June, you'll be focusing on professional goals and establishing your reputation. It's easy to become immersed in your work, but by July at the latest you should take advantage of the opportunity to enjoy a long-distance trip or several short jaunts. Information you acquire both at home and away seems random, but in September you're able to connect the dots—and the pattern that results helps you direct your path over the balance of the year. Neptune encourages you to help older friends and relatives. Another planet influences you this year. Pluto, which is in Capricorn (your fourth house), affects property, domestic affairs, home improvement, and retirement planning. Expect to see significant transformations in at least some of these areas. Saturn, meanwhile, is giving you a crash course in fiscal responsibility. Throughout the year, some of your friendships and other partnerships may be alternately unpredictable, funny, and competitive. But be careful not to lean toward exaggeration—it can challenge your credibility. On a related note, you tend to overdo many things and could be lifting too much. Your back is vulnerable, so be cautious and avoid lower back strain in particular. You of all people need to remember that everything must be balanced, physically and emotionally.

January

Your keywords for the month ahead: immediate action, deferred gratitude.

Key Days
Romance: Jan. 2, 13, 21, 29
Friends and family: Jan. 4, 16, 24, 31
Career and status: Jan. 7, 15, 23, 30
Finance: Jan. 8, 16, 25, 31

Week of the 1st–6th
The first week sets the tone of a take-charge year. You can soon activate an interest that you put aside in 2012. Get a head start on making resolutions. You can conquer a phobia and are ready to confront an issue that you've been ignoring.

Week of the 7th–13th

Family dynamics begin to change, thanks your more assertive attitude. Watch out for a tendency to overdo things and worry too much. People you've been trying to connect with are suddenly free. There is an emphasis on romance's traditional side, so think about planning an old-fashioned date night.

Week of the 14th–20th

People rarely intimidate you, and this week is no exception. While others kowtow to a demanding individual, you assert yourself and, by Friday, assume a position of authority. Your financial picture improves when you discover ways to cut costs. No matter what you say, a relative will be easily offended.

Week of the 21st–27th

You continue to make a contribution to your work or community, but don't expect instant accolades. Your timing may be off-kilter, so be cautious on Monday or Tuesday that you don't offend a colleague. Expect to spend some hours alone on the weekend, an excellent time to consider your next move in an on-again, off-again relationship.

Week of the 28th–31st

You're projecting a relaxed vibe, and people respond well to your calm aura. Gather additional details before making a major purchase or significant commitment of your time. Small changes in your home decor can be highly effective, but resist any urge to do a major overhaul.

February

Your keywords for the month ahead: shrewdness, self-reliance, reflection.

Key Days
Romance: Feb. 2, 15, 22, 27
Friends and family: Feb. 5, 10, 19, 26
Career and status: Feb. 4, 13, 20, 25
Finance: Feb. 3, 12, 21, 28

Week of the 1st–10th
People are impressed with your knowledge, and they line up for your ideas. At the same time, you're an important advocate for someone in a vulnerable position. The result is that, even though you don't actually seek it, your prestige gets a boost.

Week of the 11th–17th
Your career path shows several peaks over the coming month and a half. The first of these takes place now, when you're highly persuasive. You're also more extroverted and romantically inclined, but tend to make the occasional rash move. You lean toward extremes and can be doing too little exercise, or too much.

Week of the 18th–24th
You need to deal with—not rush into—a family situation that's been making you uncomfortable. Watch out as well for a tendency to go on a spending spree. Don't feel pressured into making an instant decision if you're asked to take on a leadership role. Weigh the pros and cons, but especially the pros.

Week of the 25th–28th

You feel someone is being secretive, and should be able to confirm your suspicions by month's end. You can be too casual with your diet or health. Keep a scarf and toque handy, avoid deceptively rich foods, and don't postpone medical appointments.

March

Your keywords for the month ahead: reflection, selectivity, compatibility.

Key Days

Romance: March 3, 8, 16, 28
Friends and family: March 6, 14, 22, 26
Career and status: March 5, 13, 20, 28
Finance: March 2, 15, 25, 28

Week of the 1st–10th

Check documents and claims before taking on a task or hiring someone. You can afford to be choosy about people you see and things you acquire. Be sure not to toss out "junk" mail—there could be a hidden treasure inside.

Week of the 11th–17th

The new moon on Monday launches a period of reflection. Look within yourself for answers. If you're going after an assignment, it pays to be one step ahead of everyone else. It's not too late to take on a winter sport that you've been eager to try.

You may reach an impasse in a relationship and need to find a middle ground.

Week of the 18th–24th
Sometimes it's good to wear the shoe on the other foot. This week, you get to view the world from a different perspective and, as a result, become more compassionate. In addition, you excel in jobs that involve both challenges and variety and you receive a response to something you applied for.

Week of the 25th–31st
Thanks to your example, a complacent person becomes motivated and a pushy one gentler and more accommodating. You're performing at your peak and, following a period of uncertainty, your professional life starts showing signs of greater stability. You're also involved in joint money and property matters.

April

Your keywords for the month ahead: motivation, expansion, acceptance.

Key Days
Romance: April 1, 10, 19, 28
Friends and family: April 5, 6, 17, 26
Career and status: April 3, 11, 23, 29
Finance: April 6, 15, 22, 30

Week of the 1st–7th

You'll be butting heads with Aries, your opposite sign. You're unusually obstinate but need to compromise to reach an agreement by Thursday. Take a more cautious approach to finances and avoid the temptation to overdo things on the weekend.

Week of the 8th–14th

Going the extra mile—and not grumbling about it—gives you the advantage in a competitive situation. Keep your cool early in the week; in the heat of the moment you could say something you'll later regret. An old friend, possibly an old flame, is trying to contact you.

Week of the 15th–21st

Variety is the spice of your life. Get out of a rut by trying a new hobby, experimenting with a new cuisine, or checking out a new destination. People don't really "get" your sense of humour right now—things you say in jest can be taken too seriously. A new acquaintance goes out on a limb for you.

Week of the 22nd–30th

Not only do you have unexpected stamina, you also epitomize self-confidence and theatricality. If you've experienced a lull in any area—especially romance—this week sees the end of a drought. Your most important work task is to help the team. You also need to evaluate a family situation before making a decision that will affect your role in it.

May

Your keywords for the month ahead: outreach, introspection.

Key Days

Romance: May 4, 12, 21, 29
Friends and family: May 2, 11, 20, 26
Career and status: May 6, 14, 23, 29
Finance: May 3, 13, 19, 25

Week of the 1st–5th

The week progresses smoothly, but there are important lessons to be learned. Think about how you respond to criticism—both positive (are you smug?) and negative (do you sulk?). Look forward to discovering a new interest.

Week of the 6th–12th

Focus on the task at hand. Think of the week as a chest of drawers, and don't open more than one drawer at a time. If you're looking for scarves, don't open the sock drawer. Your eye for detail isn't as sharp as you think, so avoid jobs that require precision. A rocky relationship is back on a steady course.

Week of the 13th–19th

TMI—that's the theme of the week. You hear more information than you need to know, or want to know, about someone you like. As much as possible, avoid snobs and stick with people who make you laugh. Continue to expand your knowledge of finance, but avoid speculation.

Week of the 20th–26th

It's an emotional week in which you receive an apology and finally hear the other side of a story. If romance starts to intrude on your professional life, let it. You can't ignore your heart. If you reintroduce an idea that fell flat earlier in the year, the response will be more enthusiastic this time around.

Week of the 27th–31st

Try to take care of legal and property matters before summer kicks in. Seek compromise in a family issue that's reached an impasse. It's a good time for updates and upgrades, but be sure to compare prices and check warranties. Recently acquired information proves very useful on the weekend.

June

Your keywords for the month ahead: flexibility, motivation, optimism.

Key Days

Romance: June 3, 13, 18, 24
Friends and family: June 6, 11, 21, 29
Career and status: June 4, 17, 25, 28
Finance: June 5, 14, 22, 26

Week of the 1st–9th

You can conquer a phobia or other fear. You're driven and determined this week. You need to concentrate on all aspects of a job and avoid shortcuts. Your partner is less distracted and, with just a little encouragement, ready to open up to you.

Week of the 10th–16th

Progress, not perfection, is the theme of the week. Continue to expand your knowledge, but concentrate on just one or a few interests. This is a good time to simplify your environment. Clear out clutter—and then resist the urge to start acquiring things all over again.

Week of the 17th–23rd

Don't take anyone—especially yourself—too seriously. Well-meaning people may offer more than they can deliver. Don't make too big a deal of tensions with a co-worker or neighbour. The flames flare up, then quickly die down. Your home provides a safe harbour throughout the weekend.

Week of the 24th–30th

Have a frank talk with a loved one—you're not doing anyone a favour by avoiding a sensitive topic. In addition, clear up a dispute with a neighbour before it blows out of proportion. This is a good week for joining a professional organization, networking, and getting together with friends for lunch.

July

Your keywords for the month ahead: protection, productivity, politics.

Key Days

Romance: July 4, 14, 24, 30
Friends and family: July 5, 12, 19, 25

Career and status: July 9, 15, 23, 29
Finance: July 4, 12, 23, 31

Week of the 1st–7th
Community-related activities are highlighted in a week that emphasizes the social side of your personality. Libra is the first of the zodiac's "we" signs, and this week you need others in your life. However, you seem to be drawn to eccentric types.

Week of the 8th–14th
A long-awaited decision is delivered by Wednesday. It's somewhat surprising—but in a good way. Fewer distractions plus a higher energy level equal a productive week. Your understanding of behind-the-scenes manoeuvring helps you pull strings and cut through the red tape.

Week of the 15th–21st
Try doing things on a smaller scale or at a slower pace. You need to cut back and focus on one or two specific tasks. The emphasis is on important relationships, especially those that you want to rebuild. Being more open to new ideas helps you determine the next steps to take in a family situation.

Week of the 22nd–31st
The full moon on Monday puts you in a protective—not possessive—state of mind. You make several missteps toward the middle of the week, but consider them learning experiences. A person you admire applauds your ideas. Don't rest on your laurels, but continue to refine and polish your work.

August

Your keywords for the month ahead: re-evaluation, encouragement, comparison.

Key Days
Romance: Aug. 6, 10, 16, 25
Friends and family: Aug. 4, 12, 20, 26
Career and status: Aug. 7, 12, 23, 29
Finance: Aug. 2, 11, 17, 27

Week of the 1st–4th
This is a good week for rethinking your strategies. You have an excellent opportunity to promote ideas—influential people are receptive and in a position to help you. A relationship is moving at an even pace. You can give it a gentle boost.

Week of the 5th–11th
An influential person is attracted to your enthusiasm, but you need to fine-tune your ideas before taking them to the next level. You find it difficult to diagnose a romantic problem, but the difficulty may be that you're analyzing it too deeply. Legal and property matters require continued attention.

Week of the 12th–18th
You're an armchair psychologist, interested in knowing what makes people tick. The information you learn this week more than satisfies your curious mind. A working relationship with someone of the opposite sex proves rewarding but can set tongues wagging.

Week of the 19th–25th

You find it easier to express yourself with someone you've grown to care about. Now it's time to be as kind to yourself as you are to others. You can count on increased responsibilities but minus the accompanying rewards. Friends are less inhibited and are eager to share what's on their minds. Be warned.

Week of the 26th–31st

While others seem frazzled, you're relaxed. Is it because you're more organized or because you're in a more spiritual world? It doesn't matter—you now have the time to pursue an interest you've been putting off. "Less is more" is a credo that suits you this week—an understated look is what gets you noticed.

September

Your keywords for the month ahead: reactivation, understatement, control.

Key Days

Romance: Sept. 3, 12, 24, 29
Friends and family: Sept. 6, 15, 22, 28
Career and status: Sept. 5, 12, 25, 30
Finance: Sept. 1, 10, 17, 26

Week of the 1st–8th

It's easy to pull yourself out of a rut, thanks to the support of an acquaintance who's just returning the favour. It also helps to get in touch with your spiritual side. Meditation, yoga, or a long solitary walk can soothe your soul. The interlude is well timed since a stalled project is reactivated.

Week of the 9th–15th
You're feeling in control. A possessive friend backs off (or moves on), and you also understand how a relationship will play out. This is a good week to help the underdog by providing encouragement. In return, you wind up with a loyal and determined ally.

Week of the 16th–22nd
Take advantage of a chance to correct mistakes. A weight is lifted from your shoulders following a serious conversation with a co-worker or neighbour. Analyze the direction a friendship is taking, and then plan your next steps. A new acquaintance helps you broaden your horizons.

Week of the 23rd–30th
Confirm plans that involve visitors. You may be surprised to learn which people—or how many—are about to show up. This is a good week to do something frivolous, either on your own or with friends. Remember, you don't have to be on your best behaviour. Emotions run high at a weekend event.

October

Your keywords for the month ahead: down to earth, up in the air.

Key Days
Romance: Oct. 6, 15, 23, 29
Friends and family: Oct. 4, 14, 22, 27
Career and status: Oct. 8, 24, 26, 28
Finance: Oct. 3, 9, 17, 24

Week of the 1st–6th

Don't turn up your nose at a job that you think is beneath you. It could provide an important learning experience. Make a point of eating sensibly, and resist the temptation to overindulge or miss a meal. On the weekend, your partner is more outspoken but also receptive to new ideas.

Week of the 7th–13th

Plans are unsettled and you're trying to please guests with unusual requirements. But restlessness and uncertainty give way to a sense of purpose. You find a sympathetic ear and, after having bottled your feelings up for a very long time, can freely vent. Higher-ups are also easier to approach.

Week of the 14th–20th

Be grateful on Thanksgiving day. You feel comfortable asking for any kind of change, and a long-missing object mysteriously appears. One new acquaintance follows you like a lost puppy, while another is surprisingly blunt. You're amused when you find out who's trying to contact you about an upcoming gathering.

Week of the 21st–27th

The more practical side of your personality is on display. Schedule medical appointments promptly, and protect your password.

Unexpected events happen close to home. If you need to confide in someone, try a member of the opposite sex. Make the weekend a "me" time and enjoy your favourite things.

Week of the 28th–31st

Your outstanding job performance may lead to tension in the work environment. You're known for your sense of fairness—now it's time to go after what's fair for you. Communications proceed smoothly once you cut through the red tape. Unconventional people brighten your week.

November

Your keywords for the month ahead: timing, breakthrough, introductions.

Key Days

Romance: Nov. 2, 11, 22, 29
Friends and family: Nov. 5, 9, 23, 26
Career and status: Nov. 4, 12, 21, 28
Finance: Nov. 1, 13, 20, 27

Week of the 1st–10th

The week is packed with surprises and frustrations. People are unpredictable and distracted. You need to get your point across promptly, so don't wait for the right moment. It's a good week for matchmaking—you have a sense of who belongs with whom.

Week of the 11th–17th

You tend to sweep unpleasant things under the carpet, but the sooner you face reality the faster you'll receive the assignment you want. You're putting in extra hours and need to seek out quiet places for reflection. Be careful not to reveal confidences—people can be sneaky on the weekend.

Week of the 18th–24th

This is an ideal week to address concerns. Send a letter to the editor or write to your Member of Parliament. Small get-togethers and picnics are better than larger gatherings. You'll also be attending cultural events or spending time with high-brow individuals.

Week of the 25th–30th

Strike a balance between work and family—you could be emphasizing one at the expense of the other. Watch for a possible communication snag on the weekend—people may not be understanding, or even receiving, your messages. The month ends with encouraging professional or financial news.

December

Your keywords for the month ahead: commitment, ingenuity, assertiveness.

Key Days

Romance: Dec. 6, 16, 23, 29

Friends and family: Dec. 7, 16, 22, 27

Career and status: Dec. 4, 13, 20, 30
Finance: Dec. 2, 11, 19, 31

Week of the 1st–8th

You're spending money wisely and should draw up a budget for the coming year. Check what you reveal in your midweek emails—you don't know who'll be reading them. Friday is the best time for getting messages across.

Week of the 9th–15th

You tend to be overly fussy. Holiday plans or late-year assignments can seem overwhelming, and you should try to join forces with someone whose talents or ideas complement your own. By the end of the week, you receive long-awaited information and can close the book on an outstanding matter.

Week of the 16th–22nd

Your current strength lies in your ability to bring people together. Late in the week, you play a role in helping a hesitant friend become more decisive. You connect with someone of the opposite sex, but the relationship is most likely platonic. Confirm plans and check your calendar before heading out to a midweek appointment.

Week of the 23rd–31st

People go to great lengths to get your attention. You need to sharpen your focus, particularly early in the week when you may be missing announcements that include important information. On the last days of the year, a friend or relative is willing to share something that you've had your eye on for a very long while.

What's Ahead for Scorpio

October 24–November 22

No, you haven't really been lost, but this is the year you find yourself. If you've been considering a change in direction—personal or professional—you're ready to move from the thinking stage and take positive action. Jupiter in your eighth house (trust, sharing, intimacy) motivates you to take relationships more seriously and not to write off small flaws or trivialize major ones. Starting in late June or early July, you're ready for adventure, exploration, and possibly, relocation. At the same time, you connect with three groups of people: advisers (such as lawyers or accountants), travellers, and those involved in communications. The first group helps you tie up a tricky transaction; this isn't something to tend to yourself. The second group, whom you meet while you're out of town or they're on your turf, helps you rearrange priorities. And the third group convinces you that something you've said or written is worthy of a broader audience. Your financial picture remains largely constant—there will be some small losses balanced by modest windfalls. Your ability to concentrate is stronger than usual—you're not trying to do as many things at one time as you often attempt. However, watch for possible lapses around April and again toward your birthday, when you can be impatient and careless. Aim to be more image-conscious, and make a point of dressing appropriately for formal occasions (there are likely to be several scattered through the year). In the area of health, you may be changing medical professionals. Research is important as you locate a new doctor or dentist. This is an excellent year to start a diet or fitness program, so long as it doesn't scream "fad."

January

Your keywords for the month ahead: commitment, compromise, integrity.

Key Days
Romance: Jan. 4, 12, 19, 26
Friends and family: Jan. 4, 15, 24, 30
Career and status: Jan. 8, 16, 24, 29
Finance: Jan. 6, 11, 21, 27

Week of the 1st–6th
Don't search for hidden answers. Check for the obvious and the familiar. Enjoy comfort foods and romantic movies, and spend time with the person who makes you laugh and feel secure. Look forward to lively detours over the weekend.

Week of the 7th–13th
Start a fitness program and stick with it. Yes, practice makes perfect is a cliché, but that's the key this week. Get a jump on the competition by brushing up your skills. A friendship launched last year starts gaining momentum. If checking out technical equipment, bring along a knowledgeable consultant.

Week of the 14th–20th
You can't resist a touch of the dramatic, and it seems that you're

adding a flourish to even the simplest statements. The result? People hang onto your every word like wallpaper. It's time to pin down someone who constantly flip-flops on an issue. Watch out for a tendency to be more adventurous but less cautious.

Week of the 21st–27th
Expansion is key this week. Increase your vocabulary, and add some new choices to your standard menu. You have difficulties convincing people of your ideas or selling a product. You may be unintentionally coming across as confrontational, so add some humour to your approach.

Week of the 28th–31st
You don't have to be stuck with an arrangement. Give it a trial run, then ask for a change if you're feeling uncomfortable. No matter what you're putting together, read instructions carefully and don't improvise. Relatives are easier to talk to and more willing to follow your suggestions.

February

Your keywords for the month ahead: insights, answers, reciprocation.

Key Days
Romance: Feb. 6, 10, 18, 26
Friends and family: Feb. 2, 14, 20, 28
Career and status: Feb. 4, 10, 20, 27
Finance: Feb. 3, 15, 21, 25

Week of the 1st–10th

You express yourself in nonverbal ways, perhaps through gift-giving. Your reputation is growing and you may be asked to promote a pet cause. Be on your toes on the 9th and 10th. One rival steps out of the picture but another is preparing to take over.

Week of the 11th–17th

You exude confidence, and this is a good time to contact someone you admire. It's easy to lose touch with family members but important to stay in the loop. By the end of the week you understand why you and a friend drifted apart. You can now start the process of getting the relationship back on track.

Week of the 18th–24th

You're the bounce-back kid. It seems that every setback makes you stronger, and this week you make major progress toward a long-term goal. You're generally shrewd in business but can be sacrificing quality just to save a few loonies. Romance may take a back seat to work but mustn't be neglected.

Week of the 25th–28th

Scorpio is the sign of extremes, and this week you jockey between doing something to the point of exhaustion and goofing off. An acquaintance may think the relationship you have is deeper than you believe it to be. Your encouragement goes a long way toward rebuilding a youngster's self-confidence.

March

Your keywords for the month ahead: open-mindedness, questions, conflict.

Key Days
Romance: March 2, 7, 18, 30
Friends and family: March 4, 12, 20, 27
Career and status: March 6, 12, 21, 26
Finance: March 3, 16, 21, 28

Week of the 1st–10th
This is an ideal time for organizing a long-term project or planning a trip, no matter how far in the future it seems to be. Arrange a date night. Whether it's a movie or a hockey game, emphasize what your partner wants to do.

Week of the 11th–17th
This is a good week for going after outstanding debts. You have an air of authority about you and are in a position to effect change. Avoid petty people who keep checklists of whose turn it is to do this and that. It's far better to surround yourself with individuals as big-hearted and gracious as you are.

Week of the 18th–24th
Mischievous people may have fun at your expense, since you can be somewhat gullible early this week. The mood turns more serious by Thursday or Friday, when someone asks you to make

a long-term commitment. Take time to process the request, even if you're dealing with an impatient individual.

Week of the 25th–31st

"I had no idea that such individuals exist outside of stories," Dr. Watson said of Sherlock Homes. This week you meet that kind of person—someone with a brilliant mind and an eccentric personality. This is a good week to overcome pessimism. You're becoming more calm, collected, and upbeat.

April

____

Your keywords for the month ahead: support, forgiveness, intuition.

Key Days

Romance: April 7, 13, 22, 29
Friends and family: April 6, 16, 21, 27
Career and status: April 3, 10, 17, 25
Finance: April 3, 14, 24, 28

Week of the 1st–7th

The week has two personalities. Early on, your skin is as thin as spring ice, and even little things can offend you. Then, starting Friday, you're more confident. A new acquaintance decides to adopt you but may soon demand more time than you're willing to give.

Week of the 8th–14th

Mars, co-ruler of your sign, is involved with drive. Pluto, the other ruler, is the planet of intuition. At this point in time you're energized, perceptive, and a force of nature. Early in the week you sense what needs to be done. Then, starting Wednesday or Thursday, you're driven to accomplish it.

Week of the 15th–21st
Your strong drive continues, but you can be leaning toward extremes early in the week. Watch for a tendency to overdo your fitness routines, eat too much good food, or be blunt and opinionated. This tendency should end by Thursday, when you're sharp as a tack and acquiring all sorts of useful information.

Week of the 22nd–30th
You need to be at your most diplomatic early in the week, when the people you deal with are irritable and annoying. The full moon on Thursday launches a period of creativity and generosity. You may be taking on a volunteer assignment by the end of the month, possibly one that involves pets.

May

Your keywords for the month ahead: variety, motivation, structure.

Key Days
Romance: May 2, 11, 17, 31
Friends and family: May 4, 12, 16, 25
Career and status: May 2, 8, 15, 29
Finance: May 7, 14, 18, 23

Week of the 1st–5th

Don't assume something's a done deal until you have the agreement in writing. You make a key contribution but, if you want to be noticed, you need to sing your own praises. A relationship that's been all over the map starts to follow a predictable path.

Week of the 6th–12th

You'll make a significant contribution to your field of work, but don't count on instant recognition. You could be entering a formal arrangement with a friend or relative. It may at first seem unnecessary, but it's smart—particularly for the relationship— to put all the terms in writing.

Week of the 13th–19th

If you need any more convincing that it's time for a change, you receive the signal this week. Someone is trying to manipulate you and can be quite crafty, especially on Wednesday and Thursday. Otherwise, things move along efficiently, and your home environment continues to be your favourite retreat.

Week of the 20th–26th

Check that you don't become too comfy at home. You benefit from a change of scene and the opportunity to meet fresh faces. You don't realize how significant your work is until an "ordinary" job garners extraordinary praise. You learn that a possession has increased in value.

Week of the 27th–31st

Find another way of looking at a problem and you'll discover the answer that's long eluded you. This is a good time to broaden

your social circle, acquire knowledge on a new subject area, and
take a more active role in a joint financial arrangement.

June

Your keywords for the month ahead: affection,
moxie, big-heartedness.

Key Days
Romance: June 3, 11, 16, 26
Friends and family: June 5, 15, 23, 28
Career and status: June 4, 12, 21, 26
Finance: June 10, 14, 22, 30

Week of the 1st–9th
Your encouragement helps a friend through a difficult patch, but
your involvement with neighbours may create friction. You have
a suspicion about who your mysterious ally is, but can't prove it.
Take a more active role in shared financial arrangements.

Week of the 10th–16th
Your outlook is more realistic and less cynical. At the same time,
you're better able to express your feelings to the people who
inspire you. A stubborn friend becomes less bull-headed. Don't
lose the opportunity to correct a misunderstanding. Continue to
polish your presentation skills.

Week of the 17th–23rd
You're struggling to stay fit, but resist the temptation to throw in

the towel. Help is on the way in the form of a new activity—and a new buddy. Around Saturday's summer solstice, your frustration or resentment about a community or other project turns into satisfaction and pride.

Week of the 24th–30th
This is a week in which you initiate action. Looking for an invitation to a cottage? Nobody's picking up any of the hints that you're dropping. Take a less subtle approach and you'll start getting results by Wednesday. Your partner is ready to take the relationship to the next level.

July

Your keywords for the month ahead: discretion, affection, generosity.

Key Days
Romance: July 3, 7, 16, 25
Friends and family: July 1, 9, 20, 29
Career and status: July 3, 11, 17, 24
Finance: July 5, 13, 22, 27

Week of the 1st–7th
A period of anxiety ends when a family member stops beating about the bush. This is a good week to strike a personal or professional alliance, but not both. Someone you like tries to ask for help but keeps hedging. Provide an opportunity.

Week of the 8th–14th

You show a possessive quality early in the week, so it's under-standable if people keep their distance. But starting Thursday, you're less overbearing. On the weekend, you're downright easy to please. Little wonder that some of your nearest and dearest are just waiting to see what you'll be like next Monday.

Week of the 15th–21st

An idea or presentation garners a standing ovation. Capitalize on the enthusiastic response by offering more of your services. A temperamental person is easier to deal with. Don't count on anything routine over the weekend. Prepare for last-minute cancellations, changes, and delays.

Week of the 22nd–31st

A friend's aggressive mood can lead to confrontation, and some-one you're getting to know stirs up suspicion. At the other end of the spectrum, relatives are supportive, generous, and even funny. Check minor technical and mechanical problems before they turn into major headaches.

August

Your keywords for the month ahead: ambition, congeniality, elegance.

Key Days
Romance: Aug. 6, 14, 20, 31
Friends and family: Aug. 6, 14, 21, 29

Career and status: Aug. 7, 15, 23, 28
Finance: Aug. 8, 17, 24, 30

Week of the 1st–4th
Clear your plate as early in the week as you can. Your upcoming project requires complete attention, so it's important to tie up loose ends. You'll be introduced to classy people on the weekend, but don't change a thing about your down-to-earth style.

Week of the 5th–11th
Something or someone triggers a memory. Along your journey to the past, you may find an answer to something you've been unable to resolve. Take a more active role in your health and finances and don't hesitate to challenge the professionals. Continue to compare prices and look for sales.

Week of the 12th–18th
A friend who switches between cantankerous and determined gets stuck in the former mode. But a wishy-washy colleague or relative becomes surprisingly decisive. Creativity is your current forte. You secure your reputation by adding a personal touch to even the most routine job.

Week of the 19th–25th
It's easy to promise more than you can deliver. Think twice before making another generous offer. You meet your match in the battle of wits, and some prize-winning zingers are exchanged through the week. Distractions surround you on the weekend. Resist all but the most fascinating ones.

Week of the 26th–31st

You may feel like you're in a different time zone. If you're usually an early bird, this week you turn into a night owl—or the reverse happens. Regardless of the time of day, you gain an appreciation of people you've taken for granted and find greater stability in a relationship.

September

Your keywords for the month ahead: transition, restoration, consolidation.

Key Days

Romance: Sept. 4, 11, 18, 26
Friends and family: Sept. 7, 15, 20, 29
Career and status: Sept. 5, 16, 24, 30
Finance: Sept. 6, 14, 22, 28

Week of the 1st–8th

Someone you deal with is so dramatic you feel he or she should be auditioning for the Stratford Festival. But your role is even more noteworthy as you find the self-confidence that lets you challenge bigots and bullies. A normally passive friend takes the initiative and makes a surprising offer.

Week of the 9th–15th

Avoid getting caught up in other people's problems. You can be sensitive and supportive while remaining objective. This is a week to focus on your personal and professional plans for the fall, which can evolve into the most productive and meaningful season of the year.

Week of the 16th–22nd

If you've been itching for a change, this is a good week to explore new interests. You're also able to come up with a novel solution to an age-old family dilemma. Thursday, with the full moon illuminating the sky, is an ideal day to evaluate your present situation and reflect on the next three months.

Week of the 23rd–30th

No question about it. You enjoy flattery and flirtations. The compliments this week are frequent and sincere—you're looking smart in the earthy, mellow colours that suit your temperament. You're also sending forth a confident aura. Just stay on top of your paperwork—it can easily get the better of you.

October

Your keywords for the month ahead: precision, discretion, intuition.

Key Days

Romance: Oct. 9, 19, 24, 30

Friends and family: Oct. 5, 14, 24, 29

Career and status: Oct. 2, 18, 24, 28

Finance: Oct. 3, 8, 20, 26

Week of the 1st–6th

You have a personality distinctly your own, which is what

endears you to someone you're getting to know. You need answers quickly, and this is not the time to be subtle. Be specific, direct, and highly persistent. Take charge in family-related finances.

Week of the 7th–13th
It's a retro-themed week. You'll be reconnecting with an old pal or visiting a locale from your youth. By Friday, however, you're more than ready to return to the present. Joint enterprises require a professional opinion. Toughen your skin for the weekend, when you can't avoid insensitive people.

Week of the 14th–20th
Long-distance travel is on your mind. Your sense of adventure is piqued, and this is a good week to check brochures and websites. As your birthday approaches, think about your changing interests, the direction your personal path is taking, and the people who've recently entered your life.

Week of the 21st–27th
You're back on the A list. VIPs want your advice, and this is a good time to pitch your ideas to people in high places. It's also a good time to launch a fitness strategy. Bring in help, however, if you're considering any kind of decorating project. It's not too late to mend fences, so watch for an opportunity to fix an old friendship.

Week of the 28th–31st
Expect a series of mix-ups—everything from getting the time wrong for an appointment, to forgetting familiar names, to putting your sweater on backwards or inside out. Offer help even

when it's not requested. Something sparks the performer in you; it's an excellent time for auditions.

November

Your keywords for the month ahead: charisma, extravagance, originality.

Key Days
Romance: Nov. 6, 11, 24, 27
Friends and family: Nov. 2, 10, 17, 26
Career and status: Nov. 7, 19, 25, 29
Finance: Nov. 1, 9, 20, 28

Week of the 1st–10th
You have a knack for drawing out secrets. The new moon on the third Wednesday coincides with your revived interest in a creative activity. Someone in your everyday world acts defensively, but for now it's best not to rock the boat.

Week of the 11th–17th
Someone you respect makes a tempting offer. Buy some time as you weigh the pros against the cons and check whether strings are attached. You can make a difference this week as you fight for a cause you believe in. Keep up with local politics and community events.

Week of the 18th–24th
Your best source of information is less than reliable, you disagree with your favourite movie critic, and you can't even

depend on your famous Scorpio instincts. However, you make an important connection with Taurus, your opposite sign, and bring out the very best in each other.

Week of the 25th–30th
It's easy to lose patience with someone who ignores your advice, but consider the way you present it. Are you being preachy? Are strings attached? Keep things on a friendly level at work—at least in a superficial way. You never know who you'll need for an ally, and you can't afford to burn any bridges.

December

Your keywords for the month ahead: opportunity, determination, loyalty.

Key Days
Romance: Dec. 10, 14, 22, 31
Friends and family: Dec. 6, 15, 21, 26
Career and status: Dec. 3, 11, 20, 30
Finance: Dec. 4, 9, 14, 27

Week of the 1st–8th
This is a significant week in which you have an opportunity to realize one of your dreams. Explore various sources of information—from old books to current websites—as you continue your research. Take a less passive role in family events.

Week of the 9th–15th
You may not know what's driving you, but now you're a force

to be reckoned with. Whether you're organizing a family meeting or an office potluck, you take charge with a vengeance. And while some find you overbearing, others very much enjoy the fun-loving and passionate side of your personality.

Week of the 16th–22nd

The hard-working side of your personality surfaces when everyone else is slowing down for the holidays. With the full moon on Tuesday, you prepare yourself for an upcoming challenge. Take a farsighted approach and look beyond the week. Focus on long-range projects and set goals for the new year.

Week of the 23rd–31st

Creativity and friendship intersect during the holiday week. Write a long, old-fashioned letter to someone you've been thinking of, or design a special gift rather than buying something impersonal. Family members are more understanding, and you can take down some of the boundaries you set up during the past year.

What's Ahead for Sagittarius

November 23–December 21

This year isn't as much about monumental changes as it is about shifts. You'll be rethinking your goals and re-evaluating your career direction, but you're not likely to make any sudden or radical moves. As 2013 begins, Jupiter, the planet of expansion, appears in your seventh house of marriage, best friends, and partnerships. This means you're more likely to add depth to the quality of your existing relationships than to widen the circle. Your seventh house also rules rivals and competitors, and while you usually don't feel threatened, you should watch out for anyone trying to gain access to your files or business secrets. Be cautious here throughout the first half of the year, but particularly in April and May. In late June, Jupiter moves into your eighth house, which covers trust and sharing. It's possible at this time—especially through the late summer and early fall months—that your joint assets will increase. For much of the year, you'll be making others feel happy—this, in fact, is one of your great pleasures: helping people feel good about themselves. It's part of your style to give someone the shirt off your back; just don't give away the whole farm during a period of ultra-generosity that strikes around October or November. It's possible that you'll be tested and challenged in areas that are linked to the past, and this year you could discover a skeleton lurking in your family closet. As for your health, the key is moderation. Two words not found in your typical vocabulary are "happy medium," but try to apply them in fitness and diet, where you veer toward extremes. Keep in mind that your sign rules the hips and the liver, and make an ongoing effort to keep your blood pressure—and everyone else's—under control.

January

Your keywords for the month ahead: vitality, diligence, compassion.

Key Days
Romance: Jan. 3, 10, 21, 31
Friends and family: Jan. 1, 11, 26, 27
Career and status: Jan. 4, 7, 16, 29
Finance: Jan. 8, 17, 24, 30

Week of the 1st–6th
The offer you've been waiting for comes through, but check the fine print before accepting it. Be aware of a tendency to hover too much. Take time to pamper someone who was especially kind to you last year and surround yourself with optimistic people.

Week of the 7th–13th
People enjoy your way with words, but a little goes a long way this week. Try not to monopolize every conversation. Be prepared to seize an opportunity that can boost your career or community standing. Get into the habit of maintaining your car, your technical equipment, and especially your health.

Week of the 14th–20th
The atmosphere turns more pleasant with the arrival of someone who makes you smile. This is also a good week to become involved in a community cause. Be a little cautious if sending out applications or attending meetings. Check forms for mistakes and your outfit for wardrobe malfunctions.

Week of the 21st–27th

Your ambitious side is front and centre. If you've been eyeing a promotion, this is the time to make your move. Your stamina is strong, but you need to take time out to recharge your batteries. Be careful on Thursday and Friday, when you can be blunt and unintentionally hurt a friend's delicate feelings.

Week of the 28th–31st

You're uncharacteristically critical of other people's ideas and have a need to be in control. Not surprisingly, some co-workers and even friends may distance themselves from you. By mid-week, you're taking yourself less seriously. Friends seek you out for support, guidance, and possibly cash.

February

Your keywords for the month ahead:
professionalism, idealism, encouragement.

Key Days

Romance: Feb. 8, 14, 22, 26
Friends and family: Feb. 3, 11, 19, 23
Career and status: Feb. 7, 18, 26, 27
Finance: Feb. 4, 10, 20, 25

Week of the 1st–10th

You need to make the first move in resolving a family conflict, and an offbeat approach may work. It's also a good time to schedule appointments. Lines of communication open up and professionals are available. Gifts arrive, but with strings attached.

Week of the 11th–17th
Valentine's week is a good time to make a fresh start in a relationship. Your more positive attitude helps you build confidence. Demanding people continue to irritate you at work, but the good news is that you've found an ally who's willing to go to bat for you.

Week of the 18th–24th
First impressions about people are strong; you're a good judge of character. A temporary assignment can turn into a long-term gig—you need to decide whether that's what you want. There's a chance, if you want it, to renew a relationship with a distant friend or an estranged relative.

Week of the 25th–28th
There are two sides of your personality at work: businesslike and playful. Just be sure to apply the right one to the right situation. The week favours one-on-one discussions rather than group meetings. A take-charge person challenges you to become even more outspoken than you usually are.

March

Your keywords for the month ahead: sociability, experimentation, creation.

Key Days

Romance: March 6, 12, 13, 29

Friends and family: March 4, 14, 23, 28

Career and status: March 7, 11, 15, 27

Finance: March 4, 13, 24, 31

Week of the 1st–10th

Act on your ideas before others do. You feel so comfortable with a new friend that you finish each other's sentences. This is a good week for physical activity, but be cautious—you don't want to show off on the rink or the slopes.

Week of the 11th–17th

You're in a mood to host a party whether or not there's something to celebrate. Rigid people are more tolerant, flexible, and generous, and Wednesday is a good day to make requests. Resolve tiffs by the weekend or they can mushroom.

Week of the 18th–24th

There's less friction in an everyday situation, thanks to the arrival of a new member of your team. You'll be making one or more family-related decisions around the spring equinox on Wednesday, and making them alone. Clarify any information involving numbers in general and money in particular.

Week of the 25th–31st

Someone's odd behaviour or inappropriate remarks can be unsettling, and your response can surprise those close to you. Your ability to concentrate is improving, and you feel more confident about making important decisions. An unexpected guest may land at your door on Saturday or Sunday.

April

Your keywords for the month ahead:
unpredictability, supportiveness, indulgence.

Key Days
Romance: April 3, 15, 20, 28
Friends and family: April 6, 14, 20, 25
Career and status: April 8, 16, 23, 29
Finance: April 4, 16, 22, 30

Week of the 1st–7th
You and a colleague share a common goal and work in tandem
to meet it. In contrast, you're not on the same wavelength as
your partner. One of you wants to stay home and watch a movie
or game; the other is ready to go out and party.

Week of the 8th–14th
You feel cranky for no real reason, and the best tonic is to spoil
yourself. You've nurtured others, and now it's time to indulge
yours truly. A small creature appears in the week's picture, and
you could be looking after a pet. Communication is strong on
the weekend. You're a pro at getting a point across.

Week of the 15th–21st
Pick up on someone's body language—it probably means more
than spoken or written words. You start running out of steam
early in the week. Take a "me" break, get back to your task, and
you'll go the distance. Keeping up with local events will come
in handy during the summer.

Week of the 22nd–30th

You project a quality of strength, and people line up for your advice and opinions. It's easy to fall behind on your own important jobs, so you need to organize priorities and stick to a schedule. There's an area, however, where you need some help. Your sense of style is off the mark and you're due for a wardrobe makeover.

May

Your keywords for the month ahead: curiosity, investigation, optimism.

Key Days
Romance: May 3, 8, 16, 29
Friends and family: May 4, 12, 19, 28
Career and status: May 6, 15, 23, 30
Finance: May 1, 10, 19, 27

Week of the 1st–5th

You're like a terrier—digging until you get to the root of an all-consuming problem. You know you're getting close, and by the end of this week or the beginning of the next, you've solved the issue that's been on your mind for a month or longer.

Week of the 6th–12th

Your ruling planet is Jupiter, associated with opportunity and optimism, and your positive outlook this week makes you an ideal candidate for a prestigious position. You seem to have a sixth sense about people and can help motivate those you care about.

Week of the 13th–19th

Quiet activities are highlighted in a week that emphasizes the spiritual side of your personality. You also take a "less is more" approach to your work and do a few jobs well rather than tackling a little of everything. Someone in a position to help you recognizes the quality of your work.

Week of the 20th–26th

You may not feel brave enough for your first barbecue of the season, but you're ready to get into shape for it. This is a good week for launching a fitness regimen. It's also a potentially strong time for forging a new relationship, so make an effort to circulate, beginning on Friday.

Week of the 27th–31st

It's a week of controversy. You initiate discussions by defending a position that's currently out of fashion. As well, you take a stand when a neighbour or co-worker starts to stir up trouble. Draw up a budget for the summer, but prepare for the reality that you need to be more frugal.

June

Your keywords for the month ahead: renewal, reconciliation, research.

Key Days

Romance: June 5, 12, 18, 27

Friends and family: June 1, 14, 22, 30

Career and status: June 4, 11, 19, 24

Finance: June 6, 14, 25, 29

Week of the 1st–9th
Whether writing a business report or a sentimental poem, you get to the heart of the subject. Try motivating someone who's become lackadaisical. Clarify financial information and check bills and statements carefully.

Week of the 10th–16th
You make minor professional gains and should celebrate by doing something frivolous. Someone you deal with puts you into an awkward spot by trying to get your support for a project. Don't automatically reject criticism—it contains a nice suggestion for self-improvement.

Week of the 17th–23rd
The week starts with a choice, and by Friday you need to make a difficult decision. Along the way, you gain insights into yourself. The full moon on Sunday marks the start of a short but intense period of reconciliation and new beginnings. Continue to get more in touch with nature.

Week of the 24th–30th
A change is as good as a rest, but this week a rest is the best antidote to the turmoil in your job or family. Update your technology and keep informed of current trends. You'd be smart to read every section of the newspaper, even the ones you usually use for lining the bird cage.

July

Your keywords for the month ahead:
self-confidence, conservatism, information.

Key Days
Romance: July 1, 14, 19, 29
Friends and family: July 6, 14, 25, 31
Career and status: July 9, 16, 24, 29
Finance: July 3, 18, 25, 30

Week of the 1st–7th
This is a transition week, as you change either your job or the approach you take to it. Be cautious about revealing personal information. There are only a few people you confide in, and this week you may want to shorten the list.

Week of the 8th–14th
Plans change by the day, and flexibility is key. Keep updated on changes in your community that could affect you over the short-term. If you're involved in a competition, including a sport, you suddenly realize you're no longer the underdog. You may want to drop out of an organization, but weigh pros against cons before making a decision.

Week of the 15th–21st
You're able to deal with a difficult situation in a logical fashion while others fly off the handle. Increased pressure proves a plus since it affords the opportunity to demonstrate your skills and try new experiences. You continue to be shrewd in business but still tend to neglect your own health.

Week of the 22nd–31st

Someone brings up something from your past, but it's something positive that can be used to your advantage. Your nurturing side is prominent, and you may be spending time looking after a friend's pet or an ailing relative. News from another city or province can affect your plans for the balance of the summer.

August

Your keywords for the month ahead: acquisition, enthusiasm, leadership.

Key Days

Romance: Aug. 5, 10, 22, 28

Friends and family: Aug. 3, 11, 23, 30

Career and status: Aug. 6, 15, 21, 28

Finance: Aug. 2, 9, 17, 27

Week of the 1st–4th

You're an excellent judge of character and can pick up on subtle changes in relationships. It's time to move your own needs to the front of the line. Treat yourself to something you've been wanting, and don't look for excuses to ignore health concerns.

Week of the 5th–11th

The new moon on Tuesday marks the start of a period of productivity and renewed energy. You can make serious progress on a job or a creative work. Your views on politics or other issues start to shift as the result of someone you recently met. The feedback you've been expecting arrives by the weekend.

Week of the 12th–18th

You learn why someone has been so uncommunicative and can now figure out how to help. At the same time, although you find it difficult to accept criticism, you should see it as a lesson in self-improvement. Don't be too eager to hear a friend's secret. Take a less haphazard approach to money and begin some serious financial planning.

Week of the 19th–25th

Procrastination changes into action—and there's nothing subtle about the transition. Arrange that dinner you've been putting off and get back to that dreary project. Put health and wellness at the top of the to-do list and start making appointments and signing up for fall fitness classes.

Week of the 26th–31st

This is an order-out-of-chaos time. Sort papers and de-clutter cupboards. It won't make for the most stimulating week, but your brain needs mindless tasks to get it into gear. While you're organizing the sock drawer, a rocky relationship moves to a steadier course and a dramatic relative becomes easier to live with.

September

Your keywords for the month ahead: partnership, empathy, control.

Key Days

Romance: Sept. 2, 9, 16, 29
Friends and family: Sept. 7, 13, 20, 30

Career and status: Sept. 4, 12, 19, 26
Finance: Sept. 6, 15, 24, 28

Week of the 1st–8th

Your bargaining power improves, and this should be a good week for deal-making. Attitudes begin to change, and people line up to take numbers to join your inner circle. Expect to do a lot of speaking and protect your voice as much as possible.

Week of the 9th–15th

Jupiter, your ruling planet, is associated with the tendency to take risks. Be particularly cautious this week—especially on Thursday the 12th and Friday the 13th. Look forward to spending time with someone who appreciates your offbeat sense of humour. Your romantic life takes a turn in the right direction.

Week of the 16th–22nd

The last days of summer are ideal for enjoying the limelight. This doesn't mean that you're performing before a crowd (although it's possible). Rather, people respond positively to your ideas and seek out your company. If you've been waiting to make any kind of pitch—professional or personal—this is the perfect week.

Week of the 23rd–30th

Although summer's behind you, this is an excellent week to plan or even take a trip. For no particular reason, you're feeling affluent. Watch out for a tendency to spend extravagantly, and where you can, hold back on making purchases till mid-October. This is a good week to become reacquainted with relatives.

October

Your keywords for the month ahead: connecting the dots, narrowing the choices.

Key Days
Romance: Oct. 3, 15, 21, 26
Friends and family: Oct. 5, 14, 21, 27
Career and status: Oct. 11, 16, 24, 30
Finance: Oct. 7, 12, 18, 25

Week of the 1st–6th
Something, or someone, you've been searching for is closer to home than you realize. The year began with an array of options, but as the countdown to 2014 begins, your choices are fewer—and the choosing more important.

Week of the 7th–13th
Put fresh air and exercise high on your priority list. The hard-working side of your personality is front and centre, and it's no surprise that the week turns into one of your most favourable times for career advancement. Enjoy some unexpected cash on Friday or the weekend, and try to bank it for 2014.

Week of the 14th–20th
You see a pattern emerge from some of the random events that have occurred over the past three months. Continue to assert yourself and the respect you've been seeking will soon follow. Your knowledge of your family's background helps solve a lingering mystery.

Week of the 21st–27th

The week seems to have a dual personality. You don't mean to be aloof, but people keep their distance from you from Monday to about Thursday. Then, starting Friday, you turn bubbly and draw crowds for no special reason. The weekend is favourable for making short-term commitments.

Week of the 28th–31st

Communication snarls create misunderstandings and cause mistakes early in the week, but by Wednesday you're enjoying well-deserved success. Continue to rely more on yourself than on people who put on a good show. A suspicion about someone's credibility is confirmed on Friday or Saturday.

November

Your keywords for the month ahead: recharging, strategy, public relations.

Key Days:
Romance: Nov. 3, 12, 24, 29
Friends and family: Nov. 2, 10, 17, 26
Career and status: Nov. 5, 13, 21, 28
Finance: Nov. 6, 15, 23, 30

Week of the 1st–10th

It feels like Monday all week. Every day, you think you're starting from scratch. By the weekend of the 9th, you can look back on a number of small accomplishments. Don't make light of the compliments you receive—accept them with grace, then take time to unwind.

Week of the 11th–17th
It's a good week for making presentations and promoting your ideas. Although your prestige increases, someone's less-than-tactful remarks can sting. You have some good retorts, but silence is your best defence. Save the prize-winning zingers for another occasion.

Week of the 18th–24th
While others react with petty jealousy, you applaud a friend's achievements. Continue to encourage a relative to be less withdrawn. People don't always know when you're pulling their leg. Your sense of humour can be subtle, so don't rely on it to get your message through.

Week of the 25th–30th
A one-time opponent sees eye to eye with you on a controversial matter. The middle of the week is an especially good time to plot out a new romantic strategy. Throughout the next weeks you're showing less interest in material possessions and begin travelling a path of intellectual pursuits.

December

Your keywords for the month ahead: judgment, control, consolidation.

Key Days
Romance: Dec. 5, 12, 21, 31
Friends and family: Dec. 4, 15, 21, 28
Career and status: Dec. 2, 10, 19, 30
Finance: Dec. 3, 11, 18, 26

Week of the 1st–8th
People know how to yank your chain, but you know how to stay in control and avoid confrontation. Be cautious, too, about taking even small risks. No matter what your age, the week initiates a period of greater maturity.

Week of the 9th–15th
The things you accomplish at the tail end of the year affect the responsibilities you'll assume in January. Travel holds greater appeal. Ask people to share stories about favourite destinations. Take a retrospective look at some of the year's high and low points as you plan a wish list for 2014.

Week of the 16th–22nd
You receive information that was requested months ago, and it's not too late to act on it. The full moon on Tuesday finds you charismatic and witty—and helps you charm yourself out of a sticky situation. Someone you like is in a jam and asks for your help. Prepare to be thanked in an unexpected way.

Week of the 23rd–31st
While others are distracted during the holiday week, you're more thorough and more focused in your work. You also take an interest in subject areas ranging from philosophy to ancient

history. Opposing sides are lobbying for your support, and you wisely keep your strong opinions to yourself.

What's Ahead for Capricorn

December 22–January 20

This is another take-charge year for Capricorn. You'll periodically be asked to oversee professional projects, while family members regularly count on you as the voice of sanity. Expansive, generous Jupiter remains in your sixth house until June 26. For the first half of the year especially, avoid taking risks with your health, look forward to improved relationships with coworkers (including new members of your team) and neighbours, and don't rule out getting a pet (or another pet). From July onward, you'll be focusing more on best friends and rivals—and keep in mind that, on occasion, they're one and the same. Review your profits and losses throughout the year and, regardless of your age, start making plans for retirement. If you've never owned real estate, this may be the year when you take the plunge; and if you're a homeowner, you could be doing some important renovations that will enhance the value of your property. During the late summer and early fall months, expect to see changes in the temperaments of people you thought you knew. A gentle individual may turn hostile for a short but disturbing time, while a friend or relative with a notorious short fuse becomes more complacent. You'll find the latter change particularly disconcerting. As a rule of thumb, give everybody, including yourself, more space. Saturn, your ruling planet, encourages you to seek out knowledge, though not in conventional places. Expect to learn major life lessons at the time of the lunar eclipse on April 25 and again at the solar eclipse on November 3. Apply the year's "take charge" approach to your health as well as to your work. You could find yourself more sedentary than usual, so it's important to keep your joints limber.

January

Your keywords for the month ahead: detours, expansion, achievement.

Key Days
Romance: Jan. 3, 10, 21, 29
Friends and family: Jan. 1, 11, 26, 27
Career and status: Jan. 4, 7, 16, 29
Finance: Jan. 8, 17, 24, 30

Week of the 1st–6th
Capricorns don't do things the easy way. You master a skill that you've been perfecting since last fall, and can ultimately turn it into a profitable enterprise. As well, your new interests can lead to a significant friendship.

Week of the 7th–13th

The week offers an unusual lineup of activities that range from sports to intellectual pursuits. You can also look forward to meeting someone who appreciates your wry sense of humour. You're suddenly bursting with inspiration, but selectivity is the key. Talk over your ideas rather than dealing with them on your own.

Week of the 14th–20th

Joint activities help get you out of a rut. The week is a work in progress. You may not complete anything, but several projects are taking shape. An Spanish proverb says that the best way to keep a secret is without help. Remember those words on the weekend.

Week of the 21st–27th

Early this week, you connect with someone of the opposite sex. It could be a common artistic interest or a shared ethical position that attracts you to each other. The full moon on Saturday indicates good financial news, if not for you then for someone you like.

Week of the 28th–31st

Make sure that you and the people you deal with are on the same wavelength. For example, you may think you're getting paid for something while your "boss" is sure you're volunteering your time. Plans are now taking shape for an out-of-town event. It's not too early to start saving your toonies.

February

Your keywords for the month ahead: self-reliance, innovation, unconventionality.

Key Days
Romance: Feb. 2, 15, 22, 27
Friends and family: Feb. 5, 10, 19, 26
Career and status: Feb. 4, 13, 20, 25
Finance: Feb. 3, 12, 21, 28

Week of the 1st–10th
The groundhog isn't the only one making a decision this week. You're faced with several choices involving a relationship. It helps if you don't dwell on this one issue. Spend time on the ski slopes or in a museum.

Week of the 11th–17th
This is a week for intellectual expansion. It's also time to activate plans and begin negotiations. You find it hard to accept help but allow someone the privilege of giving you a hand. Let another relative keep the peace at a family function. Diplomacy isn't one of your current strong points.

Week of the 18th–24th
The week is divided into two parts. During the first three days, you're highly persuasive and quick to share your strong opinions. At the same time, expect disruptions in your home life.

Things are less hectic starting Thursday. The mood becomes calmer, and you take a neutral approach to family and workplace politics.

Week of the 25th–28th
There's a fun side to the week, and you play a part in lightening up the atmosphere. Recent tensions can flare up again, so closely monitor situations. You consider doing volunteer work. Although it may involve pets, it can lead to an enjoyable interaction with fellow human beings.

March

Your keywords for the month ahead: conscience, spontaneity, originality.

Key Days
Romance: March 1, 9, 19, 28
Friends and family: March 4, 15, 20, 31
Career and status: March 5, 12, 21, 27
Finance: March 3, 11, 20, 29

Week of the 1st–10th
You're hoping to spread your wings but should have a plan in place before taking flight. Your status will go up a notch thanks to the work you did late last year. It's a good week to connect with family members, including ones you barely know.

Week of the 11th–17th

Thinking outside the box can work both for and against you. Your professional ideas are innovative and provide a refreshing change. But if you're seeking a new look, your thinking can be too extreme. Best to bring along a more traditional friend if you want to reinvent yourself.

Week of the 18th–24th

Your great strength is determination, and this week you can expect to put in long hours. Friends share secrets—even if you don't want to hear them—but feel no need to reciprocate. It's a good time to review service agreements and evaluate the work of the professionals you deal with.

Week of the 25th–31st

Family-related tensions are building, and everyone benefits from a timeout. Despite the impression you're under, you're being favourably evaluated and there is the possibility of advancement. Does absence make the heart grow fonder? You'll find out this week, when you or your partner is called out of town.

April

Your keywords for the month ahead: fine-tuning, sharing, re-evaluation.

Key Days

Romance: April 6, 11, 19, 26
Friends and family: April 4, 12, 20, 27

Career and status: April 3, 9, 18, 30
Finance: April 2, 10, 21, 28

Week of the 1st–7th

Keep an eye on spending habits, including your own. Be cautious about making snap decisions on Monday and Tuesday, when you're easily influenced. Share your concerns and feelings directly with the person involved.

Week of the 8th–14th

There's no shortage of suggestions this week, but the best ones seem to come from unlikely sources. This is a good time to concentrate on health and diet; you'll want to be fit for spring. Things only appear to be slowing down at work or in a relationship. In fact, they're just starting to rev up.

Week of the 15th–21st

You're involved in two major projects this week. The first deals with figures and hard facts. The second concerns creativity and the arts. And while project number two seems more inspiring, you need to focus your attention equally on both.

Week of the 22nd–30th

Your gift for dealing with different personalities comes in handy. You'll be working with a Jekyll and a Hyde—possibly the same person. A project moves from the back to the front burner, and you'll scramble to reorder priorities. You could be dealing with forgetful people, so confirm appointments.

May

Your keywords for the month ahead: compromise, exploration, investigation.

Key Days
Romance: May 5, 11, 20, 28
Friends and family: May 6, 18, 25, 31
Career and status: May 2, 9, 16, 29
Finance: May 3, 12, 25, 30

Week of the 1st–5th
There is an emphasis on the arts. You express yourself through painting, music, or writing, and you may find someone who shares your interest in one of these fields. Be willing to make concessions if you want to remove a roadblock on the path to romance.

Week of the 6th–12th
Continue to review and fine-tune your plans and projects. The finishing touches make your work exceptional. Be careful not to cramp someone's style by dispensing too many well-meaning comments. In fact, at this point in time you're a far better listener than an orator.

Week of the 13th–19th
Mid-May is a good time to explore new ideas and investigate your past. Investments may not pay off for a while, so watch your cash flow. Consider taking up a new routine. You may want to start your day earlier, or you could add a walk to your lunch hour.

Week of the 20th–26th

Ask a foolish question—or even a smart one—and you'll likely get a sarcastic answer. You're best doing your own research and coming up with your own solutions. Business and languages are current strengths. Before long, people will figure out how accomplished you are in these areas.

Week of the 27th–31st

You have your hands full, so remember that you can't pick up one more thing unless you set something down. You may have to examine and evaluate areas of your life, but try to hold back on initiating important actions. Someone you compete with is about to become a staunch ally.

June

Your keywords for the month ahead: expansion, expression, persuasion.

Key Days

Romance: June 5, 12, 23, 29
Friends and family: June 1, 11, 18, 30
Career and status: June 4, 13, 19, 27
Finance: June 3, 12, 21, 25

Week of the 1st–9th

You know how to get what you want, but you need to figure out what it is that you're after. Expect to be dealing with impulsive individuals. As you look after the welfare of someone you love, be sure to tend to your own health needs.

Week of the 10th–16th

Teamwork is essential—it allows you to blame someone else. Unfortunately, you may be the one in the hot seat, so set the record straight. Check your appointment book regularly. The weekend is a good time to introduce people, especially those who, on the surface, don't seem to have much in common.

Week of the 17th–23rd

This is a good week to do things on a large scale. Look at the big picture too, and continue to aim high. You won't consistently reach the mark, but your confidence will grow immensely. Two strong people you know can clash with each other. It's hard not to take sides, but resist the urge.

Week of the 24th–30th

Give serious thought to a non-serious issue. For example, if you're planning a party, make every effort to guarantee it goes off without a hitch. Your plate finally starts to clear, but don't start piling it up again. Head out instead and give yourself a smart, stylish look for the summer.

July

Your keywords for the month ahead: public relations, structure, evaluation.

Key Days

Romance: July 5, 11, 21, 28

Friends and family: July 1, 14, 23, 30

Career and status: July 8, 19, 25, 29

Finance: July 6, 17, 20, 28

Week of the 1st–7th

This is a good week to scale down, concentrate on the essentials, and avoid distractions. There's an international theme at play; you may sign up for a language course or perhaps you meet someone from another country.

Week of the 8th–14th

Someone's unexpected news may catch you off guard, and your reaction may not be quite what the person had in mind. You find a key piece of a puzzle that involves friends or family, and when you put it into place everything makes sense. You're feeling antsy. Keep reminding yourself that patience is a virtue.

Week of the 15th–21st

You feel like you're a member of the official opposition. Your greatest role this week is to keep people on their toes by challenging plans and playing devil's advocate. You fire off some memorable one-liners and certainly make an impression. The weekend is a good time to take up volunteer work and meet people.

Week of the 22nd–31st

You're better able to express your emotions. In fact, you have a special kind of radar and know when someone could use a hug. You and your partner agree on small things—like favourite hockey players or performers. Politics is a different matter—a topic to be avoided on the weekend.

August

Your keywords for the month ahead: diversification, resourcefulness, optimism.

Key Days
Romance: Aug. 6, 13, 19, 25
Friends and family: Aug. 3, 11, 19, 28
Career and status: Aug. 2, 13, 20, 27
Finance: Aug. 1, 10, 19, 26

Week of the 1st–4th
A neighbour or co-worker is stirring up trouble and plays both sides of the fence. In contrast, a friend or relative has your interests at heart. A quick thinker, you may get ahead of yourself this week and jump to a wrong conclusion.

Week of the 5th–11th
You're in motion but need to stop and be alone with your thoughts. Legal or property-related matters move smoothly. Continue to ask questions till you're entirely satisfied. Avoid a midweek confrontation with a person in authority. Late week finds you bonding with someone you meet in a social setting.

Week of the 12th–18th
Plans are in limbo. Friends are difficult to pin down, and

each time you try to finalize a project it gets the better of you. Direct attention to old investments. Be careful what you send out, especially what's being sent in your name. There are changes in your environment and possible news of an upcoming move.

Week of the 19th–25th

After a few weeks of back and forth, a project gets the go-ahead. A protective friend or relative becomes overprotective, and then starts clinging. It's time for a serious talk. Look forward to an unexpected invitation or gift. You could feel a little vulnerable on the weekend, so take added health precautions.

Week of the 26th–31st

A tempting opportunity presents itself on Monday or Tuesday. Weigh the pros and cons before making your decision, especially if it involves other people. You'll see a few role reversals this week. For example, someone you think is passive assumes a take-charge position.

September

Your keywords for the month ahead: versatility, thrift, balance.

Key Days

Romance: Sept. 4, 11, 19, 28
Friends and family: Sept. 1, 10, 21, 29

Career and status: Sept. 3, 11, 20, 27
Finance: Sept. 6, 16, 25, 30

Week of the 1st–8th

You're dealing with various personalities. There's the temperamental type, the snob, and your favourite—the person as flaky as a good butter tart. Two cautions: First, your spending can get out of control. Second, be careful to not to make commitments that you're likely to regret.

Week of the 9th–15th

It's good to be aware of your strengths and play them up without being boastful. Balance is important. Be generous with your praise, but offer constructive criticism where appropriate. Career activities start heating up late in the week. On the weekend, you have a chance to indulge someone you care about.

Week of the 16th–22nd

Being generous is who you are, but right now you tend to be generous to a fault. You'll be dealing with the public, and you show a knack for salesmanship. You're open to new ideas but need to ask hard questions. Late in the week you may learn that the value of a possession has increased.

Week of the 23rd–30th

You're evenly matched, and a competition you're involved in can go either way. The key is to be sure you're physically as well as mentally prepped. Family matters weigh on your mind. Monday and Tuesday are good for reflecting on your next move. Thursday and Saturday see you implementing plans.

October

Your keywords for the month ahead: analysis, collaboration, perseverance.

Key Days
Romance: Oct. 3, 12, 19, 27
Friends and family: Oct. 5, 14, 26, 30
Career and status: Oct. 1, 9, 22, 28
Finance: Oct. 2, 10, 21, 29

Week of the 1st–6th
You may be feeling trapped in a situation. Choices are key. Contemplate at least a plan A and a plan B. Pay little attention to people who say your expectations are unrealistic. On Friday, you find out where someone stands on a key issue.

Week of the 7th–13th
News can be unreliable, or perhaps you're not absorbing it completely. In either case, clarify information before making your next move. It's a good week for innovation. You can apply creative touches to even the most mundane project, taking it from the realm of the ordinary to the exceptional.

Week of the 14th–20th
People are less dependent on you and starting to think for themselves. But much of the week is like a bar of soap. Once you think you've got hold of something, it slips away. Be more open to new ideas. You'll discover that you thrive on change and unearth some surprising information.

Week of the 21st–27th

People you don't know well take offence easily and may not be used to your wry sense of humour. The week starts sluggishly, and then it quickly picks up the pace. You treasure your privacy, so be certain to get time to yourself—even if it means delegating some of your favourite jobs.

Week of the 28th–31st

Your quick reflexes work in your favour—you pick up on vibes and respond right away. Just be sure you don't react too quickly and put your foot in your mouth. Continue to keep your nose to the grindstone and your recent feelings of uncertainty will be replaced by a sense of satisfaction.

November

Your keywords for the month ahead: initiative, inclusiveness, expansion.

Key Days
Romance: Nov. 2, 10, 18, 26
Friends and family: Nov. 5, 13, 23, 28
Career and status: Nov. 6, 20, 25, 29
Finance: Nov. 3, 11, 21, 27

Week of the 1st–10th

If you feel left out of the loop, consider it a blessing. You need time to yourself to set a new project in motion. Check your guest list for an upcoming event and include some fresh faces along with the old, familiar ones.

Week of the 11th–17th

Surround yourself with calm people and, until the full moon on Sunday, do your best to avoid confrontation. It's a hectic week— no sooner do you finish one task than you begin another major job. It's best to let family problems sort themselves out—your involvement will only add fuel to the fire.

Week of the 18th–24th

You can be somewhat thoughtless early in the week. Be sure not to take anyone's generosity for granted and to give youngsters encouraging doses of vitamin P (praise). A new interest steps into your life. You might meet through a professional organization, and you share an interest in an unusual hobby.

Week of the 25th–30th

Use your initiative and drive to turn this week into one of the year's most productive times. Regardless of your age, you're earning respect as a family leader. Relatives look to you for guidance. Expect delays and other snags in money matters. Check that your goals are consistent with reality.

December

Your keywords for the month ahead: perception, trust, ethics.

Key Days

Romance: Dec. 4, 12, 21, 31

Friends and family: Dec. 8, 17, 24, 29

Career and status: Dec. 2, 11, 16, 23

Finance: Dec. 3, 10, 18, 27

Week of the 1st–8th

One person you deal with seems distant but is in fact pre-occupied. Another shares private information and personal thoughts. End the year by contemplating new possibilities rather than dwelling on missed opportunities.

Week of the 9th–15th

It appears you've been hanging around a Scorpio or two, because you've picked up some of that sign's most notable traits. You're intuitive and can read people like an open book. But you can also be a little too secretive for your own good, especially late in the weekend.

Week of the 16th–22nd

A Capricorn without a plan is like a Maple Leafs fan without a hope. This is a good week to outline your goals for the first half of the new year. With the winter solstice on Saturday, you're feeling less inhibited and can share some private thoughts with a person you're starting to trust.

Week of the 23rd–31st

Take the scenic route as you journey to the end of the year. The detours and distractions make for a memorable week. Your ideas about a relationship continue to evolve, and you don't find it easy to hide your feelings. People respect your strongest asset: your conscience.

What's Ahead for Aquarius

There are a few "new" themes to the year—new opportunities, new relationships, and new destinations. From January till late June, expansive Jupiter is in your fifth house (Gemini), which rules friendship and hobbies. This is a time to build on existing relationships and explore interests that have long intrigued you. Then, when Jupiter moves into your sixth house (Cancer), you'll find yourself putting in more hours at work, paying greater attention to fitness, and spending more time with pets. You'll do better this year in solo or partnership arrangements. June–September is a time for consolidation and change. You may find yourself considering a new job (something connected with your current work rather than anything radically different). Those same months, when most people are distracted by warm weather and vacations, are good for you to concentrate on finances. You'll be able to put your mind to fiscal matters, explore investment ideas, and make sensible plans for the future—not just for the balance of the year, but also for retirement. This doesn't mean you won't be wandering. On the contrary; extending the "new" theme, you may have the chance to visit a place you've always hoped to see. Other planetary influences affect your relationships with neighbours, brothers and sisters, and aunts and uncles and cousins. Your involvement with these individuals mixes compassion with healthy competition. You pick up information that helps you see one person in a new light, while another person challenges your intellect. Your verbal skills are exceptional toward the end of the year. You may not be creating anything original, but will instead help others express their thoughts. While your love life flourishes, especially toward the end of the year, you can't take your partner—or anyone else—for granted. Although much of the year will see you enriching other people's lives, be cautious not to neglect your own health. Aquarius rules the circulatory system and the ankles. Look for activities that benefit both areas—but don't confine yourself to a lonely treadmill. You don't like to feel hemmed in and routines bore you, so keep trying till something clicks. Work your way through the alphabet, and don't stop till Zumba.

January

Your keywords for the month ahead: discretion, motivation, assessment.

Key Days
Romance: Jan. 2, 13, 21, 29
Friends and family: Jan. 4, 16, 24, 31
Career and status: Jan. 7, 15, 23, 30
Finance: Jan. 8, 16, 25, 28

Week of the 1st–6th

Albert Einstein said that anyone who has never made a mistake has never tried anything new. This sums up your week—trial and error, and key lessons learned along the way. A friend tries to trick you into revealing a secret.

Week of the 7th–13th

Be sure you understand the value of your time—you tend to give too much of it away. Someone tries to force you into making a decision or supporting their cause. Seek advice and make sure you're comfortable with anything you agree to, verbally or in writing.

Week of the 14th–20th

It's a socially lively week, and you're easily distracted. Keep an eye on your priorities, especially on Thursday and Friday, when you're tempted to sneak out for a long lunch. You may have to deliver some important news and need to be sure that your tone is appropriate.

Week of the 21st–27th

Avoid the possessive, tactless, and jealous people who seem to surround you all week. You need calm surroundings, positive role models, and supportive friends. Good financial news arrives by Thursday or Friday, but don't broadcast any details until the money is in the bank.

Week of the 28th–31st

Assess professional and personal relationships while the year is young. This is a good week to express your feelings through your personal style. Pick out a scarf and toque in bold or earthy colours, according to the mood you want to project. Help a friend overcome doubts and insecurities.

February

Your keywords for the month ahead: discovery, renewal, diplomacy.

Key Days
Romance: Feb. 6, 15, 23, 27
Friends and family: Feb. 3, 7, 14, 26
Career and status: Feb. 6, 15, 22, 25
Finance: Feb. 4, 13, 20, 28

Week of the 1st–10th
Jot down your best thoughts and ideas. You have keen insights this week and never know when the inspiration will strike. A budding relationship continues to develop, but you may be clashing with an old friend over an ancient issue that needs to be resolved once and for all.

Week of the 11th–17th
There's no shortage of opinions this week, so make yours count and resist the need to please others. Expect to land a new assignment by Thursday or Friday. A friend calls on you for moral support. Provide a broad, comforting shoulder, but don't feel you need to dish out advice.

Week of the 18th–24th

You're dealing with babies, but they're probably over thirty years old. Friends or relatives are hard to handle when they don't get their way. Stick to your principles in a neighbourhood dispute. Though you won't win a popularity contest, you'll sleep better at night.

Week of the 25th–28th

With the full moon on Monday, you help make things happen from a behind-the-scenes position. They say you might be Canadian if someone accidentally steps on your foot and you apologize—and that's how you tend to react this week. Caution: don't take the blame for someone else's mistake.

March

Your keywords for the month ahead: generosity, tenacity, empathy.

Key Days

Romance: March 3, 10, 16, 28

Friends and family: March 6, 14, 22, 26

Career and status: March 5, 13, 20, 28

Finance: March 2, 14, 27, 28

Week of the 1st–10th

When we misplace something—our keys, for instance—it's generally within a mere three feet or so of where it should be. The answers to your questions are closer than you realize. On

Wednesday or Thursday, a postponement gives you a work or social reprieve.

Week of the 11th–17th

You're devoting long hours to a family situation, but exercise and relaxation should be at the top of your priority list. A minor dispute can get out of control, so watch closely for signs of trouble. Keep your eyes open for bargains and free stuff. Don't hesitate to drop hints if there's something you'd like.

Week of the 18th–24th

Uranus, your ruling planet, is connected to discovery. Around the spring equinox on Wednesday, you uncover facts about your family history and learn about new destinations. On Thursday or Friday, you run into someone you've been trying to contact. The weekend sees you finalizing agreements.

Week of the 25th–31st

You're dealing with self-absorbed people plus a co-worker or neighbour who's in the mood for battle. It helps that you can express your feelings rationally and that you're highly resourceful this week. Take your health as seriously as you take the well-being of the people you look after.

April

Your keywords for the month ahead: boundaries, service, solitude.

Key Days
Romance: April 8, 13, 20, 28
Friends and family: April 6, 14, 23, 29
Career and status: April 4, 10, 19, 25
Finance: April 3, 11, 17, 26

Week of the 1st–7th
A partnership is on a steadier course and, thanks to your diplomatic skills (little wonder you're called the voice of sanity), a tense work situation is narrowly avoided. In family matters, however, let someone else play the peacemaker.

Week of the 8th–14th
Perhaps because you value your privacy so highly, you're cautious making commitments at this time. Pay little attention to anyone saying your expectations are unrealistic. You're willing to do what it takes to meet your goals by Friday, but check your reports and emails carefully. A typo could land you in hot water.

Week of the 15th–21st
It's always nice to hear from your fans, and this week a surprise admirer sings your praises. You're not easily shocked, but on Wednesday a colleague's actions may leave you speechless. You have a chance to acquire something of beauty. Regardless of its value, you're not interested in making a profit.

Week of the 22nd–30th
You deal with people who have no idea how to make a long story short. Of course, you provide a few useful tips. You learn that the value of something you own has increased. There's conflict

between your social schedule and your increased workload. Assume you'll rearrange the former to accommodate the latter.

May

Your keywords for the month ahead: expansion, gumption, discretion.

Key Days
Romance: May 5, 16, 27, 31
Friends and family: May 7, 17, 24, 30
Career and status: May 6, 14, 23, 29
Finance: May 4, 9, 22, 31

Week of the 1st–5th
Make joint plans and decisions early in the week. You lean toward extremes on Wednesday and Thursday and tend to do or say too much. Your talent for bringing the right people together makes this an excellent weekend for entertaining at home.

Week of the 6th–12th
You don't handle restrictions well and may feel frustrated on Monday and Tuesday. Think about what you can change for the better and concentrate on those areas. You could be tapped for a job that involves travel or out-of-province clients. A close friend could use a hug—from you—on the weekend.

Week of the 13th–19th
Continue to check information carefully before investing either your time or your cash. You and your partner may not be seeing

eye to eye, but the key is to agree to disagree. This is a good time to get exercise by enjoying sports with friends—you may want to join a table tennis league or a softball team.

Week of the 20th–26th
You love nature, and even if you're not a gardener this is a good time to grow things. Watch that you don't take responsibility for other people's blunders, and go out of your way to set the record straight. You're in charge of arrangements. Try not to offer your committee too many choices.

Week of the 27th–31st
This is not the best week to criticize people you care about. Wait till you learn more about what's going on in their lives. But it's a good time to host a party or other event. You're hospitable and witty, and your style is nothing but deluxe. You meet someone who's eccentric and idealistic—likely a fellow Aquarian.

June

Your keywords for the month ahead: objectivity, versatility, balance.

Key Days
Romance: June 3, 9, 18, 28
Friends and family: June 1, 8, 20, 30
Career and status: June 4, 12, 19, 26
Finance: June 6, 11, 22, 29

Week of the 1st–9th

You procrastinate early in the week, but things click into place and by Wednesday you're super-productive. Your imagination can become overly fertile this weekend as you read too much into what somebody tells you.

Week of the 10th–16th

Defer making important decisions if you're feeling uncertain or just tired. You have an opportunity to become close again with a friend who drifted away. You and your partner's schedules are finally in sync, so consider a date night. Look forward to meeting your intellectual match.

Week of the 17th–23rd

It's hard to gain ground at work, but at least you manage to catch up. It's a good week for making travel plans, especially if you're considering a new destination. It's easy for you to pick up on vibes, so aim to be around upbeat rather than moody types. Something you asked for some time ago arrives on the weekend.

Week of the 24th–30th

This is a good week to lead by example. Your managerial skills are your strong suit, but leave them at the office. Take a less structured and more democratic approach to your personal life. A home improvement project becomes complicated.

July

Your keywords for the month ahead: clarification, expansion, self-improvement.

Key Days
Romance: July 6, 16, 25, 30
Friends and family: July 7, 13, 23, 29
Career and status: July 3, 10, 22, 28
Finance: July 5, 11, 20, 27

Week of the 1st–7th
You start the week with a blank canvas and can accomplish some of the jobs and social activities that you've put on hold. Your research skills prove invaluable as you ferret out useful facts involving work or family.

Week of the 8th–14th
You have a chance to shine in your area of expertise. Submit a poem for publication or a painting for display. Enjoy the pleasure of indulging someone you care about. Monday's new moon sees you experimenting with a new look. There's no need to consult the fashion police—your sense of style is impeccable.

Week of the 15th–21st
People you deal with seem moody, and it's easy to pick up on a negative vibe. Try to see the humour in a situation. It may not be easy, especially when dealing with a nonstop talker, but laughter is your secret weapon. You also need to devote time to a project involving creativity and originality.

Week of the 22nd–31st
There's a side of you that seeks revenge, but don't act in the heat of the moment. Your perspective will gradually change as you learn from other people's examples and mistakes. At the end of

the month you have a reason to feel lucky, but don't leave things to chance.

August

Your keywords for the month ahead: selectivity, activation, intuition.

Key Days
Romance: Aug. 2, 10, 22, 29
Friends and family: Aug. 3, 14, 24, 28
Career and status: Aug. 6, 12, 21, 30
Finance: Aug. 8, 17, 25, 31

Week of the 1st–4th
You can be easily misled—perhaps intentionally—and someone may take advantage of your generosity. Concentrate on what keeps you happy, and keep your distance from petty people and trivial disputes. At work, you make a transition from routine tasks to something more creative.

Week of the 5th–11th
You receive good financial news or encouraging career information, but don't broadcast any of it this week. Drawing people together is a special knack. This is a good week for organizing events coming up in the fall, making travel arrangements, and hosting a small dinner party.

Week of the 12th–18th
Someone seems dull, but your first impressions are slightly off kilter. Your new acquaintance proves far more entertaining than

you expected. Leo, your opposite sign, may try to take over a shared activity. The weekend sees you acquiring knowledge and donating some of your material possessions.

Week of the 19th–25th
Be cautious about stretching the truth—it could come back to haunt you. You have an opportunity to work with someone you admire, but don't let anyone think they're doing you a favour. Don't feel pressured into making decisions, especially ones that involve finance or property.

Week of the 26th–31st
The end of the month is deceptively calm, but behind-the-scenes happenings will make for a lively September. Count on receiving invitations and family-related announcements, and check for possible conflicts. Although ruled by the planet of originality (Uranus), you should opt for an understated fall look.

September
___

Your keywords for the month ahead: responsibility, multi-tasking, advancement.

Key Days
Romance: Sept. 4, 11, 18, 26
Friends and family: Sept. 7, 15, 20, 29
Career and status: Sept. 5, 16, 24, 30
Finance: Sept. 6, 14, 22, 28

Week of the 1st–8th

The combination of good planning and good luck leads to a highly productive week. Satisfy your desire to roam by perusing brochures and visiting travel websites. This is a good time to hunt for antiques and check out garage sales for a future family heirloom.

Week of the 9th–15th

This is a good week to pare down as well as to renovate. Whether dealing with people is part of your work or not, you're superb at public relations. You know how to handle the self-absorbed individuals you're involved with daily. Reflect on a difficult friendship this weekend, and learn from past experience.

Week of the 16th–22nd

Seek out activities that can reduce some of the recent stress you've been under. Communications are a strong point, and a public-speaking performance helps restore your self-confidence. Continue to tend to someone else's health needs, but don't ignore any of your own.

Week of the 23rd–30th

Success always appears in private and failure in plain view. But this doesn't happen to you this week. An influential person takes note of your accomplishments and watches how you handle "failures." You also have a much-needed calming influence on relatives.

October

Your keywords for the month ahead: distraction, interaction, progress.

Key Days
Romance: Oct. 2, 11, 19, 25
Friends and family: Oct. 2, 13, 24, 30
Career and status: Oct. 8, 15, 24, 29
Finance: Oct. 1, 8, 20, 28

Week of the 1st–6th
People are hard to pin down, but continue to persevere. By Friday, you'll hear from your elusive friend or an escape-artist relative. A touchy family matter requires your firm hand. Think again before saying no to what sounds like a mundane invitation.

Week of the 7th–13th
Enjoy your time in the limelight. You excel in a leadership position and earn plaudits for your innovative ideas. A friend's or relative's appearance takes you by surprise on Wednesday or Thursday. Do you really want to let a co-worker or family member off the hook for bad behaviour? Think twice before giving anyone a pass.

Week of the 14th–20th
You're the type of person who buys a book about dealing with procrastination—and then can't get around to reading it. But this week you're highly motivated to catch up on your workload. And on Saturday or Sunday, you receive a long-awaited response from a fellow procrastinator.

Week of the 21st–27th

After a brief period of self-imposed isolation, your social life takes an upturn. You're rubbing shoulders with original, intelligent, eccentric people. You have your eye on a job or an activity; go after it without appearing grabby. It's easy to forget an important birthday, anniversary, or other occasion.

Week of the 28th–31st

There's something romantic about being Canadian, k.d. lang said. You would think she was talking about you. This week, you're sentimental, fun, and inventive. Job-related information can be unreliable, or perhaps you're not absorbing it completely. Seek clarification before making your next move.

November

Your keywords for the month ahead: expansion, experimentation, gathering.

Key Days

Romance: Nov. 8, 19, 22, 29
Friends and family: Nov. 6, 10, 20, 27
Career and status: Nov. 3, 11, 19, 28
Finance: Nov. 4, 13, 21, 30

Week of the 1st–10th

Your partner or a close associate becomes less withdrawn. You in turn are preoccupied from about Tuesday to Friday. There is an emphasis on creativity on the weekend as you experiment with a new technique or medium.

Week of the 11th–17th

Friction in a family situation eases when you take a more forceful approach. Sometime this week you become involved in a secret arrangement. You continue to juggle responsibilities but think about joining forces—possibly with a Libra—and you'll soon see a glimmer of light at the end of the tunnel.

Week of the 18th–24th

You'll be dealing with one or a pair of self-centred individuals. You need a balancing influence, and this is a good week to join forces with a Libra. Don't try too hard to please someone new in your life. An understated style suits you best, both in manner and in appearance.

Week of the 25th–30th

Expect to form a powerful alliance—professional or personal, but not likely both—with Leo, your opposite sign. Together you're certainly stronger than alone. Avoid being argumentative, although someone is trying to bait you. You love diversity and will be all over the map on the weekend.

December

Your keywords for the month ahead: selectivity, assertiveness, new ideas.

Key Days
Romance: Dec. 5, 9, 18, 27
Friends and family: Dec. 7, 17, 24, 29

Career and status: Dec. 2, 10, 23, 27
Finance: Dec. 11, 19, 23, 31

Week of the 1st–8th
Three's a crowd, or the more the merrier? You'll be surrounded with people and, depending on the day and your mood, will either love it or be irritated. This is a good week to upgrade technical equipment and pursue scientific interests.

Week of the 9th–15th
Expect conflict in your everyday environment, but choose your battles. Some things are worth changing, others are not. People thank you for past kindnesses in a meaningful way. Try to hide your reaction to the surprising news that you hear through the week. Business ideas are brightest on the weekend.

Week of the 16th–22nd
The week looks like a buffet table. You need to decide among a confounding number of selections. Don't overload your plate with side dishes, and be sure to leave room for the best desserts. Information easily goes AWOL, so be sure to make copies and back up your files.

Week of the 23rd–31st
Activities that were stalled are reactivated. Don't be modest if you're asked to take a lead role in a project. You're up for the challenge and more qualified than you realize. People make it all about them, which is fine with you. All you really want to do is get on with your interesting work.

What's Ahead for Pisces

February 20–March 20

Neptune, the most spiritual of the planets, is connected with creativity, imagination, and deception. This year, it has a particularly strong influence on your sign. It will promote sharing—you'll be more selective in the people with whom you share your ideas and confidences, and you'll also be the beneficiary of an unknown person's largesse. Another planet that influences you this year is Uranus, which will promote two qualities not generally associated with your sign: tenacity and competitiveness. These traits, which emerge early in the summer and become more intense throughout the year, will surprise the people who know you well and attract those who'd like to know you better. Travel to new destinations, particularly local places, is a theme, and during your journeys you'll find answers that have evaded you. Your financial picture is brightest around February and again in October–November. This doesn't mean you'll be flush at those times; rather, you'll appreciate that money allows you to be more independent. Throughout the year, you continue to bring out the best in others. These people reciprocate by introducing you to new areas of interest, including something athletic. As mentioned, Neptune not only rules your sign but has specific meaning for you. That planet's position will help you unlock your potential, but there's another side to the coin. You can be gullible, and it's comfortable to escape into the past.

These tendencies can be exaggerated this year. You're a slippery fish and can slide into a moody spell. Some of the places you visit can be dark ones, so it's important to surround yourself with upbeat but realistic people. Continue to surprise yourself with newfound confidence and a passion for work, and get used to the feeling. Neptune won't be going anywhere till 2025.

January

Your keywords for the month ahead: alliance, versatility, implementation.

Key Days
Romance: Jan. 5, 11, 20, 26
Friends and family: Jan. 2, 9, 18, 27
Career and status: Jan. 9, 12, 18, 28
Finance: Jan. 5, 11, 21, 30

Week of the 1st–6th
Surround yourself with upbeat people and include them in your plans. Make the first move in repairing a friendship that was strained late last year. Don't feel pressured into making a decision, especially if it involves a close relative.

Week of the 7th–13th
You're inclined to be critical of those you love while letting strangers off the hook for bad behaviour. You need to figure out what's wrong with this picture. Intuition is strongest late in the

week. Combine your financial hunches with research, and review the latest trends.

Week of the 14th–20th

You feel ready to move forward. You're open to new ideas, so don't limit your prospects. You also find you're better able to concentrate, likely because of fewer temptations. As a result of recent discussions or the influence of something you read, you're rethinking a cause that you once defended.

Week of the 21st–27th

Information overload can be a challenge. You're bombarded with facts and need to separate the helpful from the useless ones. This also applies to the humans you're dealing with—some are inspiring, others a drain on your energy. Pick up some culture on the weekend with a trip to a museum or gallery.

Week of the 28th–31st

You do everyone a favour by taking an unexpected hard-nosed approach to a family situation. You lean toward impatience during the middle of the week, but stamina is all-important as you prepare to finish a long job. Your partner or best friend is in a playful, mischievous mood, so have fun.

February

Your keywords for the month ahead: innovation, experimentation, re-evaluation.

Key Days
Romance: Feb. 8, 14, 22, 26
Friends and family: Feb. 3, 11, 19, 23
Career and status: Feb. 7, 18, 26, 27
Finance: Feb. 4, 10, 20, 25

Week of the 1st–10th
You have little patience for self-serving types who expect prefer-ential treatment, but you seem to attract a number of them. On the brighter side, your ideas about decor are smart, and it's an excellent time to make over your favourite place.

Week of the 11th–17th
If at first you don't succeed, then skydiving isn't for you. But this week, continue to perfect an idea or a technique through trial and error. Enjoy a new sense of freedom on Thursday, when a clingy acquaintance finds somebody else to hang onto.

Week of the 18th–24th
You're concerned with two things this week. One has to do with someone's decision to pull out of a project, and the other in-volves your role in a relationship. Avoid extremes in areas such as diet and dress, and try not to be ultra-sensitive on the week-end. Friends are critical but well-meaning.

Week of the 25th–28th
You tend to do things a bit backwards right now. For example, you react to a situation before analyzing the events leading up to it. The week offers a lineup of choices. Select a couple that

allow you to spend time with some of the people you've been neglecting.

March

Your keywords for the month ahead: caution, reflection, planning.

Key Days
Romance: March 2, 15, 21, 28
Friends and family: March 3, 14, 24, 30
Career and status: March 4, 13, 25, 29
Finance: March 2, 9, 22, 26

Week of the 1st–10th
You bring more imagination to a relationship. Expect some mid-week confusion at work because of mixed messages. You may think it superficial, but appearance makes a difference in how people perceive you. You're overdue for a snazzier, more professional look.

Week of the 11th–17th
Evaluate your skills and see how you can apply them in a new way. Your ruling planet, Neptune, is connected with imagination and sensitivity, two qualities you draw on as you look for a solution to a family dilemma. Avoid sudden changes as much as possible, and be cautious about your spending on the weekend.

Week of the 18th–24th

A family event weighs on your mind, and Monday through Wednesday are ideal for reflecting on your next move. Continue to try new approaches as you attempt to reconcile with a friend or get friends to reconcile with each other. A breakthrough is close. Your work, however, favours more traditional methods.

Week of the 25th–31st

Your overwhelming generosity may put someone in an uncomfortable position. In fact, you lean toward excess in several areas and need to cut back on everything from overtime hours to rich foods. On the weekend, take a break from the routine and enjoy an adventure or two.

April

Your keywords for the month ahead: nostalgia, ethics, progress.

Key Days

Romance: April 1, 10, 19, 28
Friends and family: April 5, 6, 17, 26
Career and status: April 3, 11, 23, 29
Finance: April 6, 15, 22, 30

Week of the 1st–7th

Despite recent accomplishments, your confidence dips. It may be because you're too involved in someone else's life. Find your own friends and look for a creative outlet. Senior colleagues seek out your opinions. On the weekend, you receive promising financial news.

Week of the 8th–14th
You'll be on the go all week, and it's important to keep track of projects, details, names, and dates. You find it easier than usual to express yourself, so take the time to share your thoughts to the people who need to hear them. On the weekend, you discover that good things come in small packages.

Week of the 15th–21st
You continue to do a jumble of jobs, but things seem to proceed in a more orderly way. An influential person observes your attention to detail. Resist any temptation to lower your high standards. You're nostalgic for some of the places from your past but must decide whether you really want to return to them.

Week of the 22nd–30th
You're unsure about how to proceed with an activity. There's nothing wrong in changing your mind about how to accomplish something that needs to be done, so long as you have a plan in place by the end of the week. You receive overdue acknowledgement for your work on a community project.

May

Your keywords for the month ahead: originality, reconciliation, renovation.

Key Days

Romance: May 4, 9, 18, 26

Friends and family: May 5, 13, 20, 31

Career and status: May 7, 15, 22, 28

Finance: May 1, 12, 17, 30

Week of the 1st–5th

This week plays like a rerun. And while it may not have the laughs of *Corner Gas*, it's filled with familiar faces and events you've lived through before. Your unique take on a family-related dilemma may appear odd, to say the least, but it brings good results.

Week of the 6th–12th

Computers are slow, emails arrive late, and you feel overdue for a mental tune-up. Take in the car, clean up the computer, and freshen your brain by surrounding yourself with stimulating people. The timing is ideal since you're about to embark on one of the most productive times of the year.

Week of the 13th–19th

People are watching your reactions, including your body language. Generally, try not to overreact to anything—even if you are shocked by some surprising news. Current relationships are favoured over developing ones. Spend time nurturing a friendship that needs a little TLC.

Week of the 20th–26th

Your energy level is high and your self-confidence strong. This week you're eager to associate with people you once thought were out of your league. Tensions with neighbours start to ease, but a relative instigates a conflict on the weekend. A missing object is closer to home than you realize and may turn up on the weekend.

Week of the 27th–31st

A number of changes are taking place around you, and you're the first to understand what's going on. Many hands make light work, but not this week. You're on a tight deadline to complete a job and do best on your own. As the month ends, you enjoy some good laughs with an older and wiser friend.

June

Your keywords for the month ahead: resilience, influence, spirituality.

Key Days

Romance: June 1, 8, 16, 25
Friends and family: June 2, 10, 18, 29
Career and status: June 5, 14, 25, 28
Finance: June 7, 13, 23, 27

Week of the 1st–9th

Setting a realistic goal is the key. You can't expect a 100 percent improvement in a relationship, for example. Settle for 60 percent and continue to work toward your long-term objective. A stubborn relative decides it's time to compromise.

Week of the 10th–16th

Your sign is represented by two fishes swimming in opposite directions, and that's how you feel this week. Plans conflict, and two people vie for your attention. But you're able to adapt and, though exhausted by the weekend, you've become a more focused, assertive, and adventurous individual.

Week of the 17th–23rd

There's a deceptive thread to the week. First, someone you had underestimated turns out to be a loyal friend. Next, a task that initially seems straightforward is full of twists, turns, and surprises. You'll also meet your share of daffy characters and hear some unusual stories about your family history.

Week of the 24th–30th

During the first part of the week, your partner seems to lack spontaneity while you're energetic and impulsive. Then, about Thursday or Friday, you're the one who wants to stay put while your other half is ready to party. Still, the chemistry is always there. Carefully review your calendar for the summer and check for possible conflicts.

July

Your keywords for the month ahead: persistence, transformation, acceptance.

Key Days

Romance: July 7, 19, 24, 30
Friends and family: July 1, 10, 21, 28
Career and status: July 9, 17, 25, 29
Finance: July 3, 9, 18, 26

Week of the 1st–7th

As the second half of the year begins, a rocky relationship is on a surer course and a stalled project is back on track. Someone you deal with regularly, at work or on a community project, is willing to go along with your unconventional ideas.

Week of the 8th–14th

The trick this week is knowing when to blend in and when to stay in the background. Watch out for a reckless stretch on Tuesday or Wednesday, when you're taking risks with finances— your own or someone else's. The weekend is a good time to make family-related requests.

Week of the 15th–21st

You're becoming more vibrant as the week progresses, and by Friday your magnetic personality attracts the attention of someone you admire. Your own partner may be more sensitive than usual, and it will be difficult to get straightforward answers. Take a more imaginative approach to the relationship.

Week of the 22nd–31st

The full moon on Monday the 22nd marks the start of a period that emphasizes endurance and perseverance. You're able to stick things out while others throw in the towel. You may not receive instant recognition, but it will come at an opportune time. Prepare for last-minute changes to weekend plans.

August

Your keywords for the month ahead:
unpredictability, competition, vigour.

Key Days
Romance: Aug. 1, 10, 18, 26
Friends and family: Aug. 3, 11, 19, 28
Career and status: Aug. 6, 14, 22, 27
Finance: Aug. 5, 14, 24, 30

Week of the 1st–4th
Your energy level is high and you can accomplish a good deal both indoors and out. This is also a week of discovery—you may find a meaningful gift or learn something significant about a friend's character. A friend backs out of a commitment—much to your relief.

Week of the 5th–11th
A rebellious streak emerges, and perhaps that's why you're attracted to someone very different from you. Plan on plenty of drama when a family instigator tries to stir up trouble this week. Reliable sources are not as dependable as usual, so don't act on information unless you're certain it's correct.

Week of the 12th–18th

If you've been waiting to introduce a controversial topic, this is the week to do so. You can speak openly and objectively, and your popularity ranking remains high. Someone you deal with is withholding key information, and this is a good time to pry it loose. The weekend marks the start of a period of renewal and reconciliation.

Week of the 19th–25th

You're a fairly uncompetitive person, but this week you play to win—no matter how minuscule the prize. Be cautious after Wednesday, when someone you deal with bends the truth and attempts to mislead you. An old acquaintance tracks you down. Don't reveal too much too soon.

Week of the 26th–31st

The week includes a sprinkling of good news. Still, you need to work further on finance (budgeting) and relationships (not letting down your guard). Your standing remains high among some family members, but others could be a little resentful. A friend recommends a book or movie that could affect you deeply.

September

Your keywords for the month ahead: tenacity, inquisition, compassion.

Key Days

Romance: Sept. 5, 12, 18, 26

Friends and family: Sept. 6, 15, 23, 29

Career and status: Sept. 3, 10, 18, 27
Finance: Sept. 4, 13, 22, 30

Week of the 1st–8th

The week is like a maze. You ultimately reach your goal, but getting there is complicated and confusing. Someone is aiming to take away one of your responsibilities, but be careful, especially on the weekend, not to relinquish control.

Week of the 9th–15th

It's time to put together a top-ten list of things you're aiming to accomplish before the year ends. Settle up shared finances by Friday. Don't stay away from a weekend event because you think it will be a snooze fest. It could provide enough stories to dine out on for several months.

Week of the 16th–22nd

You reveal an assertive side to your personality that few people know, and the shock value alone helps you achieve your desired results. The fall equinox on Sunday launches a period that sees you sprucing up your environment and your wardrobe. Warm tones complement your nurturing personality.

Week of the 23rd–30th

You're about to be acknowledged for your hard work and appreciated for the imagination that you bring to a job. Think twice before turning down an invitation this week. The event could provide an important opportunity for networking. The weekend looks good for closing a deal.

October

Your keywords for the month ahead: imagination, resourcefulness, decisiveness.

Key Days
Romance: Oct. 5, 12, 22, 29
Friends and family: Oct. 1, 12, 21, 26
Career and status: Oct. 9, 18, 24, 30
Finance: Oct. 6, 15, 19, 28

Week of the 1st-6th
As famous Pisces Albert Einstein said, imagination is more important than knowledge. Take a page from Albert's book and add creative touches to a wide range of projects. Expect some tension over a family power play, but avoid making even mild threats.

Week of the 7th-13th
It's tempting to act on a whim, especially early in the week, but take a more conservative approach to finance. In contrast, a personal relationship gets a boost when you add a dash of spontaneity to your routine. Get in touch with friends and family members who've been keeping an uncharacteristically low profile.

Week of the 14th-20th
Your ruling planet, Neptune, is associated with compassion, confusion, and creativity. Your compassion this week is extended to youngsters and animals. There's confusion over a financial

arrangement (don't sign anything without a second opinion). Creativity is boundless. You experiment with a new medium and have a chance to sell your work.

Week of the 21st–27th

Nothing is trivial this week. You may think your role is inconsequential or your ideas unimportant, but your contribution is far greater than you realize. Your playful nature makes you fun to be around, especially on Friday and Saturday. Weekend snoop alert: you need to guard your privacy—including your passwords.

Week of the 28th–31st

You tend to be reclusive but should be out there circulating, meeting people, and getting things done. Tangled lines of communication become unsnarled, and your interest in human nature and romance makes you a favourite guest. Willpower is strong, too, and it's an excellent week to improve your eating habits.

November

Your keywords for the month ahead:
breakthroughs, reconciliation.

Key Days

Romance: Nov. 8, 19, 23, 30
Friends and family: Nov. 7, 11, 21, 25
Career and status: Nov. 5, 14, 25, 29
Finance: Nov. 4, 12, 21, 27

Week of the 1st–10th

This is a time for second chances. If you missed out on an opportunity earlier this year—a prize assignment, perhaps, or a chance to travel—you can try again. Be willing to help others, but avoid people who don't have your interests at heart.

Week of the 11th–17th

If this week had a title, it would be *The Great Balancing Act*. You seem to be splitting your time between a major family responsibility and a professional project. The good news is that help is on the way. An idea that you pitched is stirring up interest.

Week of the 18th–24th

As the year draws to a close, you begin branching out. This is a good week to learn about foreign cultures, take an interest in local politics, or sign up for a course. Although you're dealing with people more assertive than you, your novel approach to a problem gives you a definite advantage on the weekend.

Week of the 25th–30th

Take an inventory of the year's highlights and trouble spots. Remember that letting go doesn't mean you're shirking your responsibilities. You're so empathetic that even pets are now drawn to you. Be willing to help out friends, but know where to draw the line. You can't afford to let other people's problems weigh you down.

December

Your keywords for the month ahead: unity, ambition, contemplation.

Key Days
Romance: Dec. 6, 15, 22, 31
Friends and family: Dec. 7, 12, 23, 28
Career and status: Dec. 4, 12, 19, 27
Finance: Dec. 2, 11, 18, 29

Week of the 1st–8th
With Monday's new moon, you're assertive and articulate—a winning combination that makes you the most persuasive person in the room. There could be some mix-ups around the middle of the week. Double check details if booking a trip at this time.

Week of the 9th–15th
The word "wrong" is rarely preceded with "I'm," but this week you need to correct a mistake. You can do it with humour. You're entrepreneurial and can come up with a sideline for the upcoming year. Thanks to your recent efforts, a family-related responsibility becomes more equitably shared.

Week of the 16th–22nd
Ever the innovative thinker, you come up with a holiday-related plan that is bound to shake things up. Saturday's winter solstice sees you assuming a take-charge approach. This is only the start of a trend that sees you acting decisive and even bossy.

Week of the 23rd–31st

Make it easier for a special someone to express feelings. Provide the right setting and don't force any issues. Give yourself more credit too, and don't pass up an opportunity because you think you're not in the running. You'll hear a hint or two about an important event being planned for the new year.

PART FOUR

THE CHINESE ZODIAC

Note: In the Chinese calendar (a lunisolar calendar), each year starts somewhat later than it does in the Western system. (The Chinese New Year begins on the second new moon after the winter solstice.) If your birthday is in January or February, check the dates carefully in the Birth Year Summaries on page 494 to determine your sign. The Year of the Snake begins February 10, 2013, and ends January 30, 2014. The forecasts that appear in this chapter also include a brief recap of the preceding year, the Year of the Dragon, to cover the start of 2014— January and the first ten days of February.

The Chinese horoscope has been in use for thousands of years. Its twelve signs are determined by the year of birth rather than the month. There are several versions of how the Chinese zodiac originated, the most popular one dating back to Buddha, who invited all the animals to join him before he departed from Earth. Twelve animals arrived to bid him farewell—the rat first (on the back of the ox), and the pig last, and Buddha named a year after each one, in order of their arrival.

The animal ruling the year in which you were born has a great influence on your life. According to a Chinese expression, "This is the animal that hides in your heart."

The Year of the Snake

The Chinese snake is different from its Western counterpart. The snake of the Chinese zodiac is no slithery devil. Rather, it's a wise, philosophical, elegant, and well-spoken creature. It bites—but its greatest weapon is its stinging tongue. It can wound with its sarcastic words.

The snake is a serpentine contradiction. It is sociable, yet private. It can be aloof but is seductive and charming. It is generous and kind, but then turns possessive. It works hard, but it also takes great pleasure in being lazy. People born in the Year of the Snake are philosophical, shrewd, and masters of timing. They rely on first impressions and have a sixth sense about people. They're judgmental (and proud of it), and can be very sore losers.

While Westerners consider the snake to be devious, the Chinese respect it for its discretion and determination. People born in the Year of the Snake are said to be born under the sign of wisdom. A snake's mind is always active. And snakes follow through on what they set out to do. They thrive on deadlines—the tighter, the better.

In general, people born in the Year of the Snake are good at business and achieve financial independence. They prefer to work alone. They place importance on money, which they manage wisely. Are snakes driven? Definitely! Are they lucky? Yes. But they make their own luck. Snakes also have impeccable taste and style. They love to read, dress impeccably, enjoy fine food and wines, and feel right at home in elegant surroundings.

Snakes are regarded as good omens. The Year of the Snake is considered a time for preparation and reflection, allowing us to catch our breath in the wake of the larger-than-life Year of the Dragon. But it's hardly a passive year. In snake years, Queen Elizabeth II was crowned, the Canadian Space Agency was created, and the Maple Leaf became Canada's national flag. Breakthroughs occur and differences are settled throughout the Year of the Snake, but we must watch for opportunities and make choices.

Snapshots of Your Chinese Zodiac Sign

The Rat (Shu)

Years of the rat: 1912, 1924, 1936, 1948, 1960, 1972, 1984, 1996, 2008

The rat is the first Chinese zodiac sign. It is most compatible with the ox, dragon, and monkey and has a difficult relationship with the goat, rooster, and horse. Rats generally enjoy sports (especially basketball) and excel at crafts. The rat is roughly equivalent to Sagittarius in the Western zodiac.

People born in the Year of the Rat are said to be:

Ambitious—sometimes overly ambitious

Creative and imaginative

Demanding—you push others hard

Disciplined—you detest waste and laziness

Forthright, upfront, often too blunt

Generous, yet occasionally greedy

Gullible—you can fall into a trap

Impatient—you take shortcuts (sometimes with bad results)

Intelligent, witty, bursting with ideas

Laid-back, outgoing, charismatic

Level-headed—you thrive in a crisis

Manipulative and envious

Not a strong leader

Protective and charitable

Prudent—with the ability to preserve wealth

Sharp—you're a quick study and have a good memory

Rat careers include:

Broadcaster

Editor

Entrepreneur

Jobs that involve creativity

Jobs that require organization

Manager

Musician

Politician

Salesperson

Writer

Some famous rats:

Playwright William Shakespeare

Composer Wolfgang Amadèus Mozart

Artist Claude Monet

Activist June Callwood

Hockey player Johnny Bower

Singer/songwriter Stompin' Tom Connors

Environmentalist David Suzuki

Actor Robert Redford

Actor Billy Crystal

Actor Michael Caine

Hockey player Bobby Orr

Composer Andrew Lloyd Webber

Actor Kathy Bates

Actor Jeremy Irons
Singer Olivia Newton-John
Prince Charles
Actor Antonio Banderas
Actor Colin Firth
Actor Julia Louis-Dreyfus
Basketball player Shaquille O'Neal
Figure skater Elvis Stojko
Hockey player Martin Brodeur
Actor Ben Affleck
Actor Gwyneth Paltrow
Prince Harry
Singer/songwriter Avril Lavigne
Actor Scarlett Johansson

Forecast for 2013:

In the Year of the Dragon you enjoyed increased prestige and made friends with people from a variety of backgrounds. Your romantic life took a back seat to your profession, but this year relationships are again in the forefront. You meet influential people as you continue to pursue an interest in politics, sales, or public relations. Property matters are generally favourable, but neighbours can be difficult. Remain alert to possible deceptions. Seek out the best professional advice as you deal with your own health and that of your loved ones. Secretive people become more upfront and encourage you to be more open as well. Explore platonic friendships and spend more time among these signs: monkey, dragon, and snake. Dealings with any of these signs require caution: pig, horse, and dog.

Five kinds of rat:

In Chinese astrology, each of the five kinds of rat is associated with an element (water, wood, fire, earth, and metal). To find out which kind you are and what that means, see the year of your birth in the summaries that begin on page 494.

The Ox (Niu)

Years of the ox: 1913, 1925, 1937, 1949, 1961, 1973, 1985, 1997, 2009

The ox is the second Chinese zodiac sign. It is most compatible with the rat, rabbit, and rooster and has a difficult relationship with the horse, goat, dog, tiger, and dragon. Oxen generally enjoy music, cooking, and gardening. The ox is roughly equivalent to Capricorn in the Western zodiac.

People born in the Year of the Ox are said to be:

Brave—not easily frightened

Calm—patience is your middle name

Cautious—you prefer to play things safe

Grudge-holding—you don't forgive easily, and you rarely forget

Hard-working—diligence, not luck, is the key to your success

Highly motivated

Literal-minded—you need to work on your sense of humour

Logical and clear-thinking—the head, not the heart, is your ruler

Materialistic—the ox symbolizes prosperity

Natural leader

Outspoken—communication skills need honing

Quick-tempered

Rigid—once your mind is made up, you rarely change it

Stubborn and obstinate—you don't really appreciate advice or
suggestions

Oxen careers include:

Actor

Archaeologist

Carpenter

Construction worker

Doctor

Horticulturalist

Mechanic

Military leader

Real estate agent

Scientist

Some famous oxen:

Artist Tom Thomson

Musician Oscar Peterson

Actor Leslie Nielsen

Actor Jack Nicholson

Actor Bill Cosby

Actor Dustin Hoffman

Swimmer Marilyn Bell

Actor Jessica Lange

Actor Meryl Streep
Guitarist Liona Boyd
Actor Richard Gere
Actor Michael J. Fox
Princess Diana
U.S. president Barack Obama
Singer/songwriter k.d. lang
Comedian/actor Jim Carrey
Hockey player Wayne Gretzky
Singer Susan Boyle
Actor Eddie Murphy
Actor George Clooney
Hockey player Eric Lindros
Singer Rufus Wainwright
Actor Neve Campbell
Supermodel/singer Kate Moss
Actor Keira Knightley
Figure skater Joannie Rochette

Forecast for 2013:

In the Year of the Dragon, you became more innovative and experimented with new ideas. You faced a series of challenges and took charge of crises. In the Year of the Snake, you need to settle differences quickly before small disagreements mushroom out of control. Seek out new interests, especially ones that challenge your mind and involve people you respect. Your financial judgment is clearer, but you need to avoid risks and seek information from reliable sources. Your communication skills improve greatly. You may be tapped for a job that involves public speaking. Romance sees you taking a more active role and becoming more attentive to your partner. Avoid extremes—balance is the key, particularly in your diet. You may be reconciling with a member of one of the following signs: rat, sheep/goat, and rooster. Be aware of hidden motives when dealing with these signs: tiger, horse, and monkey.

Five kinds of ox:

In Chinese astrology, each of the five kinds of ox is associated with an element (water, wood, fire, earth, and metal). To find out which kind you are and what that means, see the year of your birth in the summaries that begin on page 494.

The Tiger (Hu)

Years of the tiger: 1914, 1926, 1938, 1950, 1962, 1974, 1986, 1998, 2010

The tiger is the third Chinese zodiac sign. It is most compatible with the dragon, horse, dog, rabbit, and pig and has a difficult relationship with the snake, rooster, ox, and monkey. Tigers generally like theatre, sports, and travel to unusual destinations. The tiger is roughly equivalent to Aquarius in the Western zodiac.

People born in the Year of the Tiger are said to be:

Charismatic—you have a magnetic personality
Competitive—you love to take on a challenge
Courageous and passionate—you fight for those you love and what you believe in
Creative and innovative

Driven and intense—you immerse yourself in whatever captures your interest

Farsighted—you look at a situation and see both the forest and the trees

Fortunate—you seem blessed with good looks

Leaders—you take chances

Moody and restless

Not materialistic—money and power mean little; loyalty and honesty mean everything

Optimistic

Resilient—you always land on your feet

Self-reliant—you enjoy companionship but don't depend on others

Skeptical—you're not easily convinced

Tactical—you're always one step ahead of the others

Vain—you adore being the centre of attention and don't like being ignored

Tiger careers include:
Activist
Actor
Advertising position
Explorer
Jobs that involve challenges
Jobs that involve variety
Leadership positions
Musician
Driver or pilot
Travel agent
Writer

Some famous tigers:

Humanitarian Dr. Norman Bethune

Actor Alec Guinness

Queen Elizabeth II

Author Margaret Laurence

Movie director Norman Jewison

Cuban president Fidel Castro

Actor Martha Henry

Singer/songwriter Gordon Lightfoot

Hockey player Bobby Hull

Journalist/governor general Adrienne Clarkson

Actor Martin Short

Musician Peter Frampton

TV host Jay Leno

Actor John Candy

Singer Jon Bon Jovi

Singer/songwriter Jann Arden

Actor Tom Cruise

Actor Steve Carell

Actor Nia Vardalos

TV host Jon Stewart

Actor Penelope Cruz

Singer/songwriter Alanis Morissette

Actor Hilary Swank

Actor Leonardo DiCaprio

Figure skater David Pelletier

Singer Lady Gaga

Actor Lindsay Lohan

Actor Lea Michele

Forecast for 2013:

In the Year of the Dragon, you became more unconventional in your dealings and discovered a playful side to your personality. The Year of the Snake is a pioneering year. You visit places for the first time, develop new interests, and make a contribution to your profession through self-taught skills. Motivation is strong, but you tend to become disillusioned with people who don't meet your sometimes impossibly high standards. Your good fortune increases, but take care to be more protective of your money-making ideas. Relationships are on a steady path, but you need to listen to what people are saying and understand what they are not saying. Business partnerships are favourable, but keep track of expenses. You take an interest in health and science, yet need to devote more time to your own well-being. Encourage relationships with these signs: dragon, rat, and other tigers. Be more guarded when dealing with these signs: ox, pig, and monkey.

Five kinds of tiger:

In Chinese astrology, each of the five kinds of tiger is associated with an element (water, wood, fire, earth, and metal). To find out which kind you are and what that means, see the year of your birth in the summaries that begins on page 494.

The Rabbit (Tu)

Years of the rabbit: 1915, 1927, 1939, 1951, 1963, 1975, 1987, 1999, 2011

The rabbit is the fourth Chinese zodiac sign. It is most compatible with the ox, snake, goat, rat, dog, and pig and has a difficult relationship with the dragon, monkey, horse, and rooster. Rabbits are chatty creatures, and they're also calm and non-confrontational. They're alert, intelligent, and intuitive—and can talk themselves out of any jam. Rabbits enjoy their possessions and are house proud. The rabbit is roughly equivalent to Pisces in the Western zodiac.

People born in the Year of the Rabbit are said to be:

Artistic—painting, music, or poetry may be among your
    interests

Careful and calm—you make your point without raising
    your voice

Confident and self-assured

Conservative—not always willing to change

Considerate . . . yet you manage to put yourself first

Lucky—among the most fortunate of all the Chinese zodiac signs

Negative—your glass tends to be half empty rather than half full

Objective—but sometimes detached

Orderly, tidy, well organized

Peaceable—you rarely make enemies

Persuasive and blessed with good communication skills

Serene and gentle

Strong-willed

Stylish—you have a flair for current trends

Thoughtful—but sometimes you think too much.

Touchy and overly sensitive

Rabbit careers include:

Actor

Artist

Communications specialist
Diplomat
Fashion designer
Politician
Public relations specialist
Teacher
Therapist
Trouble-shooter
Writer

Some famous rabbits:
Artist Emily Carr
Singer/songwriter Judy Collins
Author Margaret Atwood
Actor Liv Ullmann
Dancer Karen Kain
Actor Geoffrey Rush
Actor Robin Williams
Hockey player Marcel Dionne
Hockey player Guy Lafleur
Singer/songwriter Sheryl Crow
Basketball player Michael Jordan
Actor Eric McCormack
Actor Mike Myers
Actor Johnny Depp
Home renovator Mike Holmes
Actor Brad Pitt
Actor Drew Barrymore
Soccer player David Beckham
Actor Angelina Jolie

Actor Tobey Maguire
Singer Michael Bublé
Actor Kate Winslett
Actor Ellen Page
Hockey player Sidney Crosby

Forecast for 2013:

The Year of the Dragon saw an increase in your good fortune. You were admired for your dedication to good causes, particularly environmental projects. In the Year of the Snake, you continue to pursue idealistic goals while also focusing on property-related matters and long-distance communications and travel. This is a better year for solo or partnership ventures than for those involving large teams or committees. You have a golden opportunity to reconcile with a relative or friend, but you need to swallow your pride and make the first move. Young people influence you in ways that are often positive, and you are a strong role model for the elderly. Personal relationships show greater stability, but family conflicts need to be settled promptly. Promote relationships with these signs: sheep/goat, snake, and other rabbits. Be super cautious when dealing with these signs: horse, ox, and dragon.

Five kinds of rabbit:

In Chinese astrology, each of the five kinds of rabbit is associated with an element (water, wood, fire, earth, and metal). To find out which kind you are and what that means, see the year of your birth in the summaries that begin on page 494.

The Dragon (Long)

Years of the dragon: 1916, 1928, 1940, 1952, 1964, 1976, 1988, 2000, 2012

The dragon is the fifth Chinese zodiac sign. It is most compatible with the rat, tiger, snake, monkey, and pig and has a difficult relationship with the rabbit, goat, ox, dog, and other dragons. Dragons have a magical quality. They are free-spirited, highly energetic, nonconforming creatures that march to their own drummer. They are larger than life and fired with enthusiasm. Generous and proud to a fault, they have trouble accepting help from their friends. The dragon is roughly equivalent to Aries in the Western zodiac.

People born in the Year of the Dragon are said to be:

Arrogant, obsessive, and demanding—you expect perfection from everyone, especially yourself

Conceited

Confident—sometimes overly confident

Domineering

Driven—you need a cause in your life

Eccentric and uninhibited

Flamboyant . . . and intimidating

Forgiving—you don't hold grudges

Logical and technical-minded

Outspoken—you don't hesitate to question authority

Protective, yet not a natural nurturer

Proud and independent to a fault

Successful—you can accomplish great things

Take-charge—you're a magnetic leader
Thrill-seeking

Dragon careers include:
Architect
Computer analyst
Doctor
Engineer
Inventor
Jobs involving perseverance
Lawyer
Nurse
Politician
Salesperson
Therapist.

Some famous dragons:
Psychoanalyst Sigmund Freud
Hockey player Gordie Howe
Author Maya Angelou
Figure skater Barbara Ann Scott
Revolutionary Che Guevara
Reverend Martin Luther King, Jr.
Racer Mario Andretti
Movie director Bernardo Bertolucci
Actor Al Pacino
TV host Alex Trebek
Beatle John Lennon
Opera singer Placido Domingo

Actor Liam Neeson
Actor Dan Aykroyd
Russian prime minister Vladimir Putin
Fashion model Elle Macpherson
Actor Russell Crowe
TV host Stephen Colbert
Actor Sandra Bullock
Actor Keanu Reeves
Singer/songwriter Diana Krall
Actor Reese Witherspoon
Football player Peyton Manning
Singer Taylor Hicks
Singer Rihanna
Actor Michael Cera

Forecast for 2013:

The Year of the Dragon inspired you to turn your attention to good causes. You overcame setbacks and made some wise financial moves. The Year of the Snake is a year for flexibility, and you learn to take a less rigid approach to your work as well as your relationships. Zero in on your finances—you need to balance your budgets and keep track of expenses. Balance, in fact, is a theme of a year that includes both an active social life and a large number of work obligations. Try to avoid being drawn into family squabbles—you're best to stay impartial. This is a year for expansion. Your circle of friends widens and, especially if you are self-employed, it is a good time to launch a new project. With so much activity, it's easy to burn up energy, so rest is essential. Enjoy interactions with these signs: rooster, rabbit, and dog. Be cautious and thorough when dealing with these signs: pig, tiger, and snake.

Five kinds of dragon:

In Chinese astrology, each of five kinds of dragon is associated with an element (water, wood, fire, earth, and metal). To find out which kind you are and what that means, see the year of your birth in the summaries that begin on page 494.

The Snake (She)

Years of the snake: 1917, 1929, 1941, 1953, 1965, 1977, 1989, 2001, 2013

The snake is the sixth Chinese zodiac sign. It is most compatible with the rabbit, dragon, rooster, rat, ox, and goat and has a difficult relationship with the tiger, horse, monkey, and pig. Snakes are private creatures, known for their intelligence, cool and confident air, pickiness, and—naturally—their bite. It has a sharp wit, quick temper, and mysterious nature. The snake is roughly equivalent to Taurus in the Western zodiac.

People born in the Year of the Snake are said to be:

Astute—you are a quick study

Cautious in business

Considered a good omen

Cunning and crafty

Deliberative—you think before taking action

Elegant and mannerly

Funny and sarcastic—with a biting wit

Goal-oriented

Intelligent and naturally wise

Mysterious—always the object of curiosity

Pensive—but you don't communicate well
Possessive—you have a jealous side
Private and independent—you prefer not to solicit advice
Skeptical—you're not easily convinced
Superstitious

Snake careers include:
Astrologer
Businessperson
Dietitian
Financier
Jeweller
Jobs involving management
Jobs involving tight deadlines
Philosopher
Private investigator
Scientist

Some famous snakes:
Humorist Stephen Leacock
Artist Pablo Picasso
Singer Ella Fitzgerald
South African president Nelson Mandela
Architect Frank Gehry
Actor Julie Christie
Singer/songwriter Bob Dylan
Governor General David Johnston
Author/publisher Martha Stewart
Singer/songwriter David Clayton-Thomas
Singer/songwriter Paul Simon

Singer/songwriter Art Garfunkel
Singer Michael Bolton
Actor Rick Moranis
TV host Oprah Winfrey
Actor Sarah Jessica Parker
Figure skater Elizabeth Manley
Singer/songwriter Shania Twain
Actor Charlie Sheen
Hockey player Patrick Roy
Hockey player Mario Lemieux
Actor Ben Stiller
Figure skater Jamie Salé
Actor Daniel Radcliffe
Singer Taylor Swift

Forecast for 2013:

The Year of the Dragon encouraged a more direct and understanding approach to your partners, with an emphasis on shared decisions and finances. In the Year of the Snake, continue to allow those close to you, especially family, to have greater input into decisions. Be alert to professional opportunities, not only in your field but especially in other areas, and keep your eye on changes that may affect the workplace as well as your community. Born in the Year of the Snake, you have the great advantage of being intuitive. You're blessed with a good memory and you understand the motives of cohorts as well as competitors. As much as you enjoy living well, inner beauty means more than material trappings, and as the year progresses, your expectations become more modest and you find yourself drawn to spiritual areas. Enjoy interactions with these signs: rabbit, rooster, and dragon. Take nothing for granted when dealing with these signs: tiger, horse, and pig.

Five kinds of snake:
In Chinese astrology, each of the five kinds of snake is associated with an element (water, wood, fire, earth, and metal). To find out which kind you are and what that means, see the year of your birth in the summaries that begin on page 494.

The Horse (Ma)

Years of the horse: 1918, 1930, 1942, 1954, 1966, 1978, 1990, 2002
The horse is the seventh Chinese zodiac sign. It is most compatible with the tiger, sheep/goat, dog, and rooster and has a difficult relationship with the ox, rat, rabbit, snake, and monkey. Horses are strong, intelligent, trustworthy, down to earth, and attractive. They like to explore new places. They can be obstinate and occasionally temperamental but are always well-meaning. The horse is roughly equivalent to Gemini in the Western zodiac.

People born in the Year of the Horse are said to be:
Agile—mentally as well as physically
Cheerful and upbeat
Earthy, not pretentious
Experimental—you enjoy trying new things
Fickle—you fall in love . . . and out of love
Independent (or, more precisely, you don't want to depend
  on others)

Manipulative

Moody and sometimes vain

Not always a logical thinker—you will jump to conclusions

Persistent and persevering

Persuasive, with a commanding presence

Self-reliant, and hesitant to seek help

Spontaneous—you enjoy taking off on a whim

Sporty—you love exercise

Verbose—you love to chat . . . and chat

Well-groomed and nice-looking

Horse careers include:

Comedian

Communications specialist

Librarian

Pilot

Poet

Politician

Public speaker

Restaurateur

Salesperson

Teacher

Tour guide

Some famous horses:

Merchant Timothy Eaton

Composer Stephen Sondheim

Actor Gordon Pinsent

Opera singer Maureen Forrester

Actor Sean Connery

Author Mordecai Richler
Singer/actor Barbra Streisand
Beatle Paul McCartney
Actor Genevieve Bujold
Actor Harrison Ford
Movie director Martin Scorsese
Actor John Travolta
Actor Jerry Seinfeld
Movie director James Cameron
Singer/songwriter Elvis Costello
Rower Silken Laumann
Figure skater Kurt Browning
Actor Adam Sandler
Actor Kiefer Sutherland
Actor Ashton Kutcher
Basketball player Kobe Bryant
Actor Rachel McAdams
Actor Katherine Heigl
Singer/songwriter Nelly Furtado
Actor/director Sarah Polley
Actor Emma Watson
Figure skater Patrick Chan

Forecast for 2013:

The Year of the Dragon saw you rely less on others and enjoy greater spontaneity. You also became more willing to compromise. In the Year of the Snake, you need be alert to opportunities but, just as importantly, you must be aware of traps. This is a good time to set the foundation for future projects. Your family responsibilities increase, and it's time to ask someone to help share the load. Projects involving the home are favoured. Local and long-distance trips are also highlighted, and you have a chance to visit a place you always dreamed of seeing. Situations change quickly this year, and expenses may arise suddenly. Beware of a tendency to act impulsively and make decisions without weighing the pros against the cons. This caution applies to several areas—health, business, and dealings with neighbours. Attempt to spend more time with these signs: dog, sheep/goat, rooster. Take a calculated approach if negotiating with these signs: snake and rat.

Five kinds of horse:

In Chinese astrology, each of the five kinds of horse is associated with an element (water, wood, fire, earth, and metal). To find out which kind you are and what that means, see the year of your birth in the summaries that begin on page 494.

The Sheep/Goat (Yang)

Years of the sheep/goat: 1919, 1931, 1943, 1955, 1967, 1979, 1991, 2003

The sheep/goat is the eighth Chinese zodiac sign. It is most compatible with the rabbit, horse, pig, snake, monkey, and other sheep/goats and has a difficult relationship with the rat, ox, dragon, and rooster. Sheep/goats are peace-loving creatures, secure and content by nature. Appearance and hospitality are both important. They are stylish dressers and wonderful hosts. They're happy to stay in the background, looking after loved ones and enjoying life's simple pleasures. The sheep/goat is roughly equivalent to Cancer in the Western zodiac.

People born in the Year of the Sheep/Goat are said to be:

Artistic—you enjoy the arts, crafts, and hobbies

Emotional and at times insecure

Forgiving—sometimes too trusting

Freedom-loving

Gullible—people can take advantage of you

Honest—but sometimes it's difficult for you to be objective

Indecisive

Kind-hearted—you're the Good Samaritan of the Chinese zodiac

Non-confrontational—you do almost anything to avoid discord

Nurturing

Peace-loving

Private—you keep your worries to yourself

Romantic—and sometimes hopelessly so

Upbeat—your glass is half full and your cheerful nature is infectious

Well-liked and popular

Sheep/goat careers include:

Artist or illustrator

Astrologer

Craftsperson

Doctor

Editor

Fashion designer

Interior designer

Musician

Salesperson

Writer

Some famous sheep/goats:

Inventor Alexander Graham Bell

Prime Minister Pierre Elliott Trudeau

Actor William Shatner

Author Alice Munro

Hockey player Jean Béliveau

Singer/songwriter Carole King

Beatle George Harrison

Skier Nancy Greene

Movie director David Cronenberg

Actor Christopher Walken

Actor Robert DeNiro

Author Michael Ondaatje

Singer/songwriter Joni Mitchell

Opera singer Joan Sutherland

Singer Keith Richards

Apple CEO Steve Jobs

Actor Bruce Willis

Microsoft chairman Bill Gates

Actor Whoopi Goldberg

Actor Howie Mandel

Actor Nicole Kidman

Actor Pamela Anderson

Actor Julia Roberts

Singer Lance Bass

Forecast for 2013:

In the Year of the Dragon you branched out and experimented with new areas of interest. Along the way, you met people in high places. The Year of the Snake is less showy. But while you won't rub shoulders with the rich and the famous, you'll meet people who inspire you to do your best work. You're a late starter, and this is the year you're motivated to write, paint, or take up a musical instrument. You find yourself laughing more, and you feel at home no matter where you find yourself. Despite this low-key approach, you have some outstanding opportunities to build up your finances. Reconciliation is a theme of the year as you realize it's never too late to mend fences with those who once played an important role in your life. The year emphasizes sharing. Some of your responsibilities will be divided among others, and many people find you a trusted confidant to whom they can reveal their secrets and concerns. Encourage interactions with these signs: rat, rooster, and monkey. Be on your toes when dealing with these signs: tiger, horse, and dragon.

Five kinds of sheep/goat:
In Chinese astrology, each of the five kinds of sheep/goat is associated with an element (water, wood, fire, earth, and metal). To find out which kind you are and what that means, see the year of your birth in the summaries that begin on page 494.

The Monkey (Hou)

Years of the monkey: 1920, 1932, 1944, 1956, 1968, 1980, 1992, 2004
The monkey is the ninth Chinese zodiac sign. It is most compatible with the rat, dragon, sheep/goat, dog, and pig and has a difficult relationship with the rabbit, horse, tiger, and other monkeys.

Monkeys are charming, clever, highly imaginative, and up to any challenge. Naturally curious creatures, they are, predictably, quick studies. They like being challenged—and they love playing games, tricks, and practical jokes. Monkeys can also be suspicious and narcissistic. The monkey is roughly equivalent to Leo in the Western zodiac.

People born in the Year of the Monkey are said to be:
Agile—mentally and physically
Artistic
Brainy—you love all sorts of puzzles
Charming, endearing, funny, sociable
Clever—you master whatever you put your mind (or hands) to
Crafty and competitive
Cunning and sneaky . . . you often look for the easy way out
Flirtatious
Game for anything
Inquisitive—curiosity is your middle name
Know-it-alls
Narcissistic . . . often with a superiority complex
Optimistic—you're seldom discouraged
Verbose—you love to gab
Vigorous, bubbly, full of life

Monkey careers include:
Accountant or bookkeeper
Banker
Businessperson
Director (movie or theatre)

Engineer
Politician
Researcher
Salesperson
Scientist
Stockbroker
Teacher

Some famous monkeys:
Author Pierre Berton
Actor Elizabeth Taylor
Pianist Glenn Gould
Singer Diana Ross
Publisher Conrad Black
TV producer Lorne Michaels
Actor Eddie Murphy
Dancer Evelyn Hart
Actor Tom Hanks
Actor Kim Cattrall
Princess Caroline of Monaco
Actor Molly Ringwald
Actor Daniel Craig
Singer Céline Dion
Actor Hugh Jackman
Actor/musician Jill Hennessy
Actor Jennifer Aniston
Tennis player Venus Williams
Singer Jessica Simpson
Actor Ryan Gosling
Actor Jake Gyllenhaal

Singer Alicia Keys
Singer Justin Timberlake
Singer Miley Cyrus

Forecast for 2013:
The Year of the Dragon encouraged an innovative approach to relationships and work. You grew intellectually and acquired some luxuries. In the Year of the Snake your relations with others improve, but you must choose your words carefully. Voicing opinions is one thing, but you need to be more diplomatic if you want to get ahead financially. The year provides an array of choices, but you must wait patiently for the right moment before activating a plan or making a request. You're inspired to seek out knowledge and may be upgrading your education. You may also wind up in a leadership role, even though you don't actively pursue it. Selectivity is important throughout the year—your health may suffer if you take on too many things. Your dealings with these signs bring out the best in you: rat, tiger, and sheep/goat. Don't monkey around when dealing with these tricky signs: rabbit, rooster, and other monkeys.

Five kinds of monkey:
In Chinese astrology, each of the five kinds of monkey is associated with an element (water, wood, fire, earth, and metal). To find out which kind you are and what that means, see the year of your birth in the summaries that begin on page 494.

The Rooster (Ji)

Years of the rooster: 1921, 1933, 1945, 1957, 1969, 1981, 1993, 2005

The rooster is the tenth Chinese zodiac sign. It is most compatible with the ox, snake, horse, and pig and has a difficult relationship with the tiger, sheep/goat, dog, rabbit, and—especially—other roosters. Roosters are flamboyant extroverts. They are natural actors and are highly motivated. They are known to be blunt—they crow it as it is. Although it can be haughty, it is never uppity. A rooster is a dependable and much-treasured friend. The rooster is roughly equivalent to Virgo in the Western zodiac.

People born in the Year of the Rooster are said to be:
Career-oriented, motivated, driven
Conservative—you prefer tried and true to new and different
Demanding
Detail-oriented
Dignified and proud
Dramatic—you love to "strut your stuff"
Fashionable, trendy, style-conscious
Humorous
Image-conscious . . . immaculately groomed
Loyal and dependable
Naive but hopeful
Overbearing but polite
Self-centred . . . never shy about promoting your achievements
Sociable—as long as you're in the limelight
Straightforward, upfront
Tidy and organized—your desk *and* your drawer are in order

Rooster careers include:

Accountant or bookkeeper

Actor

Banker

Dancer

Detective

Doctor

Insurance agent

Journalist

Nurse

Restaurateur

Stockbroker

Some famous roosters:

Feminist Nellie McClung

Prime Minister Lester B. Pearson

Author Farley Mowat

Hockey player Maurice "Rocket" Richard

Comedian/actor Carol Burnett

Hockey coach Scotty Bowman

Prime Minister Jean Chrétien

TV host Don Cherry

Singer/songwriter Eric Clapton

Singer Anne Murray

Actor Steve Martin

Violinist Yitzhak Perlman

Singer/songwriter Neil Young

Astronaut Roberta Bondar

Actor Diane Keaton

Actor Daniel Day-Lewis

Journalist/governor general Michaëlle Jean

Actor Ellen DeGeneres

Actor Javier Bardem

Actor Renée Zellweger

Actor Jason Priestley

Actor Catherine Zeta-Jones

Singer Nikki Yanofsky

Singer Justin Bieber

Forecast for 2013:

In the Year of the Dragon, you enjoyed modest financial gains through a combination of hard work and good timing. The Year of the Snake continues to be about "us" rather than "me." Partnership activities are favoured, both in your professional and your personal life. You may be forming an alliance with someone who will become a lifetime friend. You'll be recognized for work that you did last year, but don't expect tangible rewards. Follow up on small problems, especially those involving money, and don't wait for them to correct themselves. Relationships with relatives thrive as a result of your more laid-back approach. Watch out for a tendency to be the first to volunteer for every job and family responsibility. You need to take a more proactive approach to health and fitness and aim to avoid stressful situations. Strengthen ties with these signs: pig, dog, and tiger. Take nothing for granted when dealing with these signs: rabbit, sheep/goat, and monkey.

Five kinds of rooster:

In Chinese astrology, each of the five kinds of rooster is associated with an element (water, wood, fire, earth, and metal). To find out which kind you are and what that means, see the year of your birth in the summaries that begin on page 494.

The Dog (Gou)

Years of the dog: 1922, 1934, 1946, 1958, 1970, 1982, 1994, 2006

The dog is the eleventh Chinese zodiac sign. It is most compatible with the tiger, horse, pig, rat, rabbit, monkey, and other dogs and has a difficult relationship with the ox, rooster, and dragon. Dogs are empathetic, loyal, and self-sacrificing. They are compassionate creatures, though sometimes too attentive. They need to spend more time tending to their own needs. Dogs like to sniff around and see what's going on—but sometimes they're plain nosy. The dog is roughly equivalent to Libra in the Western zodiac.

People born in the Year of the Dog are said to be:

Anxious—you worry about those you love and can overwhelm them

Decisive and wise

Discreet—you know how to keep a secret

Fair—you always pull your own weight

Open-minded and non-judgmental

Outspoken—you say what you mean and don't mince words

Perceptive—you can see through others and read their motives like a book

Responsible and reliable

Self-sacrificing—you place the well-being of others ahead of your own

Short-tempered

Snoopy

Tenacious . . . you dig and dig until you find what you're
   seeking

Too trusting of others

Truthful and upfront—never deceptive or sly

Well-liked and popular

Dog careers include:
Critic

Doctor

Editor

Teacher

Interior designer

Judge

Police officer

Politician

Scientist

Social worker

Some famous dogs:
Prime Minister John A. Macdonald

British prime minister Winston Churchill

Author Lucy Maud Montgomery

Singer Judy Garland

Anthropologist Jane Goodall

Actor Shirley MacLaine

Actor Donald Sutherland

Actor Sophia Loren

Singer/songwriter Leonard Cohen

Actor Judi Dench
Actor Maggie Smith
Singer/actor Elvis Presley
Singer Liza Minnelli
Magnate Donald Trump
General Roméo Dallaire
U.S. president Bill Clinton
Actor Eugene Levy
Movie director Steven Spielberg
Singer David Bowie
Actor Andrea Martin
Humanitarian Terry Fox
Singer Madonna
Singer Michael Jackson
Comedian Tina Fey
Figure skater Isabelle Brasseur
Actor Matt Damon
Singer Adam Lambert
Prince William, Duke of Cambridge

Forecast for 2013:

Your reputation rather than your finances grew during the Year of the Dragon. In the Year of the Snake, thanks to the groundwork you set, your fiscal picture brightens as a result of your recent work-related innovations. This is also a good year to become more protective of your time and more selective in choosing the people with whom you wish to share your life. Pursue new recreational interests, including ones that challenge your mind. This is also a year for making commitments and resolutions. You follow through on your plans. Be proactive with your health and avoid a tendency to brush things off. You'll be standing up for the rights of others, but learn to assert yourself, too. Some people you deal with are rude and abrasive, and you need to let them know that you won't accept their bad behaviour. Encourage friendships with these signs: ox, horse, and other dogs. When dealing with these signs, check their motives: tiger, dragon, and rooster.

Five kinds of dog:

In Chinese astrology, each of the five kinds of dog is associated with an element (water, wood, fire, earth, and metal). To find out which kind you are and what that means, see the year of your birth in the summaries that begin on page 494.

The Pig (Zhu)

Years of the pig: 1923, 1935, 1947, 1959, 1971, 1983, 1995, 2007

The pig is the twelfth Chinese zodiac sign. It is most compatible with the rabbit, sheep/goat, dog, rat, tiger, dragon, monkey, and rooster and has a difficult relationship with other pigs and—especially—the snake. The pig is fun to be around, and it is always hospitable (and usually a great cook). Pigs are generous and creative. They throw excellent parties, and everyone wants to be on a pig's A-list. However, if you offend its family, a pig can turn into a beast. The pig is roughly equivalent to Scorpio in the Western zodiac.

People born in the Year of the Pig are said to be:

Fair—you listen to all sides of a story

Good teachers, good students

Gullible—you believe the best in people but are sometimes too trusting

Hot-tempered—you will fiercely defend your family

Inspiring—you bring out the best in others

Lucky—you enjoy good fortune . . . the pig is one of the luckiest signs (possibly *the* luckiest sign)

Materialistic—but your generosity extends to others

Naive—you often take things for granted

Patronizing

Pranksters—you love practical jokes

Selfless

Stylish—you have a fine design sense

Supportive—you don't mind being in the background while someone else hogs the limelight

Trustworthy

Well liked—you're a popular travel companion

Pig careers include:

Artist, sculptor, potter

Caterer or restaurateur

Entertainer

Innkeeper

Interior designer

Jobs involving detailed work

Jobs involving finance

Salesperson

Social worker

Veterinarian

Some famous pigs:

Author Ernest Hemingway

Movie director Alfred Hitchcock

Actor Lucille Ball

Supreme Court Justice Bertha Wilson

Actor Al Waxman

The Dalai Lama

Actor Donald Sutherland

Actor Julie Andrews

Opera singer Luciano Pavarotti

Actor Woody Allen

Prime Minister Kim Campbell

Actor Glenn Close

Singer/songwriter Elton John

Singer/songwriter Emmylou Harris

TV host David Letterman

Author Salman Rushdie

Duchess of Cornwall Camilla Parker Bowles

Actor David Hyde Pierce

Actor Paul Gross

Prime Minister Stephen Harper

Basketball player Magic Johnson

Singer/songwriter Bryan Adams

Actor Tracey Ullman

Actor Minnie Driver

Actor Ewan McGregor

Forecast for 2013:

The Year of the Dragon encouraged new and renewed relationships. You discovered some ways to earn money and other ways to spend it. Ambition is highlighted in the Year of the Snake. Define your goals carefully and work diligently to meet them. You develop good business strategies and excel at negotiations, but be cautious, too—you tend to be gullible. Your environment is especially important and should emphasize tranquility. You continue to feel secure in your relationships but need to be more supportive and empathetic. Although you generally shun the limelight, this year is an exception—you want to be the centre of attention. Events that take place behind the scenes lead to a boost in your prestige late this year or early in the next one (the Year of the Horse). Knowledge acquired now proves beneficial in the future, so keep informed of changes and trends. You're passionate about everything you take on this year, but you tend to overdo things. You need to cut back and get sufficient rest. Relationships with these signs need more attention: horse, tiger, and rabbit. Take little at face value when interacting with these signs: rooster, monkey, and dog.

Five kinds of pig:

In Chinese astrology, each of the five kinds of pig is associated with an element (water, wood, fire, earth, and metal). To find out which kind you are and what that means, see the year of your birth in the summaries that begin on page 494.

The Chinese Zodiac
Birth Year Summaries

Note: In the Chinese calendar (a lunisolar calendar), each year starts somewhat later than it does in the Western system. If your birthday is in January or February, check the dates carefully. You may need to look at the previous year in the chart.

1913

Water ox year:
February 6, 1913–January 25, 1914
Those born in the Year of the Ox are dependable, straightforward, and strong . . . as an ox. They're tolerant, considerate, and down to earth, and they display a sense of justice. *The water ox is quick on its feet and always ready to help a friend or relative. It is methodical and patient. It enjoys its independence but is easy to deal with and makes a good team player and leader. It is often the beneficiary of good fortune.*

1914

Wood tiger year:
January 26, 1914–February 13, 1915
Those born in the Year of the Tiger have high standards for others and, especially, for themselves. Tigers are often stubborn, always loyal, and renowned for their bravery and courage. *The wood tiger is a pioneer, eager to brave trails and lead the way. It*

prefers teamwork to solo efforts and plays well with others. Its attention span may be limited, but it is generous with its time and possessions. It sometimes displays a calculating side.

1915

Wood rabbit year:
February 14, 1915–February 2, 1916
Those born in the Year of the Rabbit enjoy their privacy. They like to work behind the scenes and play a supportive role. Rabbits appreciate a serene environment and avoid confrontation. They are quick-witted and excellent communicators. *The wood rabbit* is a compassionate creature but can be oversensitive and take things personally. It looks more at the big picture than at the details of life. A generous soul, it has trouble saying no.

1916

Fire dragon year:
February 3, 1916–January 22, 1917
Those born in the Year of the Dragon (a symbol of good fortune) are free-spirited, gifted, driven, and often very successful at what they do. The dragon is an innovator and is famous for its flamboyance, to say nothing of its ego. *The fire dragon* is brave, outgoing, and always up for a challenge. It plays fair—and its dragon glass is always half full. It strives for perfection (perfectionism is both its strength and its weakness) and at times displays a reckless streak.

1917

Fire snake year:
January 23, 1917–February 10, 1918

Those born in the Year of the Snake are intuitive, crafty, business-oriented, and restless. They are competitive and materialistic—enjoying the good things in life. And they maintain an air of secrecy. *The fire snake* takes charge of any situation with an air of confidence and determination. It is an opinionated creature—and a highly persuasive one. It is also extroverted and has a possessive streak.

1918

Earth horse year:
February 11, 1918–January 31, 1919

Those born in the Year of the Horse are active, popular, sophisticated, independent, and impulsive. They keep up with changing trends and enjoy multi-tasking—but they don't always finish what they start. *The earth horse* thinks logically and sets its sights on a goal. Slow but steady is its approach. It is a reliable, adaptable friend—and has a wonderful sense of humour.

1919

Earth sheep/goat year:
February 1, 1919–February 19, 1920

Those born in the Year of the Sheep/Goat are the caregivers of the Chinese zodiac. They keep a low profile and are modest—but, in fact, are more accomplished than many, including they themselves, realize. *The earth sheep/goat* has all four feet on the ground. It is practical and secure, handles money well, is not fond of surprises, and prefers the established to the new.

1920

Metal monkey year:
February 20, 1920–February 7, 1921

The monkey is a clever creature that thrives on stimulation. It is innately curious, interested in what happens in its own world as well as the world at large. It has an excellent memory, is upbeat and fun to be around, and needs to be the centre of attention. *The metal monkey* is stylish and affectionate. It is highly independent, preferring to work alone. It is ambitious, but sometimes takes shortcuts and has been known to stretch the truth.

1921

Metal rooster year:
February 8, 1921–January 27, 1922

The rooster is in charge of the barnyard—flamboyant, proud, bossy. Everything is about image. Although overbearing, the rooster is polite, staunchly loyal, and makes a devoted friend. It aims high—and generally gets there. *The metal rooster* is an intense creature that strives to get to the root of every problem. It is funny, too, and talented—often musically. It tends to dominate conversations but is always around to help a friend or relative in need.

1922

Water dog year:
January 28, 1922–February 15, 1923

Those born in the Year of the Dog are loyal and devoted. They are observant (and nosy)—always on the lookout. Dogs are fiercely protective and are supportive friends. They are methodical, liking to finish what they start. *The water dog* is worldly—it keeps informed and knows a lot about many things. It has an open mind and is flexible and philosophical. It is also playful, intuitive, and a good listener. But it needs to be more prudent with finances.

1923

Water pig year:
February 16, 1923–February 4, 1924

Those born in the Year of the Pig are generous, modest, compassionate, hospitable—and occasionally gullible. They prefer to fend for themselves rather than asking for help, and they take their commitments seriously. *The water pig* is persevering and spiritual. It is persuasive—but can be easily swayed as well. It is a party animal and enjoys helping others.

1924

Wood rat year:
February 5, 1924–January 24, 1925

Those born in the Year of the Rat are sociable, creative, and high achievers. They're attracted to money. They can be difficult to deal with when things don't go their way. *The wood rat* is inquisitive (translation: nosy), adaptable, well liked, and a nonconformist. It sometimes lacks self-confidence. It detests waste. A gentle, gracious, hospitable creature, it is admired by a large circle of friends.

1925

Wood ox year:
January 25, 1925–February 12, 1926

Those born in the Year of the Ox are dependable, straightforward, and strong . . . as an ox. They're tolerant, considerate, and down to earth, and they display a sense of justice. *The wood ox* keeps up with the times and is eager to accept new ideas. Wood oxen are self-confident creatures with strong leadership abilities. They are quick-witted types, and they're sometimes quick-tempered as well.

1926

Fire tiger year:
February 13, 1926–February 1, 1927

Those born in the Year of the Tiger have high standards for others and, especially, for themselves. Tigers are often stubborn, always loyal, and renowned for their bravery and courage. *The fire tiger* is a diva with a flair for drama. It is also a powerful speaker and can be very funny. The least patient among the tigers, it is enthusiastic and wins friends easily. It is persuasive, forceful, and optimistic—and sometimes eccentric.

1927

Fire rabbit year:
February 2, 1927–January 22, 1928
Those born in the Year of the Rabbit enjoy their privacy. They like to work behind the scenes and play a supportive role. Rabbits appreciate a serene environment and avoid confrontation. They are quick-witted and excellent communicators. *The fire rabbit* is something of a mystery. Full of adventure—and often mischievous—it is curious, fun-loving, charming . . . and sometimes superficial. It does its best to avoid conflict but will definitely respond if provoked.

1928

Earth dragon year:
January 23, 1928–February 9, 1929
Those born in the Year of the Dragon (a symbol of good fortune) are free-spirited, gifted, driven, and often very successful at what they do. The dragon is an innovator and is famous for its flamboyance, to say nothing of its ego. *The earth dragon* is a romantic creature. It is also calm (for a dragon), trustworthy, and a born manager. It relishes its independence yet is a loyal and loving friend and partner.

1929

Earth snake year:
February 10, 1929–January 29, 1930

Those born in the Year of the Snake are intuitive, crafty, business-oriented, and restless. They are competitive and materialistic—enjoying the good things in life. And they maintain an air of secrecy. *The earth snake* takes a casual approach to life. It appears friendly—but its friends (and definitely its enemies) should not let down their guard. It is a sophisticated creature with an aristocratic bearing.

1930

Metal horse year:
January 30, 1930–February 16, 1931

Those born in the Year of the Horse are active, popular, sophisticated, independent, and impulsive. They keep up with changing trends and enjoy multi-tasking—but they don't always finish what they start. *The metal horse* loves exercise, freedom, and variety. It values friendship over possessions, and its friends and relatives know that it can always be trusted. It enjoys entertaining others and being entertained.

1931

Metal sheep/goat year:
February 17, 1931–February 5, 1932

Those born in the Year of the Sheep/Goat are the caregivers of the Chinese zodiac. They keep a low profile and are modest—but, in fact, are more accomplished than many, including they themselves, realize. *The metal sheep/goat* is a cultured animal—it loves the arts and is talented in one or more of them. It projects a tough exterior but has a gentle soul.

1932

Water monkey year:
February 6, 1932–January 25, 1933

The monkey is a clever creature that thrives on stimulation. It is innately curious, interested in what happens in its own world as well as the world at large. It has an excellent memory, is upbeat and fun to be around, and needs to be the centre of attention. *The water monkey* is the nosiest of the monkeys. It picks up useful information as it goes about its business—but it likes to meddle. It has a knack for making others smile, and it is sensitive to criticism.

1933

Water rooster year:
January 26, 1933–February 13, 1934

The rooster is in charge of the barnyard—flamboyant, proud, bossy. Everything is about image. Although overbearing, the rooster is polite, staunchly loyal, and makes a devoted friend. It aims high—and generally gets there. *The water rooster* is the least flashy among the roosters. It knows how to get a point across in an effective but low-key way. It's a stylish creature, with an eye for fashion. It is detail-oriented and sometimes misses seeing the bigger picture.

1934

Wood dog year:
February 14, 1934–February 3, 1935

Those born in the Year of the Dog are loyal and devoted. They are observant (and nosy)—always on the lookout. Dogs are fiercely protective and are supportive friends. They are methodical, liking to finish what they start. *The wood dog* has a generous heart and enjoys experimenting with new things. It prefers to be one of the family rather than the leader of the pack. It is fair-minded, resilient, and a good provider.

1935

Wood pig year:
February 4, 1935–January 23, 1936

Those born in the Year of the Pig are generous, modest, compassionate, hospitable—and occasionally gullible. They prefer to fend for themselves rather than asking for help, and they take their commitments seriously. *The wood pig* is an ambitious creature, but it plays well with others. Its highest priority is to help those who need it—friends, relatives, and even strangers.

1936

Fire rat year:
January 24, 1936–February 10, 1937

Those born in the Year of the Rat are sociable, creative, and high achievers. They're attracted to money. They can be difficult to deal with when things don't go their way. *The fire rat* is a spontaneous, impulsive creature that loves a challenge and is bored by routine. It's lively and competitive, and it thrives on change (change of address, change of job, and change of mood). It is charitable, cordial, bursting with energy—and highly popular.

1937

Fire ox year:

February 11, 1937–January 30, 1938

Those born in the Year of the Ox are dependable, straightforward, and strong . . . as an ox. They're tolerant, considerate, and down to earth, and they display a sense of justice. Everything about *the fire ox* is dynamic and powerful. It enjoys taking charge and excels in a leadership role. It is a fair-minded and loyal creature. But it is highly impulsive and its temper is easily ignited.

1938

Earth tiger year:

January 31, 1938–February 18, 1939

Those born in the Year of the Tiger have high standards for others and, especially, for themselves. Tigers are often stubborn, always loyal, and renowned for their bravery and courage. *The earth tiger* is the realistic tiger. It is highly responsible, persevering, and doesn't take itself as seriously as the other tigers do. It enjoys spending money—and, fortunately, can be lucky with money.

1939

___

Earth rabbit year:
February 19, 1939–February 7, 1940

Those born in the Year of the Rabbit enjoy their privacy. They like to work behind the scenes and play a supportive role. Rabbits appreciate a serene environment and avoid confrontation. They are quick-witted and excellent communicators. *The earth rabbit* is a highly practical and down-to-earth creature. It enjoys beautiful surroundings, as long as they're free of clutter. It's extremely sociable and is a born chatterbox. And it makes others feel safe and secure.

1940

___

Metal dragon year:
February 8, 1940–January 26, 1941

Those born in the Year of the Dragon (a symbol of good fortune) are free-spirited, gifted, driven, and often very successful at what they do. The dragon is an innovator and is famous for its flamboyance, to say nothing of its ego. *The metal dragon* has a magnetic presence. It is action-oriented and fights bravely for whatever cause it believes in. It is a conceited creature, yet a charismatic one, with the power to attract others. Not surprisingly, it excels in politics.

1941

Metal snake year:
January 27, 1941–February 14, 1942

Those born in the Year of the Snake are intuitive, crafty, business-oriented, and restless. They are competitive and materialistic—enjoying the good things in life. And they maintain an air of secrecy. *The metal snake* is a goal-oriented creature. It makes its moves quietly as it advances toward its goals. It is ostentatious—it loves to show off its possessions. But it is also generous and protective.

1942

Water horse year:
February 15, 1942–February 4, 1943

Those born in the Year of the Horse are active, popular, sophisticated, independent, and impulsive. They keep up with changing trends and enjoy multi-tasking—but they don't always finish what they start. *The water horse* is either adaptable or indecisive—depending on your point of view. A cheerful creature, its optimism is infectious. It is competitive but in a friendly, even sociable, way.

1943

___

Water sheep/goat year:
February 5, 1943–January 24, 1944

Those born in the Year of the Sheep/Goat are the caregivers of the Chinese zodiac. They keep a low profile and are modest—but, in fact, are more accomplished than many, including they themselves, realize. *The water sheep/goat* is a good-natured creature. It is witty, charming, and gets along with nearly everyone—as long as it gets its way. It doesn't care to wander, preferring the familiarity and comforts of home.

1944

___

Wood monkey year:
January 25, 1944–February 12, 1945

The monkey is a clever creature that thrives on stimulation. It is innately curious, interested in what happens in its own world as well as the world at large. It has an excellent memory, is upbeat and fun to be around, and needs to be the centre of attention. *The wood monkey* is witty, hard-working, and adaptable. It knows its audience and communicates easily, regardless of the situation. It has a scientific mind and is a great problem-solver.

1945

Wood rooster year:

February 13, 1945–February 1, 1946

The rooster is in charge of the barnyard—flamboyant, proud, bossy. Everything is about image. Although overbearing, the rooster is polite, staunchly loyal, and makes a devoted friend. It aims high—and generally gets there. *The wood rooster* is a team player. It is idealistic, working hard to make the planet a better and more environmentally friendly place. Its heart is in the right place, but it can overextend itself—promising more than it can always deliver.

1946

Fire dog year:

February 2, 1946–January 21, 1947

Those born in the Year of the Dog are loyal and devoted. They are observant (and nosy)—always on the lookout. Dogs are fiercely protective and are supportive friends. They are methodical, liking to finish what they start. *The fire dog* is born to lead. It has a sense of adventure and a sense of fun, and is the most popular among dogs. It is attractive and charismatic, but—if provoked—can be fierce.

1947

Fire pig year:
January 22, 1947–February 9, 1948

Those born in the Year of the Pig are generous, modest, compassionate, hospitable—and occasionally gullible. They prefer to fend for themselves rather than asking for help, and they take their commitments seriously. *The fire pig* is a complex creature—affectionate and stubborn, emotional and distracted. It is larger than life—bold, passionate, and creative—and often a big spender.

1948

Earth rat year:
February 10, 1948–January 28, 1949

Those born in the Year of the Rat are sociable, creative, and high achievers. They're attracted to money. They can be difficult to deal with when things don't go their way. *The earth rat* is a quick-witted creature that thrives on stability and security. It prefers to follow a plan rather than act spontaneously. It has a realistic outlook and is home-oriented and thrifty (occasionally stingy).

1949

Earth ox year:

January 29, 1949–February 16, 1950

Those born in the Year of the Ox are dependable, straight-forward, and strong . . . as an ox. They're tolerant, considerate, and down to earth, and they display a sense of justice. *The earth ox* is never afraid of hard work. As a result of its diligence, it is accomplished in its chosen field and often financially successful. It is a gracious, generous, and compassionate creature, frequently the backbone of its family.

1950

Metal tiger year:

February 17, 1950–February 5, 1951

Those born in the Year of the Tiger have high standards for others and, especially, for themselves. Tigers are often stubborn, always loyal, and renowned for their bravery and courage. *The metal tiger* is assertive, competitive, and extremely spontaneous. It is a quick thinker but sometimes pounces to conclusions without weighing the cons against the pros of a situation.

1951

Metal rabbit year:
February 6, 1951–January 26, 1952

Those born in the Year of the Rabbit enjoy their privacy. They like to work behind the scenes and play a supportive role. Rabbits appreciate a serene environment and avoid confrontation. They are clever and excellent communicators. *The metal rabbit* is an ambitious and intense creature that can lose itself in a task. It is passionate about everything and demonstrates a quick wit.

1952

Water dragon year:
January 27, 1952–February 13, 1953

Those born in the Year of the Dragon (a symbol of good fortune) are free-spirited, gifted, driven, and often very successful at what they do. The dragon is an innovator and is famous for its flamboyance, to say nothing of its ego. *The water dragon* is enterprising, brave, and action-oriented but without the arrogance and impatience of the other dragons. It is a loving and protective friend.

1953

Water snake year:
February 14, 1953–February 2, 1954

Those born in the Year of the Snake are intuitive, crafty, business-oriented, and restless. They are competitive and materialistic and enjoy the good things in life. And they maintain an air of secrecy. *The water snake* is not a modest creature. It enjoys not only success but also the luxuries and the recognition that go with it. Although it does not always display it, it does have an affectionate side.

1954

Wood horse year:
February 3, 1954–January 23, 1955

Those born in the Year of the Horse are active, popular, sophisticated, independent, and impulsive. They keep up with changing trends and enjoy multi-tasking—but they don't always finish what they start. *The wood horse* is the epitome of determination and perseverance. It hates wasting time, and it works—and plays—well with others. Its standards are extremely high, both for itself and the rest of the world.

1955

Wood sheep/goat year:
January 24, 1955–February 11, 1956

Those born in the Year of the Sheep/Goat are the caregivers of the Chinese zodiac. They keep a low profile and are modest—but, in fact, are more accomplished than many, including they themselves, realize. *The wood sheep/goat* is a social creature, happiest among friends and family members. It has an instinct for nurturing people and gardens but sometimes neglects to look after itself.

1956

Fire monkey year:
February 12, 1956–January 30, 1957

The monkey is a clever creature that thrives on stimulation. It is innately curious, interested in what happens in its own world as well as the world at large. It has an excellent memory, is upbeat and fun to be around, and needs to be the centre of attention. *The fire monkey* has charisma, strength, and tremendous drive. It sets high but realistic goals for itself. Exuding self-confidence, it believes it knows best. It communicates easily, has a scientific mind, and is a great problem-solver.

1957

Fire rooster year:
January 31, 1957–February 17, 1958

The rooster is in charge of the barnyard—flamboyant, proud, bossy. Everything is about image. Although overbearing, the rooster is polite, staunchly loyal, and makes a devoted friend. It aims high—and generally gets there. *The fire rooster* is narcissistic and theatrical. But it is dependable and strong-willed. When someone needs to take charge, it steps up to the plate and leads the way.

1958

Earth dog year:
February 18, 1958–February 7, 1959

Those born in the Year of the Dog are loyal and devoted. They are observant (and nosy)—always on the lookout. Dogs are fiercely protective and are supportive friends. They are methodical, liking to finish what they start. *The earth dog* is a complicated creature. It is supportive, inspiring, fair-minded, and practical. But there are times when it can be unpredictable.

1959

Earth pig year:
February 8, 1959–January 27, 1960

Those born in the Year of the Pig are generous, modest, compassionate, hospitable—and occasionally gullible. They prefer to fend for themselves rather than asking for help, and they take their commitments seriously. *The earth pig* enjoys the pleasures of home and is happiest in the company of family and friends. It encourages fairness and is responsive to other opinions. It enjoys cooking and eating, with a taste for rich foods.

1960

Metal rat year:
January 28, 1960–February 14, 1961

Those born in the Year of the Rat are sociable, creative, and high achievers. They're attracted to money. They can be difficult to deal with when things don't go their way. *The metal rat* is a take-charge and very intense creature, possessing great foresight. It knows what it wants—and will do whatever it takes to get it.

1961

Metal ox year:

February 15, 1961–February 4, 1962

Those born in the Year of the Ox are dependable, straightforward, and strong . . . as an ox. They're tolerant, considerate, and down to earth, and they display a sense of justice. *The metal ox* is a hard-working, goal-oriented, and driven creature. At times it can be ruthless. It is also modest and never a show-off, and it keeps its feelings to itself.

1962

Water tiger year:

February 5, 1962–January 24, 1963

Those born in the Year of the Tiger have high standards for others and, especially, for themselves. Tigers are often stubborn, always loyal, and renowned for their bravery and courage. Of all the tigers, *the water tiger* is the most tranquil, the most considerate, and the least decisive. It looks before it leaps—but is known to deliberate a little too long before taking necessary action.

1963

Water rabbit year:
January 25, 1963–February 12, 1964
Those born in the Year of the Rabbit enjoy their privacy. They like to work behind the scenes and play a supportive role. Rabbits appreciate a serene environment and avoid confrontation. They are quick-witted and excellent communicators. *The water rabbit* is a laid-back creature—sociable and funny. It makes love, not war. It is supportive and understanding, and a good listener as well as a good speaker. Others sometimes take advantage of its kindness and generosity.

1964

Wood dragon year:
February 13, 1964–February 1, 1965
Those born in the Year of the Dragon (a symbol of good fortune) are free-spirited, gifted, driven, and often very successful at what they do. The dragon is an innovator and is famous for its flamboyance, to say nothing of its ego. *The wood dragon* is goal-oriented, creative, and outspoken. It has a taste for the unusual and the offbeat and is often drawn to astrology. The word *subtle* is not in its vocabulary, preferring everything to be larger than life.

1965

Wood snake year:
February 2, 1965–January 20, 1966

Those born in the Year of the Snake are intuitive, crafty, business-oriented, and restless. They are competitive and materialistic—enjoying the good things in life. And they maintain an air of secrecy. *The wood snake* is not the show-off that the other snakes are. It has a small but extremely devoted circle of friends. Although not demonstrative, it is a loyal and loving companion.

1966

Fire horse year:
January 21, 1966–February 8, 1967

Those born in the Year of the Horse are active, popular, sophisticated, independent, and impulsive. They keep up with changing trends and enjoy multi-tasking—but they don't always finish what they start. *The fire horse* loves showing off and performing. It has unbridled energy and is a born extrovert. It loves to jump . . . to conclusions. It is passionate about people and ideas, and has a short fuse.

1967

Fire sheep/goat year:
February 9, 1967–January 29, 1968

Those born in the Year of the Sheep/Goat are the caregivers of the Chinese zodiac. They keep a low profile and are modest—but, in fact, are more accomplished than many, including they themselves, realize. *The fire sheep/goat* is not as thin-skinned as the others in its flock. It is independent and lively, with a flair for anything theatrical. If it has troubles, it keeps them to itself.

1968

Earth monkey year:
January 30, 1968–February 16, 1969

The monkey is a clever creature that thrives on stimulation. It is innately curious, interested in what happens in its own world as well as the world at large. It has an excellent memory, is upbeat and fun to be around, and needs to be the centre of attention. *The earth monkey* is a humanitarian. As it goes about its business, it stops to help its friends and relatives. It strives to better the world and is environmentally responsible. It doesn't seek praise, but it expects respect.

1969

Earth rooster year:
February 17, 1969–February 5, 1970

The rooster is in charge of the barnyard—flamboyant, proud, bossy. Everything is about image. Although overbearing, the rooster is polite, staunchly loyal, and makes a devoted friend. It aims high—and generally gets there. *The earth rooster* is a born planner—organized, motivated, and prone to be fussy. It excels at multi-tasking. It expects others to pull their weight and will definitely let them know if they don't.

1970

Metal dog year:
February 6, 1970–January 26, 1971

Those born in the Year of the Dog are loyal and devoted. They are observant (and nosy)—always on the lookout. Dogs are fiercely protective and are supportive friends. They are methodical, liking to finish what they start. *The metal dog* has high moral standards and will fight for what it believes is right and fair. It is not a spontaneous creature, preferring to follow a well-thought-out plan. It is always hospitable but often inflexible.

1971

Metal pig year:
January 27, 1971–February 14, 1972

Those born in the Year of the Pig are generous, modest, compassionate, hospitable—and occasionally gullible. They prefer to fend for themselves rather than asking for help, and they take their commitments seriously. *The metal pig* is an outspoken creature. It is hard-working and fair, inspires others through its example, and gives out healthy doses of vitamin P (praise). It likes to show off and can be bossy.

1972

Water rat year:
February 15, 1972–February 2, 1973

Those born in the Year of the Rat are sociable, creative, and high achievers. They're attracted to money. They can be difficult to deal with when things don't go their way. *The water rat* is shrewd, intelligent, intuitive, and unconventional—and it loves to solve riddles. It is respected for its kindness, generosity, and ability to take charge.

1973

Water ox year:

February 3, 1973–January 22, 1974

Those born in the Year of the Ox are dependable, straightforward, and strong . . . as an ox. They're tolerant, considerate, and down to earth, and they display a sense of justice. *The water ox* is quick on its feet and always ready to help a friend or relative. It is methodical and patient. It enjoys its independence but is easy to deal with and makes a good team player and leader. It is often the beneficiary of good fortune.

1974

Wood tiger year:

January 23, 1974–February 10, 1975

Those born in the Year of the Tiger have high standards for others and, especially, for themselves. Tigers are often stubborn, always loyal, and renowned for their bravery and courage. *The wood tiger* is a pioneer, eager to blaze trails and lead the way. It prefers teamwork to solo efforts and plays well with others. Its attention span may be limited, but it is generous with its time and possessions. It sometimes displays a calculating side.

1975

Wood rabbit year:
February 11, 1975–January 30, 1976

Those born in the Year of the Rabbit enjoy their privacy. They like to work behind the scenes and play a supportive role. Rabbits appreciate a serene environment and avoid confrontation. They are quick-witted and excellent communicators. *The wood rabbit* is a compassionate creature but can be oversensitive and take things personally. It looks more at the big picture than at the details of life. A generous soul, it has trouble saying no.

1976

Fire dragon year:
January 31, 1976–February 17, 1977

Those born in the Year of the Dragon (a symbol of good fortune) are free-spirited, gifted, driven, and often very successful at what they do. The dragon is an innovator and is famous for its flamboyance, to say nothing of its ego. *The fire dragon* is brave, outgoing, and always up for a challenge. It plays fair—and its dragon glass is always half full. It strives for perfection (perfectionism is both its strength and its weakness) and at times displays a reckless streak.

1977

Fire snake year:
February 18, 1977–February 6, 1978

Those born in the Year of the Snake are intuitive, crafty, business-oriented, and restless. They are competitive and materialistic—enjoying the good things in life. And they maintain an air of secrecy. *The fire snake* takes charge of any situation with an air of confidence and determination. It is an opinionated creature—and a highly persuasive one. It is also extroverted and has a possessive streak.

1978

Earth horse year:
February 7, 1978–January 27, 1979

Those born in the Year of the Horse are active, popular, sophisticated, independent, and impulsive. They keep up with changing trends and enjoy multi-tasking—but they don't always finish what they start. *The earth horse* thinks logically and sets its sights on a goal. Slow but steady is its approach. It is a reliable, adaptable friend—and has a wonderful sense of humour.

1979

Earth sheep/goat year:
January 28, 1979–February 15, 1980

Those born in the Year of the Sheep/Goat are the caregivers of the Chinese zodiac. They keep a low profile and are modest—but, in fact, are more accomplished than many, including they themselves, realize. *The earth sheep/goat* has all four feet on the ground. It is practical and secure, handles money well, is not fond of surprises, and prefers the established to the new.

1980

Metal monkey year:
February 16, 1980–February 4, 1981

The monkey is a clever creature that thrives on stimulation. It is innately curious, interested in what happens in its own world as well as the world at large. It has an excellent memory, is upbeat and fun to be around, and needs to be the centre of attention. *The metal monkey* is stylish and affectionate. It is highly independent, preferring to work alone. It is ambitious but sometimes takes shortcuts and has been known to stretch the truth.

1981

Metal rooster year:
February 5, 1981–January 24, 1982
The rooster is in charge of the barnyard—flamboyant, proud, bossy. Everything is about image. Although overbearing, the rooster is polite, staunchly loyal, and makes a devoted friend. It aims high—and generally gets there. *The metal rooster* is an intense creature that strives to get to the root of every problem. It is funny too, and talented—often musically. It tends to dominate conversations but is always around to help a friend or relative in need.

1982

Water dog year:
January 25, 1982–February 12, 1983
Those born in the Year of the Dog are loyal and devoted. They are observant (and nosy)—always on the lookout. Dogs are fiercely protective and are supportive friends. They are methodical, liking to finish what they start. *The water dog* is worldly—it keeps informed and knows a lot about many things. It has an open mind and is flexible and philosophical. It is also playful, intuitive, and a good listener. But it needs to be more prudent with finances.

1983

Water pig year:

February 13, 1983–February 1, 1984

Those born in the year of the pig are generous, modest, compassionate, hospitable—and occasionally gullible. They prefer to fend for themselves rather than asking for help, and they take their commitments seriously. *The water pig* is persevering and spiritual. It is persuasive—but can be easily swayed as well. It is a party animal and enjoys helping others.

1984

Wood rat year:

February 2, 1984–February 19, 1985

Those born in the Year of the Rat are sociable, creative, and high achievers. They're attracted to money. They can be difficult to deal with when things don't go their way. *The wood rat* is inquisitive (translation: nosy), adaptable, well-liked, and a nonconformist. It sometimes lacks self-confidence. It detests waste. A gentle, gracious, hospitable creature, it is admired by a large circle of friends.

1985

Wood ox year:
February 20, 1985–February 8, 1986

Those born in the Year of the Ox are dependable, straight-forward, and strong . . . as an ox. They're tolerant, considerate, and down to earth, and they display a sense of justice. *The wood ox* keeps up with the times and is eager to accept new ideas. Wood oxen are self-confident creatures with strong leadership abilities. They are quick-witted types, and they're sometimes quick-tempered as well.

1986

Fire tiger year:
February 9, 1986–January 28, 1987

Those born in the Year of the Tiger have high standards for others and, especially, for themselves. Tigers are often stubborn, always loyal, and renowned for their bravery and courage. *The fire tiger* is a diva with a flair for drama. It is also a powerful speaker and can be very funny. The least patient among the tigers, it is enthusiastic and wins friends easily. It is persuasive, forceful, and optimistic—and sometimes eccentric.

1987

Fire rabbit year:
January 29, 1987–February 16, 1988
Those born in the Year of the Rabbit enjoy their privacy. They like to work behind the scenes and play a supportive role. Rabbits appreciate a serene environment and avoid confrontation. They are quick-witted and excellent communicators. *The fire rabbit* is something of a mystery. Full of adventure—and often mischievous—it is curious, fun-loving, charming . . . and sometimes superficial. It does its best to avoid conflict but will definitely respond if provoked.

1988

Earth dragon year:
February 17, 1988–February 5, 1989
Those born in the Year of the Dragon (a symbol of good fortune) are free-spirited, gifted, driven, and often very successful at what they do. The dragon is an innovator and is famous for its flamboyance, to say nothing of its ego. *The earth dragon* is a romantic creature. It is also calm (for a dragon), trustworthy, and a born manager. It relishes its independence, yet is a loyal and loving friend and partner.

1989

Earth snake year:
February 6, 1989–January 26, 1990

Those born in the Year of the Snake are intuitive, crafty, business-oriented, and restless. They are competitive and materialistic—enjoying the good things in life. And they maintain an air of secrecy. *The earth snake* takes a casual approach to life. It appears friendly—but its friends (and definitely its enemies) should not let down their guard. It is a sophisticated creature with an aristocratic bearing.

1990

Metal horse year:
January 27, 1990–February 14, 1991

Those born in the Year of the Horse are active, popular, sophisticated, independent, and impulsive. They keep up with changing trends and enjoy multi-tasking—but they don't always finish what they start. *The metal horse* loves exercise, freedom, and variety. It values friendship over possessions, and its friends and relatives know that it can always be trusted. It enjoys entertaining others and being entertained.

1991

Metal sheep/goat year:
February 15, 1991–February 3, 1992

Those born in the Year of the Sheep/Goat are the caregivers of the Chinese zodiac. They keep a low profile and are modest—but, in fact, are more accomplished than many, including they themselves, realize. *The metal sheep/goat* is a cultured animal—it loves the arts and is talented in one or more of them. It projects a tough exterior but has a gentle soul.

1992

Water monkey year:
February 4, 1992–January 22, 1993

The monkey is a clever creature that thrives on stimulation. It is innately curious, interested in what happens in its own world as well as the world at large. It has an excellent memory, is upbeat and fun to be around, and needs to be the centre of attention. *The water monkey* is the nosiest of the monkeys. It picks up useful information as it goes about its business—but it likes to meddle. It has a knack for making others smile, and it is sensitive to criticism.

1993

Water rooster year:
January 23, 1993–February 9, 1994

The rooster is in charge of the barnyard—flamboyant, proud, bossy. Everything is about image. Although overbearing, the rooster is polite, staunchly loyal, and makes a devoted friend. It aims high—and generally gets there. *The water rooster* is the least flashy among the roosters. It knows how to get a point across in an effective but low-key way. It's a stylish creature, with an eye for fashion. It is detail-oriented and sometimes misses seeing the bigger picture.

1994

Wood dog year:
February 10, 1994–January 30, 1995

Those born in the Year of the Dog are loyal and devoted. They are observant (and nosy)—always on the lookout. Dogs are fiercely protective and are supportive friends. They are methodical, liking to finish what they start. *The wood dog* has a generous heart and enjoys experimenting with new things. It prefers to be one of the family rather than the leader of the pack. It is fair-minded, resilient, and a good provider.

1995

Wood pig year:

January 31, 1995–February 18, 1996

Those born in the Year of the Pig are generous, modest, compassionate, hospitable—and occasionally gullible. They prefer to fend for themselves rather than asking for help, and they take their commitments seriously. *The wood pig* is an ambitious creature, but it plays well with others. Its highest priority is to help those who need it—friends, relatives, and even strangers.

1996

Fire rat year:

February 19, 1996–February 6, 1997

Those born in the Year of the Rat are sociable, creative, and high achievers. They're attracted to money. They can be difficult to deal with when things don't go their way. *The fire rat* is a spontaneous, impulsive creature that loves a challenge and is bored by routine. It's lively and competitive, and it thrives on change (change of address, change of job, and change of mood). It is charitable, cordial, bursting with energy—and highly popular.

1997

Fire ox year:
February 7, 1997–January 27, 1998

Those born in the Year of the Ox are dependable, straight-forward, and strong . . . as an ox. They're tolerant, considerate, and down to earth, and they display a sense of justice. Everything about *the fire ox* is dynamic and powerful. It enjoys taking charge and excels in a leadership role. It is a fair-minded and loyal creature. But it is highly impulsive and its temper is easily ignited.

1998

Earth tiger year:
January 28, 1998–February 15, 1999

Those born in the Year of the Tiger have high standards for others and, especially, for themselves. Tigers are often stubborn, always loyal, and renowned for their bravery and courage. *The earth tiger* is the realistic tiger. It is highly responsible, persevering, and doesn't take itself as seriously as the other tigers do. It enjoys spending money—and, fortunately, can be lucky with money.

1999

Earth rabbit year:
February 16, 1999–February 4, 2000

Those born in the Year of the Rabbit enjoy their privacy. They like to work behind the scenes and play a supportive role. Rabbits appreciate a serene environment and avoid confrontation. They are quick-witted and excellent communicators. *The earth rabbit* is a highly practical and down-to-earth creature. It enjoys beautiful surroundings, as long as they're free of clutter. It's extremely sociable and is a born chatterbox. And it makes others feel safe and secure.

2000

Metal dragon year:
February 5, 2000–January 23, 2001

Those born in the Year of the Dragon (a symbol of good fortune) are free-spirited, gifted, driven, and often very successful at what they do. The dragon is an innovator and is famous for its flamboyance, to say nothing of its ego. *The metal dragon* has a magnetic presence. It is action-oriented and fights bravely for whatever cause it believes in. It is a conceited creature, yet a charismatic one, with the power to attract others. Not surprisingly, it excels in politics.

2001

Metal snake year:
January 24, 2001–February 11, 2002

Those born in the Year of the Snake are intuitive, crafty, business-oriented, and restless. They are competitive and materialistic—enjoying the good things in life. And they maintain an air of secrecy. *The metal snake* is a goal-oriented creature. It makes its moves quietly as it advances toward its goals. It is ostentatious—it loves to show off its possessions. But it is also generous and protective.

2002

Water horse year:
February 12, 2002–January 31, 2003

Those born in the Year of the Horse are active, popular, sophisticated, independent, and impulsive. They keep up with changing trends and enjoy multi-tasking—but they don't always finish what they start. *The water horse* is either adaptable or indecisive—depending on your point of view. A cheerful creature, its optimism is infectious. It is competitive but in a friendly, even sociable, way.

2003

Water sheep/goat year:
February 1, 2003–January 21, 2004

Those born in the Year of the Sheep/Goat are the caregivers of the Chinese zodiac. They keep a low profile and are modest—but, in fact, are more accomplished than many, including they themselves, realize. *The water sheep/goat* is a good-natured creature. It is witty, charming, and gets along with nearly everyone—as long as it gets its way. It doesn't care to wander, preferring the familiarity and comforts of home.

2004

Wood monkey year:
January 22, 2004–February 8, 2005

The monkey is a clever creature that thrives on stimulation. It is innately curious, interested in what happens in its own world as well as the world at large. It has an excellent memory, is upbeat and fun to be around, and needs to be the centre of attention. *The wood monkey* is witty, hard-working, and adaptable. It knows its audience and communicates easily, regardless of the situation. It has a scientific mind and is a great problem-solver.

2005

Wood rooster year:
February 9, 2005–January 28, 2006

The rooster is in charge of the barnyard—flamboyant, proud, bossy. Everything is about image. Although overbearing, the rooster is polite, staunchly loyal, and makes a devoted friend. It aims high—and generally gets there. *The wood rooster* is a team player. It is idealistic, working hard to make the planet a better and more environmentally friendly place. Its heart is in the right place but it can overextend itself—promising more than it can always deliver.

2006

Fire dog year:
January 29, 2006–February 17, 2007

Those born in the Year of the Dog are loyal and devoted. They are observant (and nosy)—always on the lookout. Dogs are fiercely protective and are supportive friends. They are methodical, liking to finish what they start. *The fire dog* is born to lead. It has a sense of adventure and a sense of fun, and is the most popular among dogs. It is attractive and charismatic, but—if provoked—can be fierce.

2007

Fire pig year:
February 18, 2007–February 6, 2008

Those born in the Year of the Pig are generous, modest, compassionate, hospitable—and occasionally gullible. They prefer to fend for themselves rather than asking for help, and they take their commitments seriously. *The fire pig* is a complex creature—affectionate and stubborn, emotional and distracted. It is larger than life—bold, passionate, and creative—and often a big spender.

2008

Earth rat year:
February 7, 2008–January 25, 2009

Those born in the Year of the Rat are sociable, creative, and high achievers. They're attracted to money. They can be difficult to deal with when things don't go their way. *The earth rat* is a quick-witted creature that thrives on stability and security. It prefers to follow a plan rather than act spontaneously. It has a realistic outlook and is home-oriented and thrifty (occasionally stingy).

2009

Earth ox year:
January 26, 2009–February 13, 2010
Those born in the Year of the Ox are dependable, straight-forward, and strong . . . as an ox. They're tolerant, considerate, and down to earth, and they display a sense of justice. *The earth ox* is never afraid of hard work. As a result of its diligence, it is accomplished in its chosen field and often financially successful. It is a gracious, generous, and compassionate creature, frequently the backbone of its family.

2010

Metal tiger year:
February 14, 2010–February 2, 2011
Those born in the Year of the Tiger have high standards for others and, especially, for themselves. Tigers are often stubborn, always loyal, and renowned for their bravery and courage. *The metal tiger* is assertive, competitive, and extremely spontaneous. It is a quick thinker but sometimes pounces to conclusions without weighing the cons against the pros of a situation.

2011

Metal rabbit year:

February 3, 2011–January 22, 2012

Those born in the Year of the Rabbit enjoy their privacy. They like to work behind the scenes and play a supportive role. Rabbits appreciate a serene environment and avoid confrontation. They are clever and excellent communicators. *The metal rabbit* is an ambitious and intense creature that can lose itself in a task. It is passionate about everything and demonstrates a quick wit.

2012

Water dragon year:

January 23, 2012–February 9, 2013

Those born in the Year of the Dragon (a symbol of good fortune) are free-spirited, gifted, driven, and often very successful at what they do. The dragon is an innovator and is famous for its flamboyance, to say nothing of its ego. *The water dragon* is enterprising, brave, and action-oriented, but without the arrogance and impatience of the other dragons. It is a loving and protective friend.

2013

Water snake year:
February 10, 2013–January 30, 2014

Those born in the Year of the Snake are intuitive, crafty, business-oriented, and restless. They are competitive and materialistic and enjoy the good things in life. They also maintain an air of secrecy. *The water snake* is not a modest creature. It enjoys not only success but also the luxuries and the recognition that go with it. Although it does not always display it, it does have an affectionate side.

APPENDIX

Locating Your
Ascendant (Rising Sign)
and the Houses of
Your Horoscope

As noted in the introduction, the twelve houses of a horoscope correspond to different areas of a person's life. Each house is ruled by a different zodiac sign. The line that divides each house is known as a cusp. The cusp, or start, of the first house is called the Ascendant. Once the Ascendant is determined, the "house rulers" can easily be identified.

Your Ascendant is the sign that was rising over the eastern horizon at the time of your birth. (That's why the Ascendant is also known as your rising sign.) This marks the moment at which you made your appearance in the world. To calculate the Ascendant sign, you need to know the location and exact time when you were born. You can then find your precise Ascendant in an advanced horoscope book or using the Internet.

However, you can use a quick method to estimate your personal Ascendant if you know the approximate time of your birth. The chart on page 551 and the instructions that precede it will guide you along.

Your Ascendant determines how others view you, not your actual nature. It indicates the manner in which you interact with people. The section on the basics of astrology includes summaries of the areas of your life that the houses govern.

(See page 3.) Here is a summary of the Ascendant in the twelve signs.

If your Ascendant is Aries, you present yourself as affectionate, courageous, adventurous, bossy, and brash. People see you as generous (but your generosity has to be acknowledged), driven, and upfront. You have a winning smile and move with a combination of determination and grace.

If your Ascendant is Taurus, others view you as calm and dependable, conservative, materialistic, and stubborn. People recognize your willingness to work hard but find you opinionated. You take pride in your appearance and dress smartly. Overall, you present a sturdy appearance.

If your Ascendant is Gemini, you give the appearance of being lively, versatile, and unpredictable. People find you witty and multi-talented and enjoy your way with words—but you also come across as inconsistent and hammy. Your eyes are alive, and you seem to be in perpetual motion.

If your Ascendant is Cancer, others perceive you as sensitive, supportive, loyal, family-loving, and imaginative. But you also reveal a melancholy side and show a possessive quality along with a lack of self-confidence. Not surprisingly, you have sympathetic eyes and an expressive face.

If your Ascendant is Leo, you come across as proud and determined, big-hearted and confident. You have a take-charge approach, but there's no hiding your ego. People find you fun-loving, passionate, and dramatic, as well as overbearing and inflexible. You have a winning smile and definite presence.

If your Ascendant is Virgo, people see you as logical, detail-oriented, and wanting to be in control. You're also viewed as a picky and precise perfectionist who's hard to please. You present an image of refinement and taste. You have a kind face, and your eyes take in everything. Chances are good that you're a lot stronger than you appear.

If your Ascendant is Libra, you present yourself as cultured, discreet, artistic, and fair-minded. You're upbeat and intuitive, but indecisive and easily distracted. You're image-conscious and are always turned out impeccably, no matter the occasion. You have a contagious laugh and mischievous eyes.

If your Ascendant is Scorpio, you immediately come across as intense, intuitive, mysterious, and curious. People are quick to grasp the fact that you like to be in control. Nor is it hard to see that you're motivated, as well as suspicious, possessive, and obsessive. Your body moves with a purpose, and your eyes are deep and passionate.

If your Ascendant is Sagittarius, you give an impression of being adventurous, curious about everything, jovial, lucky, funny, and generous—to a fault. But there's no denying you're blunt, irresponsible, and prone to exaggeration. You have a restless manner about you and project a quality of strength. You often express yourself best through body language.

If your Ascendant is Capricorn, others see you as ambitious, brave, cautious, funny, industrious, and organized. But you also may come across as overbearing, calculated, rigid, and grumpy. You find it difficult to show your feelings, so first impressions of you aren't always on target. Your eyes show determination, and you have a welcoming smile.

If your Ascendant is Aquarius, others view you as active and lively, logical and fair-minded. They quickly grasp that you're idealistic, and know at a glance that you're a genuine eccentric. First impressions of you vary. Some see you as aloof, others as outgoing; some find you big-hearted, others think you're cranky. You have kind eyes and a gentle smile. Your dress style can be elegantly simple or downright gaudy.

If your Ascendant is Pisces, people see you as artistic, romantic, imaginative, compassionate, and deeply sensitive. But you also have a melancholy side, and can be impractical, easily distracted, vague, and secretive. Not surprisingly (because you're a water sign), you move with a fluid grace. There's always a hint of mystery in your eyes.

To estimate your Ascendant sign, you first need to know the approximate time at which you were born. Don't forget to allow for Daylight Saving Time (by subtracting one hour from your birth time). And remember that, in Canada, the date on which Daylight Saving Time begins has changed over the years, and the starting time may differ according to the province where you were born. (You can find this information on the Internet.)

To locate your Ascendant, look at the diagram on page 551.

Find the segment in the celestial wheel that covers the time of your birth.

Write down your Sun sign at the outside edge of this segment. As an example, let's say your Sun sign is Libra and you were born at 1 a.m. So go to the segment that covers midnight to 2 a.m. and label it Libra. You'll then see that Libra rules your third house.

Now proceed around the wheel, moving *counter-clockwise* and following the established order of the zodiac signs. Using the same example, you'll see that Scorpio rules your fourth house; Sagittarius your fifth; Capricorn your sixth; Aquarius your seventh; Pisces your eighth; Aries your ninth; Taurus your tenth; Gemini your eleventh; Cancer your twelfth; Leo your first; and Virgo your second.

Your first house is the same as the position of your Ascendant, which means that your Ascendant is Leo.

As mentioned, this technique isn't precise. If the sign that appears as your Ascendant doesn't match the description given on pages 548–550, look at the signs immediately before and after the one you located. (For example, if your calculation shows your Ascendant is Leo, read the descriptions for Cancer and Virgo.) You may find that either of these signs more accurately describes the impression that you make.

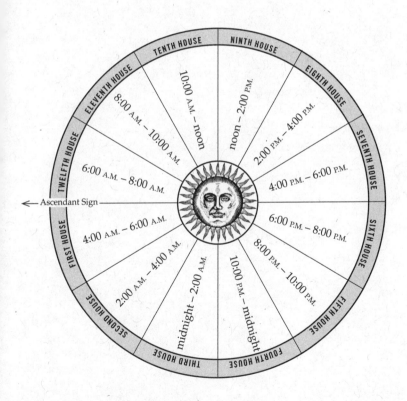

Acknowledgements

I sincerely thank all those who have contributed to the publication of this book. I begin with my friend Clifford Collier (Sagittarius) who, many years ago, opened my eyes to the extraordinary possibilities of astrology. I also extend my appreciation to the excellent team at HarperCollins, particularly senior editor Brad Wilson, who encouraged me to write this book and constantly helped me to "make it better." Production editor Allegra Robinson and managing editor Noelle Zitzer expertly navigated the manuscript through its various stages. I also thank Heather Sangster for her thoughtful copy editing and Kathryn Exner and Tilman Lewis for their fine proofreading. Meaghan Beverly provided helpful editorial assistance; Jeremy Rawlings made matters contractual a pleasant experience; and Norma Cody, the welcoming face and voice of HarperCollins, never put me on hold. I appreciate how important it is to capture the tone of a book through its design, and I acknowledge David Gee for his wonderful cover and Alan Jones for his inviting layout. I am also grateful to my friends Lan and Yu for providing helpful insights into Chinese astrology; to Ann Woollcombe for her valuable suggestions; and to Karen Worek for her careful reading of the manuscript. Marni Weisz at *Famous* magazine helped me refine my style over the years, and I appreciate the opportunity that she and Salah Bachir gave me. Finally, I thank my partner, Gord, for his good humour, great patience, and nourishing and delectable meals throughout the writing process.

Dan Liebman
August 2012